I0029327

NORMALIZING OCCUPATION

NORMALIZING OCCUPATION

The Politics of Everyday Life in the West Bank Settlements

Edited by Marco Allegra, Ariel Handel,
and Erez Maggor

Indiana University Press

Bloomington and Indianapolis

This book is a publication of

Indiana University Press
Office of Scholarly Publishing
Herman B Wells Library 350
1320 East 10th Street
Bloomington, Indiana 47405 USA

iupress.indiana.edu

© 2017 by Indiana University Press

All rights reserved

No part of this book may be reproduced or utilized in any form or
by any means, electronic or mechanical, including photocopying
and recording, or by any information storage and retrieval system,
without permission in writing from the publisher. The Association
of American University Presses' Resolution on Permissions
constitutes the only exception to this prohibition.

⊗ The paper used in this publication meets the minimum
requirements of the American National Standard for Information
Sciences—Permanence of Paper for Printed Library Materials, ANSI
Z39.48-1992.

Manufactured in the United States of America

Library of Congress Cataloging-in-Publication Data

Names: Handel, Ariel, editor | Allegra, Marco, editor. |
    Maggor, Erez, editor
Title: Normalizing occupation : the politics of everyday life in the
    West Bank settlements / edited by Ariel Handel, Marco Allegra,
    and Erez Maggor.
Description: Bloomington : Indiana University Press, 2017. |
    Includes bibliographical references and index.
Identifiers: LCCN 2016025307 (print) | LCCN 2016040106 (ebook) |
    ISBN 9780253024732 (cloth : alk. paper) | ISBN 9780253024886
    (pbk. : alk. paper) | ISBN 9780253025050 (ebook)
Subjects: LCSH: Land settlement—West Bank. | Jews—West Bank. |
    Jews—West Bank—Social conditions. | Palestinian Arabs—West
    Bank—Social conditions.
Classification: LCC DS110.W47 N67 2017 (print) | LCC DS110.W47
    (ebook) | DDC 956.95/3044—dc23
LC record available at https://lccn.loc.gov/2016025307

1 2 3 4 5 22 21 20 19 18 17

Contents

Part III—Forced Coexistence: Palestinians and Jewish Settlers

Acknowledgments

THE INITIAL IMPETUS for this project was the workshop Settlements in the West Bank (1967–2014): New Perspectives, which was held at the Minerva Humanities Center in Tel Aviv University on June 2014. Our gratitude goes out to the Minerva Humanities Center as well as to the French Research Institute in Jerusalem and the Van Leer Institute in Jerusalem for their generous support of the workshop. We extend our sincere appreciation to the workshop's participants and audience, and especially to the sessions' discussants: Ian Lustick, Hadas Weiss, Sandi Kedar, Dani Filc, and Ronen Shamir, who provided important feedback and comments. Rebecca Tolen of Indian University Press displayed great confidence in the project even when it was only in its initial stages, and we are indebted to her for helping us getting it off the ground. Also at Indiana University Press, we would like to thank Dee Mortensen, Paige Rasmussen and Jennika Baines for their generous assistance throughout the editing process. We thank Mary C. Ribesky for overseeing the copyediting stage, Alexander Trotter for his help with creating the index, and Alessandro Colombo, who was kind enough to help us in producing the maps. The timely financial support we received from the Department of Sociology at New York University is also greatly appreciated. Most of all, we are greatly indebted to the book's contributors, without which this collection would not have been possible.

Finally, we would like to commemorate the memory of our former colleague, Michael Feige, who was one of the four victims of the terror attack that took place in Tel Aviv on June 8, 2016. Michael, an admired teacher and a renowned scholar of Israeli society, was trained at the Hebrew University of Jerusalem and taught at Ben-Gurion University, where he most recently served as the head of the Israel Studies program. A scholar of the national-religious settler movement and author of several key studies on Gush Emunim, Michael was among the most vibrant participants of the workshop held at the Minerva Humanities Center in 2014; his death came as a shock and represents a great loss for us all.

Abbreviations

CBS—Israeli Central Bureau of Statistics

FSU—Former Soviet Union

HCJ—Israeli High Court of Justice

HRW—Human Rights Watch

IDF—Israeli Defense Forces

ILO—International Labor Office

JIIS—Jerusalem Institute for Israel Studies

NLT—Israeli National Labor Tribunal

OT—Occupied Territories

PNA—Palestinian National Authority

WB—West Bank

YESHA—Judea Samaria and Gaza Council

NORMALIZING OCCUPATION

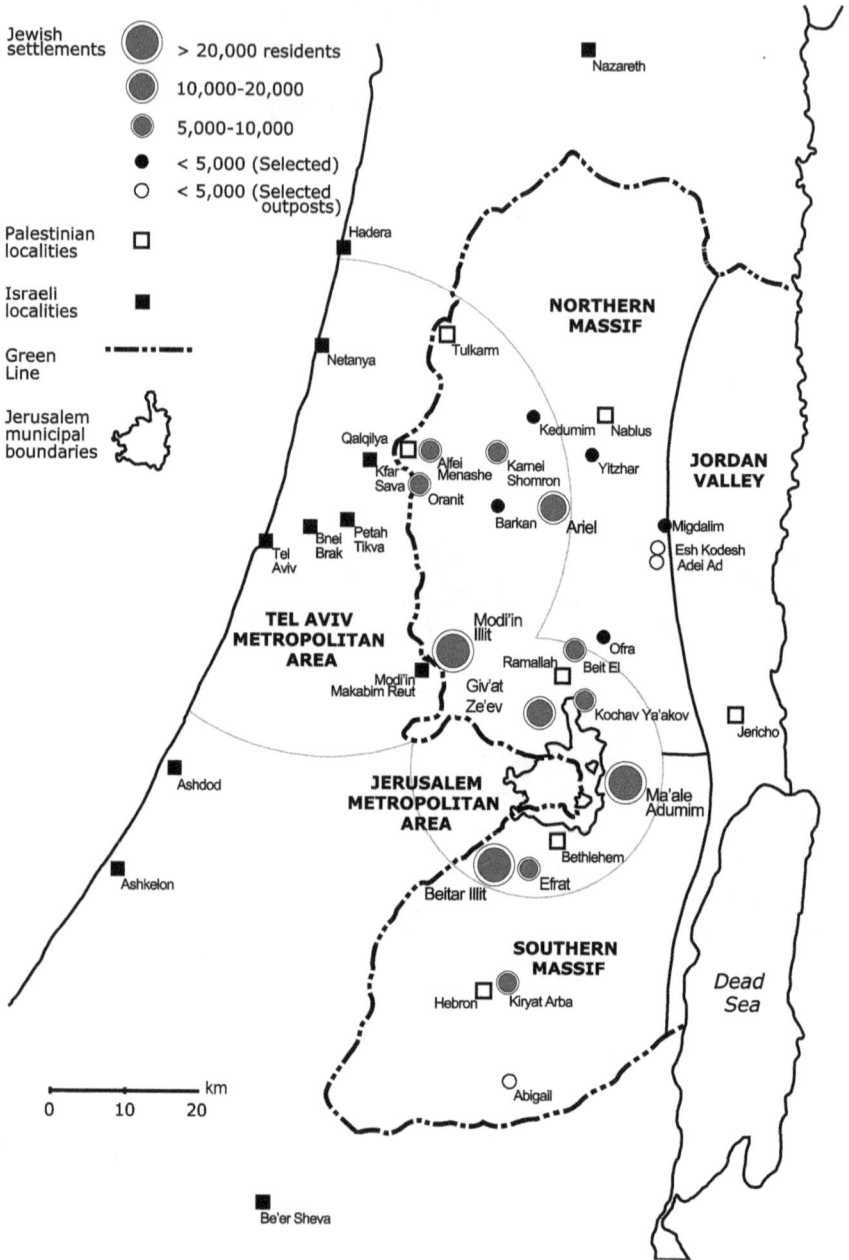

Map 1. Selected localities in the West Bank and Israel. All the settlements that had five thousand or more residents at the end of 2011 have been included in the maps. In addition, all the localities in Israel/Palestine that have a special relevance for the arguments developed in one or more chapters have also been included. Map by Marco Allegra and Alessandro Colombo, based on B'Tselem, 2013, "Settlement Population, XLS," *B'Tselem* website, accessed January 31, 2016, www.btselem.org/download/settlement_population.xls; and Meron Benvenisti and Shlomo Khayat, 1988, *The West Bank and Gaza Atlas* (Jerusalem: West Bank Data Base Project/The Jerusalem Post), 8.

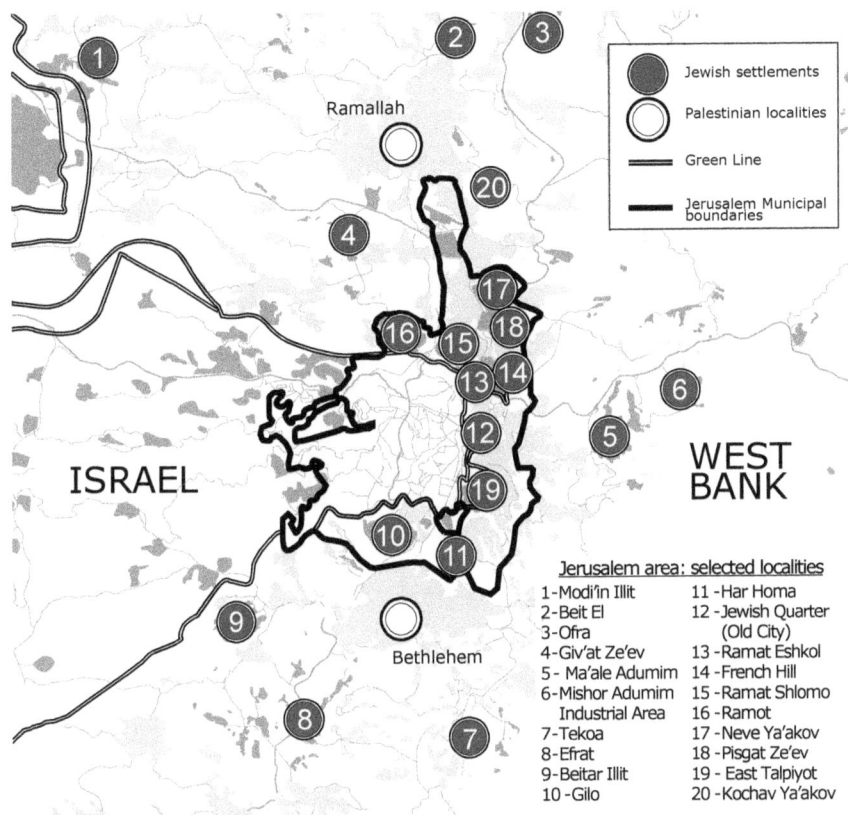

Map 2. Selected localities in the Jerusalem area, including the settlements established inside the municipal boundaries of the city. (For additional information about the demography and the political geography of the settlements, see the appendix in this volume.) Map by Marco Allegra and Alessandro Colombo, based on B'Tselem, 2013, "Settlement Population, XLS," *B'Tselem* website, accessed January 31, 2016, www.btselem.org/download /settlement_population.xls; and Shai Efrati and B'Tselem, 2014, "The West Bank: Settlements and the Separation Barrier," *B'Tselem* website, accessed January 31, 2016, http://www.btselem .org/download/201411_btselem_map_of_wb_eng.pdf.

Introduction

The Politics of Everyday Life in the West Bank Settlements

Marco Allegra, Ariel Handel, and Erez Maggor

In january 2016, this flat in the Jewish settlement of Ma'ale Adumim was presented in the popular website Airbnb: "Amazing beautiful and spacious house, in a beautiful quiet suburban city 15 minutes to central Jerusalem. 4 big bedrooms, well equipped kitchen and large and cozy living room with panoramic view to the desert mountains."[1] Nothing in the advertisement hints at the fact that the Israeli town is located beyond the Green Line, in a territory that was occupied in the 1967 war. The controversial status of the location is obscured by a rather conventional description of the apartment, echoing that of tens of thousands of other Airbnb listings: the quality of the facilities available (at $60 a night) to guests, the beauties of the immediate surroundings, and the possibility of a fast, uncomplicated access to major commercial and touristic sites. The banality of the attributes listed by Airbnb hosts, however, illuminates some of the fundamental traits of Israel's settlement project. As a matter of fact, most of the housing units built in the settlements are quite similar to the apartment depicted above and would therefore not appear out of place among the over two million properties in thirty-four thousand cities that Airbnb lists in its website.[2] The fact that the apartment in Ma'ale Adumim, as well as others in settlements such as Ariel, Karnei Shomron, or Efrat are presented on the website as being in Israel is also telling, as it points to the role that seemingly prosaic activities such as renting an apartment have in shaping the political and human geography of a contested territory. Indeed, the history of Israel's settlement project has been by and large the history of the normalization of Jewish presence in the West Bank, a history in which the advent of Airbnb to the region represents just the latest episode. The process of normalization, i.e., the ongoing incorporation of the settlements into Israel's social, economic, and administrative fabric underlying the development of Israel's settlement policy is the topic of this volume.

Israel's settlement policy—and its political, territorial, and demographic implications—has been subject to intense debate in the local and international media for decades. The settlements have represented a continuous source of friction in Israeli-Palestinian relations, and an apparently insurmountable obstacle for negotiation. Their steady growth in the last five decades transformed them into what is widely considered as the most significant "fact on the ground" established by Israel in the territories it conquered in 1967; indeed, today, approximately six hundred thousand Israelis (out of a total of eight million) live in the West Bank—two hundred thousand of which in East Jerusalem.[3]

While nobody would seriously dispute the importance of the issue for the past, the present, and the future of Israel/Palestine, the scholarly literature on the settlements has remained surprisingly scarce. Indeed, almost any book dealing with the Israeli-Palestinian conflict devotes some attention to Jewish settlements; however, only a limited number of contributions have specifically addressed the issue so far. Among the few contributions that have done so, most follow a few established lines of inquiry, focusing on the national-religious settler movement (and its most well-known organization, Gush Emunim) and on the supposed symbiosis between the latter and Israel's political establishment.[4]

Furthermore, conventional wisdom on the settlements—as expressed by international media and, to a certain extent, by the scholarly contributions on the subject—is often misleading rather than illuminating. As Erez Tzfadia (chapter 6) comments, web searches for "Jewish settlers" or "Israeli settlers" typically return images of bearded, armed men (or women), usually depicted during demonstrations or tense confrontations with Palestinians or the Israeli Defense Forces. Often, as David Newman (chapter 2) notes, settlements are depicted as "small hilltop communities, populated only by groups of settlers imbued with a radical ideology." This stereotypical image of the settlers is reinforced in the scholarly literature, which has by and large looked to the expansion of settlements as driven almost exclusively by religious ideology and strategic considerations—or, less often, restrained by diplomatic concerns.

This deeply entrenched framework, however, fails to adequately account for the prevailing pattern of settlement development and the steady growth of the settler population. A clear indication of this is the fact that the majority of development efforts in the West Bank have remained concentrated near or around the Green Line border, while construction in the heart of the region advocated for by the leadership of the national-religious settlers has remained relatively scarce. Furthermore, as many of the contributions of this book clearly demonstrate, most settlers, as well as many among the key agents of Israel's settlement policy, do not partake in the ideology of the settler movement.

In contrast to the common emphasis of religious ideology and messianic faith, this volume will argue that the best way to understand the development of

Israel's settlement project is to consider its development as an ongoing and dynamic process of *normalization* that was not produced by one specific agent, but rather shaped by larger processes and changes that originated from within Israeli society. Making sense of this process requires paying attention to the actual dynamics and modalities that produced the settlements, which this collection will place front and center.

Our concept of normalization entails several issues. First, we are interested not so much in the specific ideology of the actors involved in the process of colonization, but rather in what are considered the more banal motivations that drew them to take part in the settlement project. Generations of activists and politicians committed to the idea of "Greater Israel" have significantly contributed to the proliferation of the settlements. Yet equally, if not more important, has been the largely overlooked contribution of state planners and bureaucrats, employers, real estate developers, and the tens of thousands of Israelis who did not necessarily care about the "redemption of the land," but choose to migrate to Jewish communities beyond the Green Line for much more banal reasons. Exploring normalization means therefore investigating the interplay between the different factors, discourses, strategies, and rationalities underlying the colonization policy, and the formation of different, often paradoxical coalitions of actors advocating for it.

Second, we do not see normalization as the end result of colonization, but rather as a driving force of the process since its inception in the aftermath of the War of 1967. The settlement enterprise has not been an exceptional phenomenon contradictory to other trends in Israeli society—something happening, politically and geographically, "outside" Israel, in a distant frontier territory. From the very start, the banalization of Jewish life in the West Bank has been a crucial feature of colonization, a historical pattern that was shaped by an array of long-term structural processes and transformations. This collection stresses, in particular, how factors such as urban and regional planning, rising inequality and the retreat of the welfare state within Israel proper, and the changing political economy of industry and employment in the region have all played a crucial yet conventionally underappreciated role in determining the ongoing expansion and resilience of Israel's settlement project. Illuminating these processes does not aim to ignore the ideological and strategic drivers behind Israel's colonization of the West Bank, but rather to place them into a wider perspective.

The concept of normalization therefore urges us to reject one-dimensional explanations of the proliferation of settlements. The history of the colonization of the West Bank cannot be reduced to the mechanical implementation of a century-old Zionist agenda, nor can it be understood as a coup, single-handedly conducted by a fundamentalist faction mobilizing in opposition and against the wishes of the otherwise sane body of the Israeli nation. More specifically, the normalization approach contributes two broad, interrelated arguments about Israel's settlement policy—about its *genesis* (i.e., the way the settlements came into existence and developed over time), and about its *reality* (i.e., the social, political, and territorial consequences it produced), respectively. Before turning back to the concept of normalization, we will first unpack these two arguments against the background of the conventional wisdom about the settlements.

From Rightist Fantasy to Historical Fact?

It is widely assumed that the establishment of Jewish settlements derives from the mobilization of the religious-messianic settler movement and/or their supporters in the Israeli establishment (both of which are usually associated with the Israeli right). This argument—the prevalence of the "ethnonational imperative," of a "pure" ideological and strategic drive toward colonization—is well entrenched both in the scholarly literature and in the popular perception. Case in point is the chapter entirely dedicated to the settlements that appears in Ari Shavit's recent bestseller, *My Promised Land: The Triumph and Tragedy of Israel*. Puzzled by the growth of settler population since the 1980s and by its political implications, Shavit tries to understand how the "folly" of the settlements has materialized: "The nightmare we [the members of Peace Now during the 1980s] envisioned turned into reality. That is why some thirty years later, I am driving to Ofra— *the mother of all settlements*—not to fight it, but to understand it. To understand how the settlements turned from rightist fantasy to historical fact" (2013, 203, our emphasis).[5]

Shavit's quest includes several dialogues with iconic figures of the leadership of Gush Emunim, with whom he discusses the nature of the settlements enterprise. In a final, dramatic crescendo, Shavit angrily blames one of his interlocutors, Pinchas Wallerstein, for the settlers' mad zealotry, which ruined the edifice that the forefathers of Israel had carefully built: "Your energy was remarkable, but on everything that matters you were utterly wrong. . . . You brought disaster upon us, Wallerstein. On our behalf, you committed an act of historical suicide" (222).

Shavit, one of Israel's leading journalists, is the heir of a long line of Israeli commentators—usually identified with the "peace camp"—that have traveled to Ofra to "understand" the settlements;[6] indeed, even a cursory survey of the existing literature makes it abundantly clear that the establishment of the first Gush Emunim settlements (such as Ofra or Kedumim) is depicted as a turning point of historic proportions.[7] In an influential contribution on the subject, Israeli anthropologist Michael Feige went as far as to argue that "it would be hardly an exaggeration to claim that [Gush Emunim] has changed the history of the Middle East" (2009, 35).

Contrary to Shavit's observation, however, Ofra was not "the mother of all settlements." Granted, after 1975 Ofra itself served as a model for several settlements founded by Gush Emunim—most of them "community settlements" (*yishuv kehilati*) located in the mountain strip of the West Bank. Needless to say, however, several settlements had been established well before the foundation of Ofra. In 1975, some twenty-five Jewish communities had already been built in the West Bank (including East Jerusalem), for a total population of about forty thousand residents. The vast majority of these settlers concentrated in the new municipal boundaries of Jerusalem that included approximately seventy square kilometers of the occupied West Bank, where the "new neighborhoods" were established—Ramat Eshkol (1968), French Hill (1969), Neve Ya'akov, Gilo, Talpiyot, and Ramot (1973).[8] Most of these neighborhoods had a distinct urban landscape, as Israeli planners were in the process of adopting a new, metropolitan model of urban development. In this period, other new settlement towns already existed (Kiryat Arba, founded in 1968) or were being planned (Ma'ale Adumim and Efrat) just outside Jerusalem's municipal boundaries. Alongside these settlements, various infrastructural and industrial projects were being implemented or planned, such as the upgrade of the Atarot Airport in East Jerusalem or the industrial area of Mishor Adumim, located right outside the municipal border. Smaller settlements had also been founded, including several moshavim in the Jordan Valley (often established in the form of agricultural-military *nahal* outposts).

The point is not that Ofra represented just one among a number of different settlement models that existed at the time, but rather that one would look in vain to Ofra to make sense of the pattern of settlement development and the steady growth of the settler population. We argue that the emphasis on Ofra and Gush Emunim attributes, as the anthropologist Hadas Weiss points out in her review of Feige's book, a "disproportionate agency to a nationalist theology" (2009, 757) and has therefore prevented gaining a thorough understanding of Israel's settlement policy. As stated, the key factor in the establishment of the settlements and in their consolidation over time has rested in the convergence of the various interests and preferences of many different actors (politicians, activists, bureaucrats, planners, developers, private enterprises, and the settlement population at large). Settlement strategies, as well as single communities, were therefore successful only to the extent that they were able to relate to a wide Israeli audience and to shepherd broad coalitions of actors in their support. In this respect, while the importance of Gush Emunim cannot be denied, it should be put in perspective. To begin with, the settler movement did not act alone but has always enjoyed the support of many allies in the Israeli establishment and bureaucracy regardless of the party or coalition in power. This is a point that several scholars have recently noted (Gorenberg 2006; Eldar and Zertal 2007; Ranta 2009, 2015); yet, even these more recent streams of studies still focus almost exclusively on the ideological and strategic drivers of the expansion of the settlements and view Gush Emunim as the main engine of this process, which other elements merely joined or supported. What is usually overlooked is the fact that the development of Israel's settlement policy emerged from the interaction between different actors, which had to negotiate with each other and often adjust their practices to better correspond with the constraints and opportunities shaped by larger processes and developments, as well as the surrounding environment.

Many contributions in this collection make this point quite clearly. For example, as David Newman (chapter 2) shows, the success of the Gush Emunim itself depended precisely on the movement's ability to exhibit flexibility by latching on to the contemporary socioeconomic trends of Israeli society and the shift in planning paradigms.[9] Danny Gutwein (chapter 1) argues that the establishment of settlements, particularly the benefits they offer in the realms of housing, education, health, taxation, infrastructure, and employment, has functioned as a compensatory mechanism in the context of an ongoing retrenchment of Israel's previously robust welfare state. The availability of otherwise shrinking opportunities for welfare, affordable housing, and social mobility at commuting distance from employment and education opportunities in the Jerusalem and Tel Aviv metropolitan areas explains, in turn, the appeal of the settlements in the eyes of the most vulnerable members of Israeli society such as immigrants from the former Soviet Union, as depicted in the work of Hadas Weiss, (chapter 5); or ultraorthodox settlers—currently the fastest growing faction in the settlements—whose massive migration to the settlements is analyzed by Lee Cahaner (chapter 7). Taken together, these studies illuminate how large scale processes and transformations that originated in Israel proper played a key role in determining settlement development patterns, and were responsible for turning run-of-the-mill settlers into central agents of colonization.

Not only do the vast majority of settlers reside in large suburban communities such as Ma'ale Adumim—this settlement alone counts some forty thousand residents, compared to Ofra's three thousand—but the suburban nature of colonization has constituted a territorial platform enabling the formation of a broad, almost universal consensus around the establishment and expansion of large planned towns and industrial zones in the metropolitan belts of Jerusalem and Tel Aviv (Allegra 2013). This consensus represented the premise for the establishment of sociopolitical partnerships and synergies that link state planners, real-estate developers, and private enterprises seeking the opportunity to profit from access to cheap land and labor, as well as various public subsidies and government funded infrastructure (Algazi 2006; Human Rights Watch 2016; Maggor 2015). This consensus also served as the common denominator for politically heterogeneous coalitions: as Allegra and Handel (2015) have shown, the establishment of the first nucleus of Ma'ale Adumim in 1975 was precisely a result of the cooperation among Gush Emunim leaders, members of both the Labor and Likud political parties, and nonaffiliated settlers, which negotiated with the Rabin government over the establishment of a nonpartisan settlement that was eventually transformed to a full-fledged city.

Suburban settlements such as Ma'ale Adumim, but also Ariel, Karnei Shomron, Alfei Menashe, Giv'at Ze'ev, and more recently Beitar Illit and Modi'in Illit have been especially successful because, by and large, they served the interests and rationalities of Israelis of (almost) every political persuasion and background. Planners saw them as the appropriate answer to the challenges of planning the development of urban regions; bureaucrats considered them an efficient way to allocate resources and services to the local communities; developers, real estate agents, and private enterprises recognized them as a new opportunity for profits; certain politicians viewed them as a mechanism through which they could compensate their constituencies; and for tens, and later hundreds of thousands, of ordinary Israelis crossing the Green Line, who viewed these new, state-subsidized localities in the West Bank as a potential springboard to upward mobility. In the context of the extreme retrenchment of public spending within the Green Line, a defining characteristic of the past three decades, migrations to the settlements should be seen as a logical decision that did not need to be driven by religious or fundamentalist ideology. At the same time, even more ideologically committed members of Israel's political establishment saw several advantages in establishing suburban communities in the West Bank. Such a choice was in part directly instrumental to their political and strategic goals, as suburban settlements could cater to a wide Israeli audience, resulting in fast-growing communities which represented solid facts on the ground.

Two Israels?

Beyond the question of the settlements' genesis lay the issues of the current reality, that is, the characteristic features of the social and territorial state of affairs created by Israel's settlement policy—and its relation with the broader landscape of Israel/Palestine. Here again, by placing great emphasis on ideological and strategic factors, the conventional wisdom about settlements tends to convey the image of a society that functions through a different logic and develops in relative isolation from the so-called Israel proper—as well as, it goes almost without saying, from the surrounding Palestinian environment. In his 2007 *New York Times* review of Akiva Eldar and Idith Zertal's (2007) *Lords of the Land*, Adam LeBor—a renowned author and journalist—rather dramatically expresses a nonetheless widespread idea, which is that the settlements form a world apart from Israel: "There are two Israels: one inside the Green Line, the 1967 border, the other an occupying power extending beyond it. The first is a vibrant democracy, with Arab members of Parliament, university professors and lawyers, beauty queens and soldiers, and even a Muslim cabinet minister. . . . Across the Green Line, the West Bank, captured in 1967, is another country, neither Israel nor Palestine, but a lawless place, where the Jewish settler, rifle in one hand and prayer book in the other, is undisputed king."

We argue, however, that the settlements are in no way an enclosed society existing outside the "rational" or "sane" body of the Israeli nation—and that they have in fact complicated relations, deeply saturated in the unequal power relations with the surrounding Palestinian West Bank. Settlements can be understood only by acknowledging their continuous interactions with the other territorial and demographic components of Israel/Palestine, as well as the complex inside/outside form of sociological, anthropological, legal, and economic "ecosystem" that those interactions create.

A first corollary of this argument is that, far from the ridiculous cartoonish image of the settler as portrayed in Lebor's quote, the settlements are home to a much more heterogeneous population than is often perceived. Overall, this population tends to mirror the diversity of the Jewish population in "Israel proper": religious and secular, Ashkenazim and Mizrahim, low, middle and even upper-middle class. A second corollary is that Israel's policy of establishing Jewish communities in the Palestinian West Bank does not create separate societies but rather new patterns of relations among the resident population of Israel/Palestine.

Anthropologists Joyce Dalsheim and Assaf Harel (2009) have compellingly argued that much of the existing literature tends to present the religious-national settlers as a homogeneous group, whose identity and practices are marked by irrational fundamentalism—a group that is politically, existentially, and spatially located "outside" the allegedly democratic, secular, sane, and rational body of Israel. The same has been often argued, as LeBor's quote shows, for the settler population as a whole. Indeed, LeBor's depiction represents a widespread, entrenched reductionist approach to the conceptualization of the Jewish settler society in the West Bank (cf. Eldar and Zertal 2007; Feige 2009). Across the Green Line, one could certainly find the messianic fanatics that LeBor and others describe. However, one cannot ignore the fact that the world beyond the Green Line includes far more than rifles, prayer books, and "godforsaken hills." To begin with, more than half of the municipality of Jerusalem—the capital of Israel and, with some 850,000 residents in 2014, the most populous city in Israel/Palestine (CBS 2015, table 2.24)—is located in the West Bank. Similarly, about three quarters of the city's metropolitan area sits east of the Green Line, including large satellite towns counting tens of thousands of residents such as Ma'ale Adumim, Modi'in Illit, or Beitar Illit. Throughout the West Bank, some ten localities count more than five thousand residents each (see the appendix). Most Jewish settlements are virtually indistinguishable, administratively speaking, from other Israeli local authorities and are serviced by modern infrastructures that connect them almost seamlessly to Israel's urban and commercial centers. Tens of Israeli educational institutions are located in the West Bank (among them, one of the country's nine universities, Ariel University, which boasts more than fourteen thousand students). Also embedded in the landscape are industrial zones that are home to both domestic and multinational manufacturing enterprises (Algazi 2006; Human Rights Watch 2016), shopping malls and, strange as it may seem, flourishing boutique vineyards (Handel, Rand, and Allegra 2015). Indeed, surveys conducted over time (Newman and Portugali 1987; Hopp 2002), as well as more qualitative evidence (Weiss 2011, Chapter 5; Allegra 2013, chapter 3), have consistently shown that the vast majority of settlers chose to relocate to the West Bank in search for affordable housing, quality education, and social services at commuting distance from the main centers of employment.

The existence of mundane pull factors for colonization has in fact expanded the audience of potential settlers far beyond the boundaries of the national-religious camp—itself a diverse community (Harel, chapter 8). The settlers population includes today a large (and growing) component of both non-Zionist *haredim* (Cahaner, chapter 7) and largely secularized immigrants from the former Soviet Union (Weiss, chapter 5)—two communities that hardly match the standard characterization of the national-religious camp. More recent scholarship has also criticized the traditional literature on the settlements for ignoring the large presence—at least since the 1980s—of a diverse Mizrahi population in various types of Jewish settlements (Dalsheim 2008; Gillis 2009; Leon 2015). Furthermore, as Erez Tzfadia (chapter 6) shows, even the category of the "illegal outpost"— usually associated to the radical, national-religious "hilltop youth"—is internally diverse and, for the most part, reproduces the dynamic of Israeli society. Finally, in an apparent paradoxical turn of events, the same mundane factors has recently determined an inflow of upwardly mobile Palestinian families (carrying either an Israeli passport or the Israeli "blue card" that identifies them as residents of Jerusalem) into selected settlements established by Israel in East Jerusalem, such as French Hill or Pisgat Ze'ev, a phenomenon described by Wendy Pullan and Haim Yacobi (chapter 11). In the rest of the West Bank, the heterogeneity of the settler population was not lost even to Palestinians, who—as is captured by Honaida Ghanim (chapter 9)—differentiate among different groups of settlers based on their history of relations with the local population.

A second reductionist, yet highly common conceptualization of the settlers is the mention of the Green Line as the boundary dividing the sane, democratic Israeli polity from the settlements' exotic, lawless, and dangerous country. It sees Israel/Palestine as composed of distinct, separate (or at least, separable with some future efforts) territorial entities. According to this argument, Israel's settlement policy created in the West Bank a distant, alien "Settlersland" that is completely removed from the reality of Israel and contradicts its fundamental values. In this view, the process of colonization of the West Bank can be treated as a sort of pressing foreign policy issue rather than an integral part of the constitutional and administrative functioning of the Israel/Palestine polity. This common treatment of the Green Line is surprisingly naïve. It overlooks the long and ongoing process of direct incorporation of large portions of the West Bank into Israel's social, economic, and administrative fabric, as well as the relationship between dynamics in the settlements and long-term developments and changes in "Israel proper" (M. Benvenisti 1976, 1984, 1989, 1995; E. Benvenisti 1990; Kimmerling 1989; Azoulay and Ophir 2013; Weizman 2007; Gordon 2008).

A striking example in this respect is the status of East Jerusalem in the literature on the settlements. In most major works on Israel's settlement policy—such as Eldar and Zertal (2007) or Gorenberg (2006)—the communities that make up Jewish East Jerusalem (the so-called new neighborhoods) are hardly mentioned and almost never discussed. Typically, the dynamics of expansion of settlements is observed "East Jerusalem excluded"—an expression that recurs countless times in the literature on the Israeli-Palestinian conflict. Therefore, the idea that the plans put forward by Gush Emunim or later by the Likud governments constituted crucial turning points in Israel's settlement policy is usually justified based on figures that demonstrate that the number of settlers remained relatively low in the West Bank ("East Jerusalem excluded") before the end of 1970s. Tom Segev, for example, in arguing against Gershom Gorenberg's (2006) claim that the Likud settlement policy after 1977 was simply an escalation of pre-existent trends, observes that "although by 1977 settlers had already started moving into the territories, at that point they numbered less than 60,000, *and about 40,000 of them lived in East Jerusalem*" (Segev 2006, 148, our emphasis).[10]

It remains unclear, however, why we should consider the creation (on Israel's unilateral initiative) of a territorial entity of "East Jerusalem," and the subsequent construction of several large Jewish planned towns and neighborhoods in the area, as an eccentric and relatively marginal episode in Israel's settlement policy—if compared, for example, with the founding of Ofra or Kedumim. For anyone interested in understanding the dynamics of Jewish settlement in the West Bank, the case of Jerusalem represents instead one of the most crucial analytical keys. First, because of the sheer dimension of the phenomenon, today, more than a third of the Jewish residents of the West Bank reside in East Jerusalem. Second, because the creation of the new neighborhoods represented the first large-scale Israeli investment in the West Bank. Third—as Israeli geographers such as David Newman, Juval Portugali and Shlomo Reichman demonstrated with their seminal contributions in the 1980s (Newman and Portugali 1987; Portugali 1991; Reichman 1986)—the inner city of Jerusalem has represented the catalyzer for the growth of a vast metropolitan area largely made up by settlements. Last but not least, East Jerusalem's settlements are the best example for the normalization process, that is, to the ways in which discursive and sociological practices were used to reproduce the occupied region as an integral part of Israel proper. In that discursive loop, the very fact that the settlements do not look like settlements contributed to legitimizing them in some spectators' eyes (see Kratsman and Ginsburg, chapter 4).

The case of the metropolitan area of Jerusalem offers perhaps the clearest example of why it is impossible to think about Israel and the settlements as separate territorial and conceptual entities. Jerusalem, however, is by no means an exceptional case in this respect. The same dynamics of suburbanization operating in Jerusalem has determined the growth of settlements located in the metropolitan area of Tel Aviv—or, as a popular marketing formula described them at the time, "five minutes from Kfar Saba"—such as Ariel, Karnei Shomron, or Alfei Menashe. The growth of the settlements as part of the metropolitan areas of Jerusalem (and, to a lesser extent, Tel Aviv) has had a considerable impact on the development of the two regions—for example, by creating urban developments for the Jerusalemite middle class such as Ma'ale Adumim (Allegra, chapter 3) or for the poor Ultraorthodox community (Cahaner, chapter 7).[11]

On the other hand, settlements are not simply the product of trends operating in Israel: their establishment has produced significant consequences for the surrounding areas of Israel/Palestine. In the West Bank, the implications of guaranteeing the existence of settlements as Jewish-only communities and their security result, most obviously, in drastic constraints placed on Palestinian access to land and resources; their establishment, however, does not simply close off land to Palestinians, but instead restructures the "use value" of the space (i.e., the way space is used by its inhabitants), thereby comprehensively reshaping the sociospatial fabric of the West Bank (Handel 2014).[12] Typically, large Jewish communities serve as important employment centers for the West Bank, for both Jewish and Palestinian labor. This is the case, for example, of Ma'ale Adumim and the attached industrial zone of Mishor Adumim where economic activities create new and seldom investigated spaces of encounters and friction (Human Rights Watch 2016; Paz-Fuchs and Ronen, chapter 10).

The Trap of Normalization

The concept of normalization is a useful analytical tool for investigating the genesis and the current reality of the West Bank's settlements; using it, however, might serve as a double-edged sword. Considering the settlements and the colonization process as part of "normal" Israel holds a double risk that we wish to avoid. The first pitfall is an ahistorical view that ties the settlements enterprise into the wider, century-old Zionist history; in other words, the colonization of the West Bank would be "normal" because Zionism has always, intrinsically been about settlement, and therefore any specific instance of colonization can be explained in a teleological manner by referring to the unchanging nature and goals of Zionism as a political movement. By refusing this approach, we certainly do not intend either to morally judge the state of Israel, or to excuse and depoliticize its actions; rather, we suggest that while there are many similarities between the settlements in the West Bank and older Zionist practices, there are more than a few important differences between them that cannot be just brushed aside.

To avoid this first trap, we choose to emphasize, from an analytical point of view, the historicity and contingency of the process of colonization, and focus on actual practices behind the proliferation of the settlements. To do so, we look to Israel proper *and* the Occupied Territories as one territorial unit (what we have called "Israel/Palestine" throughout this introduction), a system of fractures and continuities whose existence is ever-changing and contested. This is exactly what we are trying to achieve through our study of normalization as an active and ongoing process.

The second risk, which seems to present an even deeper problem, relates to the politics of Israel/Palestine. In other words, the risk is that by discussing the settlements' normalization, we ourselves turn to be agents of normalization. If we describe the settlers' population as heterogeneous and rational, and if the book argues that the settlements are part of general rurbanization and suburbanization phenomena—then, goes the argument, we swallowed the bait: the settlers wanted to normalize themselves and their communities, and we contribute to their cause with this academic collection.

This is why we need to stress that describing the process of normalization aims not to legitimize it, but rather expose its underlying mechanisms and dynamics. Doing so, we believe, allows illuminating the everyday or banal violence that exists in the "normal" settlements and is most often concealed. Here again East Jerusalem may serve as a good example. The new neighborhoods, those that "do not look like settlements," have no less of an impact on the Palestinian population and on the present and future of the geopolitics of Israel/Palestine. These modern and well-designed neighborhoods are still sitting on lands that were expropriated from Palestinian owners, and their very existence still nulls the ability to divide Israel/Palestine into two viable political entities. While the book deals mainly with the Jewish population of the West Bank, one should not forget that even the most "normal" and quiet settlement has an impact on its Palestinian surrounding. Guaranteeing the security of Jewish settlers requires the permanent presence of thousands of Israeli soldiers, hundreds of checkpoints, and maintenance of a sophisticated system of surveillance in the West Bank. For the sake of settlers' mobility, an entire system of dedicated roads has been created—which effectively separate the movement of the two populations, with a severe impact on Palestinian's freedom of movement and daily lives (Handel 2014). Last but not least, the fact that only a minority of settlers engage in violent actions against Palestinians communities is no consolation for the victims of this violence; indeed, the existence of a large mass of normal settlers indirectly legitimizes the presence of extremist groups by shielding them from the perspective of a future, large-scale evacuation of the West Bank.

Conclusion

As we have argued throughout this introduction, Israel's settlement policy can only be understood by investigating how many different factors determined its development over time and by acknowledging the connection existing between the settlements and the social, political, and economic fabric of Israel/Palestine.

Adopting an approach based on the idea of normalization entails two crucial analytical and empirical challenges—to which this volume represents a first, partial answer. In the first place, where conventional wisdom offers a teleological explanation of Israel's settlement policy—interpreting it as the product of a straightforward, conscious exercise of socioterritorial engineering inspired by the ideological underpinnings of Zionist political thought and practice—we should focus instead on the actual dynamics underlying the expansion of the settlements. Second, where most of the discourse on Israel's settlement project revolves around an effort to measure the degree of integration between Israel and the West Bank, and assess its implications for the perspectives of conflict resolution (usually associated to "two-states solution") or for the nature of Israel as a "Jewish democratic state," we should focus on the role of settlements in reframing the relations between different places and communities in Israel/Palestine.

To do so, we choose to adopt a more holistic approach to the study of the settlements. The establishment of Jewish communities in the West Bank, we believe, should be analyzed as a multifaceted process of transformation, or as Brenner and Elden would put it, of "production of territory" (2009; Allegra 2013) rather than as the imposition of the colonizer's abstract rationality (e.g., the notion of "Greater Israel" or of "defensible borders") onto the pre-existent indigenous landscape. In this respect, the mundane and banal routines and artifacts that make up the daily life of the residents of Israel/Palestine—building yourself a career, commuting to work, shopping at the mall, sending the kids to schools, visiting friends and families, driving on the highway, obtaining a mortgage—are no less consequential than active campaigns or straightforward strategies. At the same time, the establishment of the settlements has not uniformly expanded Israeli territory into the West Bank, but has thoroughly reformulated the administrative, infrastructural, and economic interactions between different territories and communities. The idea of normalization suggests that we should not see the settlements as marking the new boundaries of Israel, but rather as one of the interfaces that regulate the interactions of individuals and groups in Israel/Palestine as a whole. As a process, rather than a fixed state, the concept of normalization points at the permanent change and fluidity of those interfaces. The territory is made and remade by the interplay of laws and regulations, planning and economic policies, political campaigns, symbols and discourses against the background of broader social, political, and economic trends. Without understanding this multifaceted and ever-changing pattern, and the variety of agents and instruments involved in it, our understanding of the region's past, present, and future will always remain incomplete and weak.

Notes

1. Airbnb website, accessed January 25, 2016, www.airbnb.com/rooms/5349142.
2. *The Guardian*, accessed January 25, 2016, www.theguardian.com/technology/2016/jan/12/airbnb-listings-illegal-settlements-israel-palestine-west-bank; Airbnb website, accessed January 25, 2016, https://www.airbnb.com/about/about-us?locale=en.
3. Twenty-one settlements, inhabited by some eight thousand Jewish settlers, were evacuated from Gaza Strip in August 2005 in what was known as the Disengagement Plan, while about thirty Jewish communities (for a total population of some twenty thousand residents) are located in the Golan Heights. This book, however, focuses on the contemporary settlement policy and reality in the West Bank. For further details on the history of the settlements enterprise, see the appendix.
4. Among the important early contributions we can mention Aran (1991), Lustick (1988), Friedman (1992), Isaac (1976), Newman (1985), Newman and Hermann (1992), Sivan (1995), Sprinzak (1991), and Weisburd (1989). For a critical review on the literature on "Jewish fundamentalism" in the settlements, see Dalsheim and Harel (2009).
5. Ofra, founded in 1975 on the initiative of Gush Emunim, is the stronghold of the national-religious settler movement, the residence of settlers' "aristocracy," and the place where the movement's main institutions (such as the Yesha Council or the magazine *Nekuda*) were originally established.
6. Amos Oz, Israel's most famous author, documented his visit to Ofra in his book *In the Land of Israel* (1983); in 1997, Gadi Taub—the author of a 2010 book on the settlements published by Yale University Press—revisited Ofra on behalf of the daily *Yediot Ahronot* to mark the fifteen year anniversary of Oz's book.
7. For example, Eldar and Zertal define the nucleus of the settlers of Elon Moreh (which later founded the community of Kedumim) as "the progenitor of the massive settlement in [the north of the West Bank]" (2007, 30).
8. While Jordanian East Jerusalem's size was only six square kilometers; the remaining sixty-four square kilometers were taken from twenty-eight different villages and towns around the city. For more on the planning of urban Jewish "neighborhoods" in occupied East Jerusalem, see Pullan and Yacobi (chapter 11).

9. Newman (chapter 2) argues that Gush Emunim leadership consciously tried to exploit the suburbanization trends operating in the Israeli society to this goal. Meron Benvenisti (1984, 57–63) and Shafir and Peled (2002, 172–74) made a similar argument about the Likud Party. As Handel, Rand, and Allegra (2015) have shown, today ideological settlers deploy sophisticated marketing strategies, modeled after the models developed by the tourism industry. The slogan *YESHA ze fun* (Judea and Samaria are fun) is designed to redefine the settlements of the West Bank as a place of leisure—and to appeal the enlightened bourgeoisie of Tel Aviv.

10. Segev's figures are, to our best knowledge, not very accurate, especially for what concerns the estimate of twenty thousand settlers residing in the West Bank outside East Jerusalem. Harris (1980, 145) counts, for example, a total of forty-seven thousand settlers in East Jerusalem at the end of 1978. Meron Benvenisti (1987, 55) counted some five thousand settlers outside East Jerusalem in 1977. Based on these sources, and with the sole purpose of producing a very raw estimate, we can place the total population figure for 1977 around fifty thousand (forty-five thousand in East Jerusalem and five thousand outside the city limits).

11. Indeed, as a few seminal studies conducted in the early 1980s (Newman 1981, 1984; M. Benvenisti 1984) pointed out, even Gush Emunim's model of "community settlement" (*yishuv kehilati*) was designed to match the lifestyle of a new class of urban, white collar national-religious activists; these communities constituted in fact suburban gated developments, with a large proportion of the local population commuting daily to Israel's main employment centers—a radical departure from the previous tradition of Zionist pioneers based on the rural, collectivist model of the moshav and the kibbutz.

12. The same argument has been made by Cédric Parizot and Stéphanie Latte-Abdallah (2015) about the "separation wall" or the permit system.

References

Algazi, Gadi. 2006. "Offshore Zionism." *New Left Review* 40: 27–37.

Allegra, Marco. 2013. "The Politics of Suburbia: Israel's Settlement Policy and the Production of Space in the Metropolitan Area of Jerusalem." *Environment and Planning A* 45 (3): 497–516.

Allegra, Marco, and Ariel Handel. 2015. "Settling the Red Hill: The Establishment of the Jewish Settlement of Ma'ale Adummim, 1968–1978." Paper presented at the European Association of Israel Studies (EAIS)—4th Annual Conference, University of Cagliari, September 6–8.

Aran, Gideon. 1991. "Jewish Zionist Fundamentalism: The Block of the Faithful in Israel (Gush Emunim)." In *Fundamentalism Observed*, edited by M. E. Marty and R. S. Appleby, 265–344. Chicago: University of Chicago Press.

Azoulay, Ariella, and Adi Ophir. 2013. *The One-State Condition: Occupation and Democracy in Israel/Palestine*. Stanford, CA: Stanford University Press.

Benvenisti, Eyal. 1990. *Legal Dualism: The Absorption of the Occupied Territories into Israel*. Boulder: Westview Press.

Benvenisti, Meron. 1976. *Jerusalem, the Torn City*. Minneapolis: University of Minnesota Press.

———. 1984. *The West Bank Data Project: A Survey of Israel's Policies*. AEI Studies. Washington, DC: American Enterprise Institute for Public Policy Research.

———. 1987. *1987 Report: Demographic, Economic, Legal, Social, and Political Developments in the West Bank*. Jerusalem: Jerusalem Post; Boulder: Westview Press.

———. 1995. *Intimate Enemies: Jews and Arabs in a Shared Land*. Berkeley: University of California Press.

Brenner, Neal, and Stuart Elden. 2009. "Henri Lefebvre on State, Space, Territory." *International Political Sociology* 3 (4): 353–377.

CBS. 2015. *Statistical Abstract of Israel 2015*. Jerusalem: Central Bureau of Statistics.

Dalsheim, Joyce. 2008. "Twice Removed: Mizrahi Settlers in Gush Katif." *Social Identities* 14 (5): 535–551.

Dalsheim, Joyce, and Assaf Harel. 2009. "Representing Settlers." *Review of Middle East Studies* 43 (2): 219–238.

Eldar, Akiva, and Idith Zertal. 2007. *Lords of the Land: The War Over Israel's Settlements in the Occupied Territories, 1967–2007*. New York: Nation Books.

Feige, Michael. 2009. *Settling in the Hearts: Jewish Fundamentalism in the Occupied Territories*. Detroit: Wayne State University Press.

Friedman, Robert I. 1992. *Zealots for Zion: Inside Israel's West Bank Settlement Movement*. New York: Random House.

Gillis, Rivi. 2009. *"Now They Are Also Settlers": The Ethnic Morphology of the Settlements*. Master's thesis, University of Tel Aviv. [Hebrew.]

Gordon, Neve. 2008. *Israel's Occupation*. Berkeley: University of California Press.

Gorenberg, Gershom. 2006. *The Accidental Empire: Israel and the Birth of Settlements, 1967–1977*. New York: Times Books.

Handel, Ariel. 2014. "Gated/Gating Community: The Settlement Complex in the West Bank." *Transactions of the Institute of British Geographers* 39 (4): 504–517.

Handel, Ariel, Galit Rand, and Marco Allegra. 2015. "Wine-Washing: Normalization and the Geopolitics of Terroir in the West Bank's Settlements." *Environment and Planning A* 47 (6): 1351–1367.

Harris, William W. 1980. *Taking Root: Israeli Settlement in the West Bank, the Golan, and Gaza-Sinai, 1967–1980*. Geographical Research Studies Series. Chichester, UK: Research Studies Press.

Hopp, Michael. 2002. "Attitudes of Settlers in the West Bank and Gaza about the Possibility of Leaving." Abridged report. Accessed January 25, 2016. peacenow.org.il/eng/sites/default/files /Settlers%20Survey%20Results.pps.

Human Rights Watch. 2016. "Occupation, Inc. How Settlement Businesses Contribute to Israel's Violations of Palestinian Rights." Accessed January 25, 2016. https://www.hrw.org/report /2016/01/19/occupation-inc/how-settlement-businesses-contribute-israels-violations -palestinian.

Isaac, Rael Jean. 1976. *Israel Divided: Idealogical Politics in the Jewish State*. Baltimore, MD: Johns Hopkins University Press.

Kimmerling, Baruch. 1989. *The Israeli State and Society: Boundaries and Frontiers*. SUNY Series in Israeli Studies. Albany: State University of New York Press.

LeBor, Adam. 2007. "Over the Line." *New York Times*, October 14. Accessed January 25, 2016. http://www.nytimes.com/2007/10/14/books/review/LeBor-t.html?_r=0.

Leon, Nissim. 2015. "Self-segregation of the Vanguard: Judea and Samaria in the Religious-Zionist Society." *Israel Affairs* 21 (3): 348–360.

Lustick, Ian. 1988. *For the Land and the Lord: Jewish Fundamentalism in Israel*. New York: Council on Foreign Relations.

Maggor, Erez. 2015. "State, Market and the Israeli Settlements: The Ministry of Housing and the Shift from Messianic Outposts to Urban Settlements in the Early 1980s." *Israeli Sociology* 16 (2): 140–167 [Hebrew].

Newman, David. 1981. "The Role of Gush Emunim and the Yishuv Kehillati in the West Bank 1974–1980." PhD diss., Durham University, Durham, UK.

———. 1984. "The Development of the Yishuv Kheillati in Judea and Samaria: Political Process and Settlment Form." *Tijdschrift voor economische en sociale geografie* 75 (2): 140–150.

———. 1985. *The Impact of Gush Emunim: Politics and Settlement in the West Bank.* London: Croom Helm.

Newman, David, and Tamar Hermann. 1992. "A Comparative-Study of Gush Emunim and Peace Now." *Middle Eastern Studies* 28 (3): 509–530.

Newman, David, and Juval Portugali. 1987. *Spatial Interaction between Israelis and Palestinians in the West Bank and the Gaza Strip.* New York: Ford Foundation.

Oz, Amos. 1983. *In the Land of Israel.* Translated by Maurie Goldberg-Bartura. London: Chatto and Windus. [Original edition, 1983.]

Parizot, Cédric, and Stéphanie Latte Abdallah. 2015. *Israelis and Palestinians in the Shadows of the Wall: Spaces of Separation and Occupation.* Farnham, UK: Ashgate Publishing.

Portugali, J. 1991. "Jewish Settlement in the Occupied Territories: Israel's Settlement Structure and the Palestinians." *Political Geography Quarterly* 10 (1): 26–53.

Ranta, Ronald. 2009. *The Wasted Decade: Israel's Policies towards the Occupied Territories 1967–1977.* PhD diss., University College London.

———. 2015. *Political Decision Making and Non-Decisions: The Case of Israel and the Occupied Territories.* Basingstoke, UK: Palgrave Macmillan.

Reichman, Shalom. 1986. "Policy Reduces the World to Essentials: A Reflection on the Jewish Settlement Process in the West Bank Since 1967." In *Planning in Turbulence*, edited by David Morley and Arie Shachar, 83–96. Jerusalem: Magnes Press.

Segev, Tom. 2006. "Bitter Prize: Israel and the Occupied Territories." *Foreign Affairs* 85 (3): 145–150.

Shafir, Gershon, and Yoav Peled. 2002. *Being Israeli: The Dynamics of Multiple Citizenship.* Cambridge: Cambridge University Press.

Shavit, Ari. 2013. *My Promised Land: The Triumph and Tragedy of Israel.* New York: Spiegel and Grau.

Sivan, Emmanuel. 1995. "The Enclave Culture." In *Fundamentalisms Comprehended*, edited by M. E. Marty and E. S. Appleby, 11–68. Chicago: University of Chicago Press.

Sprinzak, Ehud. 1991. *The Ascendance of Israel's Radical Right.* New York: Oxford University Press.

Taub, Gadi. 2010. *The Settlers and the Struggle over the Meaning of Zionism.* New Haven: Yale University Press.

Weisburd, David. 1989. *Jewish Settler Violence: Deviance as Social Reaction.* University Park: Pennsylvania State University Press.

Weiss, Hadas. 2009. "Settling in the Hearts: Jewish Fundamentalism in the Occupied Territories by Michael Feige." *Cultural Anthropology* 24 (4): 755–757.

———. 2011. "On Value and Values in a West Bank Settlement." *American Ethnologist* 38 (1): 36–46.

Weizman, Eyal. 2007. *Hollow Land: Israel's Architecture of Occupation.* London: Verso.

PART I

ACROSS THE GREEN LINE: SUBURBANIZATION, PRIVATIZATION, AND THE SETTLEMENTS

1 The Settlements and the Relationship between Privatization and the Occupation

Danny Gutwein

THE SETTLEMENTS ARE the meeting point and the culmination of two major processes that have shaped the character of Israeli society in the past four decades: neoliberal privatization and the perpetuation of the occupation. The underlying interdependence of privatization and occupation has comprised the political logic of the Israeli Right and informed its hegemony. The gradual liquidation of the Israeli welfare state and the commodification of its services have expanded economic inequality in Israel and exacerbated its damaging social ramifications that have disproportionately affected Israel's lower classes. These same lower classes served as the political power base of Israel's political Right. In order to counterbalance the detrimental effects of privatization and protect its constituents, the Right has developed a series of compensatory mechanisms that supplied partial substitutes to the commodified services that they could not afford. One of these compensatory mechanisms has been the settlements project in the Occupied Territories.

As a compensatory mechanism, the settlements worked to intensify the lower classes' bonds with the political Right, alienated them from the Left—that opposed the settlements—and created the social and political basis for the perpetuation of the Occupation. The Right's rhetoric, however, has constantly blurred the causal relation between occupation and privatization by separating between politics and society. This false separation, typical to neoliberal reasoning, became an essential part of the power relations that guaranteed the persistent hegemony of the Right.

Exposing the causal relation between privatization and the Occupation—between the systematic dismantling of the welfare state and the continuous growth of the settlements as a compensatory mechanism—should have been at the forefront of the Israeli Left's political struggle against the rising hegemony of the Right. However, despite its ongoing and growing failure to enlist the support of the lower classes in its peace policy, the Left—which represents mainly the established middle classes—not only abstained from exposing the relationship between privatization and the Occupation, but it further obscured it by advancing an opposing casual explanation: it is the Occupation and particularly the growing public investment in the settlements, the Left maintained that are responsible for Israel's increasing economic and social inequalities; the obvious conclusion that the Left inferred from this inversion was that the struggle for social justice should be subjected to the struggle for peace. By this inversion, the Left has duplicated the Right's false separation between politics and society and used it to justify and advance its own neoliberal agenda.

The Left has repeatedly argued that the lower classes' support for the Right, despite its avowed neoliberal policies that contradict their interests, is a result of irrational ethnoreligious Jewish sentiment that informs their support of the Occupation and the settlements. It is this irrationality on the part of the lower classes, the Left has further maintained, that renders any attempt to fight it practically impossible. The Left has adopted, then, an idealistic and patronizing interpretation that denies the economic and social basis of the Right's hegemony, the disproving of which is a precondition for any political struggle against the Occupation. It appears that more than positing the Occupation as a source of the social gaps in Israel, the Left has used the Occupation as an excuse for affirming the privatization regime and the economic inequality it has advanced, which, in fact, have reproduced the necessary prerequisite for the Right's hegemony and the continuation of the Occupation. The Left's paradoxical support of the neoliberal power structure that guarantees the consolidation and perpetuation of the Right's hegemony is inherent in the no less shortsighted support of the established middle classes—the Left's political base—of the privatization policy, which has emerged as a decisive factor in the perpetuation of the Occupation (Gutwein A).

This chapter discusses the role of the settlements as the culmination of the Israeli privatization regime and as a meeting place of the dismantling of Israel's universal welfare state and the enduring persistence of the Occupation. It suggests a socioeconomic perspective that considers the interests of the lower and middle classes in the context of ongoing privatization and Occupation. Of course, the socioeconomic analysis proposed here highlights only a part of the complex factors that are responsible for the persistence of the Occupation. Yet its conspicuous absence from both academic and public discourse—as a reflection of the neoliberal hegemony—adversely hinders the understanding of the interrelationship between the settlements and the Occupation on the one hand, and the continued privatization and growing inequality within Israeli society on the other, not to mention the ability to challenge it.

On the False Separation between Occupation and Privatization

The separation between politics and society that informs the Left's attitude toward the settlements reflects the adoption of neoliberal ideology and the erosion of social responsibility on the part of its mainly established middle-class supporters following the loss of power to the Right in 1977. The class logic that informed this separation had most glaringly been expressed in the slogan Peace Now, which became the ethos of the Israeli Left in the 1980s. The moral devotion that the Peace Now ethos instilled in the struggle against the settlements only illuminated the middle classes' indifference to the growing social and economic inequality in Israel and to the social hardships experienced by Israel's lower classes. Thus, the Peace Now ethos exposed the contradiction between the pious rhetoric of the Left and the class-based interests of its voters. The Peace Now ethos has further unveiled the cultural contempt of the old hegemony, mainly of the labor movement, to the coalition of the "others," comprised mainly of the lower classes—either the Mizrahi (Oriental) Jews or the ultraorthodox—who have kept the Right in power since 1977. More than anything, the Peace Now ethos disclosed the vain frustration of the old establishment: as they lost their control over Israeli politics, they were determined to preserve their privileged status through an indirect strategy, that of circumventing politics. This strategy would gradually lead the Left to adopt a privatization policy of its own, one which transferred power from politics and the state to the market and the professional establishments, arenas where the middle classes still retained their power.

The other slogan of the Left—"money for the slums, not for the settlements"—ostensibly expresses an awareness of the causal relation between economic inequality and the perpetuation of the Occupation. But this slogan co-opts the politics-society relationship only to negate it, all the while revealing the class-based interests that reproduce and sustain the separation between the two. Under the guise of concern for the poor, by this slogan, the Left suggested a zero-sum game paradigm, which makes investment of money in poor neighborhoods conditional on the cessation of its flow to settlements, thus adopting the neoliberal logic that further legitimizes economic inequality and normalizes the settlements.

The Left's neoliberal logic of "Occupation first" is the underlying assumption of Adi Ophir's introduction to the edited collection of essays, *Real-Time: The Al-Aqsa Intifada and the Israeli Left* (2001). According to Ophir, the Occupation is "the starting point, the mold of power and social relations" in Israel (11), and its termination serves as the prerequisite for both peace and social justice. Thus, the Left's support for any social issue, just and worthy as it is, like opposing privatization or the raising of the minimum wage, must be "conditional upon its contribution to the struggle against the continuation of the Occupation" (18). It seems, however, that the consecutive electoral failures of the Left suggest an alternative logic and diametrically opposite conclusion: in order to put an end to the Occupation, the social relations upon which it is based first need to be abolished; in other words, postponing the struggle against economic and social inequality affirms the very power relations that guarantee the continuation of the Occupation.

The emphasis the Left placed on the Occupation and settlements, as the main sources of the economic hardships of the lower classes, obscured the crucial role played by neoliberalism in the rise of inequality and poverty. This obfuscation, which erased the dismantling of the welfare state from the Israeli political discourse, allowed the middle classes to set the conscious conditions necessary for fostering the privatization process. The separation between Occupation and privatization blurred the fact that these two policies were merely two sides of the same coin. As a result, this separation further conceals the only real alternative to both: a policy that simultaneously resists the liquidation of the welfare state and struggles against settlements. Only a policy that would seek to provide social justice and invest in the poor neighborhoods through a universal welfare state would constitute the necessary sociopolitical preconditions for terminating the Occupation by eliminating the dependence of the lower classes—the main reservoir of right-wing supporters—on the compensatory mechanism provided through the settlements.

The Compensatory Mechanism of the Settlements

Together, the settlement project and the growing economic inequality in Israel have served as complimentary foundations of the hegemony of the Right. Ever since its ascent to power in 1977, the Right has used Thatcher-like policies such as privatization and commodification of social services in order to liquidate the universal welfare state that used to be one of the main sources of power of the Left. Naturally, this policy—which turned social services from civic right into market commodities—initially affected mainly Israel's lower classes. Accordingly, in order to offset the losses it inflicted on its voters, the Right constituted a series of compensatory mechanisms, the most common of which were the sectors. The sectors are hybrid organizations that developed since the mid-1980s, combining political parties with nongovernmental organization–based service-supply systems, financed mainly by the government as well as by private donors. Employing identity politics, the sectors use their electoral power to secure for its supporters palliatives to the social services that they could not afford to acquire in the private market on an individual basis, as their purchasing power continued to dwindle. To secure their necessity, these sectoral organizations supported the dismantling of the welfare state that further expanded the vacuum that was replaced by privatized services and sectoral substitutes. This strategy stimulated the political institutionalization of the sectors, a process that has turned the Right into a coalition of rival sectoral interest groups.

The settlement project best exemplifies the essential interrelationship between privatization, sectoralization, and Occupation: while the universal welfare state was liquidated in Israel proper, an alternative sectoral welfare state was constructed in the Occupied Territories. The enormous budgets and benefits that the settlement project offers in housing, education, municipal services, taxation, infrastructure, and employment have become a mechanism that compensates the lower classes for the damages inflicted upon them by the dismantling of the welfare state and the privatization of the social services in sovereign Israel. These material benefits spurred most of the migration to the settlements: when the Left lost power in 1977, there were about 5,000 settlers (Jerusalem not included); a decade later, in 1986, their number had risen roughly to about 50,000; today, it has reached about 500,000. The settlements offered the lower classes symbolic capital as well: inclusion into the new Israeli elite of the settlers. The lower classes' political support of the Right, and their ideological identification with the vision of "Greater Israel" blurred the economic and social motives for their migration into the settlements. The importance of the opportunities for social and economic mobility that the settlement project opened up for the lower classes—to those who emigrated to the settlements, as well as for those who remained in Israel and have not yet taken advantage of them—increased as the ongoing privatization of the welfare state further exacerbated the growing social and economic inequality in Israel. These opportunities contributed to the eradication of the 1967 border between Israel and the Occupied Palestinian Territories more than the political and religious ideologies of Greater Israel. Thus, it was economic logic rather than ideological visions that shaped the lower classes' hawkish views. Given the economic suffering, which were created by the privatization regime, and considering their deteriorating situation, the lower classes' support of the Right—in contrast to the repeated fashionable complaints of the Left regarding their "False consciousness"—should be viewed as a completely "rational" decision. With the liquidation of the welfare state in sovereign Israel, the lower classes viewed the investment in settlements as an investment in them and their future. As such, they rejected as false the opposition between the slums and the settlements offered by the Left. The compensatory mechanism of the settlements mitigated the detrimental effects of the cutbacks in social services and their commodification, thereby facilitating the liquidation of the Israeli welfare state and intensifying the advancement of privatization, as well as bolstering the lower classes' dependence on, and support of, the Right. Thus, just as the Occupation created the settlements, privatization created the settlers.

The compensatory mechanism of the settlements has influenced the ideologies of both the lower and middle classes. Given the close relations between social status and voting patterns in Israel, the lower classes considered the Left's attacks on the settlements as driven by social more than by political motives. They deemed these attacks to be an attempt on the part of the middle classes to obstruct the opportunities that the compensation mechanism of the settlements provided them to cope with the growing inequality and to improve their economic and social status. At the same time, identifying the settlements with state intervention helped the Lefts' middle-class supporters to renounce the social-democrat commitment to a universal welfare state and gave them a "moral" excuse to abandon all values of social solidarity and turn to Thacherite neoliberalism. The privatization of the welfare state turned the settlements into the "promised land" of the lower classes and, as the border line between Israel and the Occupied territories gradually lost its political significance, privatization imparted to it a new social meaning.

The Janus face of the Occupation and the settlements, as a catalyst of privatization and as a compensatory mechanism for the lower classes from the repercussions of the liquidation of the welfare state, was also revealed in the labor market. The Occupation exposed Israel's lower classes to an uneven competition with Palestinian workers from the Occupied Territories, whose advantage grew as they adapted to the particular demands of the Israeli labor market, all the while willing to accept lower wages than those paid to the Israeli worker. This competition was later used as a whip by which to advance the privatization of the labor market and to break up organized labor in Israel. Under the privatization regime, the Occupation not only accelerated the breakup of organized labor, but moreover it has gradually become a false alternative to unionism as defense for low-wage workers. The frequent border closures, which prevented Palestinians from regular attendance in their workplaces, reduced their profitability, on one hand, and the fears of Jewish employers to hire Palestinian workers, on the other hand, constantly increased the competitive edge of Jewish workers. The Occupation therefore contributed to transforming the Jewishness of the lower classes from a religious or national identity into a political and economic asset that granted the Jewish worker a way to counteract the structural advantage of the Palestinian worker. Maintaining this political advantage, which compensated for the decreasing of the economic competiveness of the Jewish worker, was conditioned on the continuation of the Occupation, and, thus, perpetuated the lower classes' support for the Right. Conversely, the Left championed the "New Middle East," as a sort of "privatized peace," with abundant cheap labor that would have weakened this political competitive advantage, and consequently increased the lower classes' aversion to peace and their alienation from the Left. The alternative to this vicious circle lies in encouraging organized labor of Israeli and Palestinian workers, thus undermining the role of the Occupation as a compensatory mechanism in the labor market. Likewise, decommodification of education in the framework of a renewed welfare state may raise the employment abilities of the lower classes. These alternatives, however, contradict the adherence of the Left middle-class supporters' to privatization of both the labor market and the education system.

The interrelationship among the Occupation, privatization, the labor market, and Jewishness was a key factor in the rise of Shas, a sectoral party that appealed mainly to the Mizrahi religious lower classes. The widespread support Shas received in the ballots cannot be explained—as most commentators agree—primarily by the limited social services it supplies. The position of its supporters in the labor market, and mainly with respect to competition with the cheap labor of Palestinians and foreign workers, points to another facet of this support: Shas identified the material advantage that Jewishness could provide the lower classes in an economy whose rules are delineated by the interplay between privatization and the Occupation. Accordingly, it rendered Jewishness, under the guise of Mizrahi ultraorthodoxy, into symbolic capital, and translated this sectoral trademark into political power. Shas grew out of the interaction between the compensatory mechanisms of the settlements and sectoralization, which increasingly merged into one another and further advanced the liquidation of the welfare state and the privatization of its services. The growing dependence of Shas's supporters on the compensatory mechanism of the settlements gradually transformed its ideology and theology, which became increasingly hawkish. This hawkish turn was most evident in Shas's attitude to the Occupation. In the 1990s Shas was considered to be a dovish party; in 1992 its spiritual leader, Rabbi Ovadia Yosef, issued a ruling that granted religious sanction to Israeli withdrawal from regions of the Holy Land—namely, the occupied territories—as part of a peace treaty with the Palestinians. But a decade later, in 2003, he cancelled this decree, arguing that the agreements with the Palestinian Authority did not achieve real peace. There may, however, be another, more likely economic reason for this significant change of mind. In 2003 the settlements had attracted many of Shas's lower-class supporters; accordingly, to retain their loyalty, Rabbi Yosef had to adjust his theology to the economic interests of his supporters.[1]

On the "Privatized Peace" of the Left

The Left actively participated in establishing the privatization regime, which, contrary to its pious peace rhetoric, is responsible for creating the social and political conditions for the continued Occupation. When it became clear to the middle-class voters of the Left that the lower classes' support of the Right secured its power and hegemony for the foreseeable future, they adopted privatization as a strategy of class reproduction that would allow them to preserve their class privileges by circumventing politics. Privatization transferred economic and social control from the state to the market and the professional establishments, in which the middle classes retained their hegemony. Thus, the Israeli middle classes endorsed what David Harvey describes in his classic *A Brief History of Neoliberalism* as a redefinition of the concept of "the state" by instigating "a radical reconfiguration of state institutions and practices" that characterizes all neoliberal regimes (2005, 64-86). The class interests of its voters had, thus, driven the Left to endorse the logic of privatization, which, in clear contradiction with its avowed peace policy, reinforced Occupation by encouraging the compensatory mechanism of the settlements. Since the 1980s, the nexus of privatization and the Occupation became the platform for establishing the regime of "governments of national unity." Thus for three decades this nexus repeatedly revealed itself in the policies of both the Right and the Left governments.

The Left advanced the peace process at the same time it deepened the Occupation; and thus the fictitious separation between politics and society was reproduced in the unification of "peace" and "occupation." In this way, the Left allowed the middle classes to reap the profits of peace without compromising the compensatory mechanism of the settlements whose importance continued to grow as the intensification of neoliberalism and privatization continued to expand social and economic inequality. Former Prime Ministers Yitzhak Rabin and Ehud Barak acknowledged the relationship between the widening economic gap and the growing support for the Right. But, as representatives of the middle classes, Rabin and Barak did not curb the privatization process; rather, they intensified it. Rabin's government signed the Oslo agreement in order to put an end to the Occupation, but during his premiership, the number of settlements continued to grow. This contradiction can be explained by another aspect of the agenda of Rabin's government: the deepening privatization of state-owned corporations and social services, in particular, education and health, and the dissolution of organized labor. Thus, with the support of Rabin, the power base of the Histadrut—Israel's trade union federation—was fundamentally undermined. The weakening of organized labor facilitated the privatization of the labor market, which increased the competitive edge of the unorganized Palestinian and foreign workers, thereby strengthening the role of the Occupation as an alternative to unionism in defending low-wage Jewish labor. Thus, the more the left advanced privatization that hurt the lower classes—whose support in its "peace policy" the Left tried in vain to acquire—the larger a role the compensatory mechanism of the settlements and of the Occupation played. This paradoxical policy of the Left explains a dichotomy that informed the Oslo agreement. Lacking sufficient public and electoral support for its peace policy, the Left created an equation, according to which withdrawal from some of the territories allowed for the continued direct or indirect occupation of other parts of the occupied West Bank—a formula that the Right gradually, and in different ways, adopted.

Privatization is, therefore, the pattern of social relations that sustains the Occupation. The "privatized peace" of the Left has both deepened economic inequality, to the short-term economic benefit of the middle classes, and strengthened the Occupation as a compensatory system for the lower classes. The mutual support of privatization on the part of both the Left and the Right was reproduced as a merger of peace and the Occupation that culminated in the Left's estrangement from the "two states solution." Accordingly, it seems that the failure of the Israeli Left in the past four decades originated in the inherent contradiction between its professed peace discourse and its neoliberal practices. Thus, it is the support of intensifying privatization on the part of the middle classes, to the detriment of the lower classes, that gradually turned the Left into a partner in perpetuating the Occupation. The Left has transformed peace from a political program to a cultural identity and a ritual of purification that ratifies both privatization and the Occupation. With the rejection of the struggle for social and economic justice, the Left has ceased serving as a viable alternative to the Right. Gradually, however, privatization has also undermined the economic security of large segments within the middle classes. As a result, the Left has ceased to represent an attractive platform for representing the interests of the eroded middle classes as well, and has therefore increasingly lost its appeal to them. These déclassé groups have exchanged "the privatized peace" for "a politics of hatred" that, as a sectoral identity, was assimilated in the Right and intensified the power structure that perpetuated its hegemony.

The Loyalty Regime: A New Compensatory Mechanism

Since 2009, under Benjamin Nentanyahu's three consecutive governments, the compensatory mechanism of the settlements has gradually eroded. At the same time, the privatization regime has further undermined the social and economic security of a growing number of Israelis and amalgamated the lower and lower-middle classes into the Israeli "precarious class," or the Precariat (Standing 2011). The Precariat forms a large segment of the Right's voters. To ensure its continuous support, the Right has developed a new compensatory mechanism: "the Loyalty Regime," which offers symbolic capital and economic benefits to the Precariat supporters of the Right (Gutwein B).

The erosion of the compensatory mechanism of the settlements is most evident in the rise of housing prices that significantly weaken the main incentive for the ongoing emigration to the Occupied Territories. In 2014, the average price of a four-bedroom apartment in the settlements reached 90 percent of the price of a similar apartment in Israel proper. Likewise, the gap between Israel and the settlements in education and municipal budgeting has also continuously narrowed. This erosion was a part of a general crisis of the sectors-system that—as its critics repeatedly warned—failed to adequately address the growing inequality, poverty and social insecurity caused by the dismantling of the welfare state. The simultaneous decline of the sector-system and the rise of the Precariat forced the Right to develop an alternative compensatory mechanism, that of the Loyalty Regime.

The origins of the Loyalty Regime can be traced back to a series of anti-democratic bills directed against Israeli-Arab citizens and the Left that were proposed in the eighteenth Knesset (2009–2012). These bills—known as the "Loyalty-Citizenship Laws"—suggested preference in government employment and subsidies in higher education to those—mainly Jews—who served in the army or in national service. Other bills subordinate democratic principles—namely, equality of the Arab citizens—to Israel's role as a Jewish state. While these bills did not become laws, they incited public debate that doubted the legal equality of the Arab citizens and subjected it to their "loyalty." The assault of the Loyalty-Citizenship Laws on the Left was more successful. Thus, the "Boycott Law" enables one to sue anyone who calls for economic, cultural, or academic boycott of Israel. The "Dismissal Law" enables the dismissal of serving MKs—namely, Arabs—who demonstrate support for the armed struggle against Israel, with a majority of ninety members of Knesset. In addition, the "NGO Law" requires NGOs—namely, left-leaning human rights organizations—that receive over 50 percent of their funding from foreign governments or organizations to openly declare this fact on all of their advertising, letters, and reports.

The public debate on the Loyalty-Citizenship Laws focuses on patriotism and democracy and thus disguises their main impact: to morally and politically prepare the ground for a new compensatory mechanism. The Loyalty-Citizenship Laws reverse Israel's liberal legislation of the 1990s and legitimize the use of Jewishness as a criterion to discriminate against the Arabs and prefer Jews in labor, housing, education and culture. Moreover, they legitimize the restriction of the political activity of the Left and the Arabs. Thus, the Loyalty-Citizenship Laws represent a promise to compensate the Jewish Precariat for the damages it suffered from the privatization regime. Likewise, the restrictions put upon human-rights oriented NGOs that are commonly associated with the Left's "old elites" turned the support for the Right into a means for improving the social status of the Jewish Precariat.

The anti-democratic notions of the Loyalty-Citizenship debate have turned the paradox of "conditioned equality" into the logic of the Israeli Right in the post-sectorial era and delineated the outlines of the Loyalty Regime. It has turned the Right into a new umbrella sector that replaces the old sectors and amalgamates all the components of the Jewish Precariat. The old sectors justified their compensation mechanisms by their ostensibly special needs; in contrast, the legitimization of the compensatory mechanism of the Loyalty Regime is the support of the Right and in practice the Likud.

An example of the *modus operandi* of the compensatory mechanism of the Loyalty Regime can be found in the words of MK Miki Zohar, the Likud's coalition whip of the Knesset finance committee, who bluntly demanded that inhabitants of periphery townships would enjoy tax cuts because they voted Likud. Likewise,

Minister of Culture Miri Regev declared that patriotism as well as performing in the periphery and the settlements would become criteria for transferring subsidies to cultural institutions. Likud Mayor of Dimonna, Benny Bitton, suggested an exact explanation to the compensatory mechanism of the Loyalty Regime. He rejected the accepted interpretation that the massive support the Likud enjoyed in the Negev in 2015 elections was due to religious or ethnic motivations, and argued instead that it represented a "gratitude vote."

The logic of the "gratitude vote" is indeed that of the Loyalty Regime: under privatization, in the absence of guaranteed universal social rights, the main venue for the Precariat to achieve these rights is through loyalty to the government as proved primarily in supporting the ruling party in the ballot box. The results of 2015 general elections demonstrate that the Israeli Precariat has adopted this logic: while the three upper income deciles voted for the Left, the lower deciles preferred the Right.

The Pricariat's preference for the Right is a well-informed one: when both the Israeli Left and the Right support neoliberalism, the compensatory mechanisms are the main socioeconomic difference that distinguishes between them. The Right suggests neoliberalism alleviated by the compensatory mechanism of the sectors, settlements and loyalty; the Left adopts neoliberalism and supports the dismantling of the welfare state, but it does not suggest any compensatory mechanism to mitigate the negative effects of the privatization of its services. On the contrary, what characterizes the Left is its principled opposition to the above-mentioned compensatory mechanism suggested by the Right, which accordingly wins the support of the Precariat.

The settlers through their political representatives—mainly the HaBayt HaYehudy party—have played a leading role in establishing the Loyalty Regime as part of their support of privatization and its ensuing compensatory mechanisms. In the post-sectorial era, the interrelationship between the settlers and neoliberalism has changed. Initially, Israeli neoliberalism used the settlements as a scaffold for privatization; now, the settlers are the most dedicated agents of neoliberalism, as they advance privatization in order to preserve the diminishing compensatory mechanism of the settlements. It is in this framework that the settlers support the Loyalty Regime: it guarantees the support of the Israeli Precariat for the continued dismantling of the remains of the welfare state, thus preserving, at least in part, the role of the settlements as a compensatory mechanism.

British Imperialism, Israeli Occupation, and the Welfare State

The interrelationship among the Occupation, privatization, and the role played by the settlements as a compensatory mechanism reconstructs the typical modus operandi of imperialism. Thus, for example, British imperialism served to guarantee the interests and hegemony of the landed aristocracy and financial bourgeoisie. By making the empire into a protected market for British goods, they turned it into a compensatory mechanism for the industrial bourgeoisie who faced no competition and could reduce its investment and for the working class whose jobs were protected (Cain and Hopkins 1993, 316–350, De Cecco 1974, 22–38). Advocates of decolonization concluded from this analysis that the struggle for British withdrawal from the empire should focus not only on its political aspects, that is to say, putting an end to the ongoing colonial rule, but on its economic and social aspects as well, namely, on its role as a compensatory mechanism for different classes in Britain. Indeed, the struggles in Britain for the liquidation of the empire—especially, in Ireland at the beginning of the twentieth century and in India in the second half—were accompanied by the establishment of the British welfare state as an alternative to the compensatory mechanism of imperialism.

The Israeli Left rejected the British, and in fact the European experience of decolonization, which regarded the establishment of the welfare state as a central means for dissolving the compensatory mechanism of imperialism and for enlisting political support in the struggle for liquidating the colonial empires. On the contrary, the more it endorsed neoliberalism, the more the Left directed its criticism at the Israeli welfare state, portraying it as an essential part of the oppressive mechanism of the state—now controlled by the Right—while depicting the market and privatization as liberating factors. Thus, despite its open and firm opposition to the Occupation, in practice, the Left has supported the very economic and social basis that determines its ongoing expansion and resilience. This paradox is evident mainly among those elements on the Left, who have adopted identity politics and cultural theories of postcolonialism but rejected the economic and social policies of decolonization.

The rejection of the historical experience of decolonization goes hand in hand with the interests of the Left's middle classes in furthering the policies of privatization, which, in turn, made the Left a partner to the perpetuation of the Occupation. The solution to this paradox lies precisely in adopting the experience of decolonization and mainly the liquidation of those economic and social conditions that comprise the basis of the Occupation. Applying the experience of decolonization means a radical change in the priorities of the Left, principally by adopting a policy of "welfare in exchange for territories": providing social security to the lower and middle classes through distributive justice institutionalized in the framework of a universal welfare state that will bridge the social and economic gaps. Such a welfare state would break the vicious circle of privatization, Occupation, and support for the Right, as well as create the political conditions for the struggle for a likely withdrawal from the territories and the end of the Occupation.

Note

1. For an empirical demonstration of this claim see Cahaner's work on the ultraorthodox settlers (Cahaner, chapter 7).

References

Cain, Peter J., and A. G. Hopkins. 1993. *British Imperialism: Innovation and Expansion, 1688–1914.* London: Addison-Wesley Longman.

De Cecco, Macello. 1974. *Money and Empire: The International Gold Standard, 1890–1914.* Totowa, NJ: Blackwell.

Gutwein, Danny. A. "Israel's Socioeconomic Debate: A New Perspective." In *Handbook of Israel: Major Debates,* edited by Eliezer Ben-Rafael, Julius H. Schoeps, Yitzhak Sternberg, and Olaf Glöckner. Berlin: De Gruyter. Forthcoming.

Gutwein, Danny. B. "Intensifing the Settlements and Undermining Democracy: Changes in the Israeli Privatization Regime, 2005–2015." *Theory and Criticism.* Forthcoming.

Harvey, David. 2005. *A Brief History of Neoliberalism.* Oxford: Oxford University Press.

Ophir, Adi. 2001. *Real-Time: The Al-Aqsa Intifada and the Israeli Left.* Jerusalem: Keter publishing. [Hebrew.]

Standing, Guy. 2011. *The Precariat: The New Dangerous Class.* London and New York: Bloomsbury Academics.

2 Settlement as Suburbanization
The Banality of Colonization

David Newman

THIS CHAPTER ANALYSES the planning dynamics of the West Bank settlement network since its inception almost fifty years ago. In particular it concentrates on what has been described elsewhere as the process of suburban colonization (Newman 1996, 2005, 2006). In particular, the chapter will show how even the success of Gush Emunim and the settlers' movement resulted from the ability of settler leaders to adapt to (and strategically exploit) the process of rurbanization and suburbanization that the Israeli society was undergoing at the time. As such, the settlement process is seen as constituting a colonization banality, through which political and ideological objectives have been implemented by latching on to the banal, and often bureaucratic, procedures of the national planning process as a means through which settlements are established in the first place and become part of the public and municipal networks that enable both the growth and the functioning of these communities over time. The chapter focuses on the settlement network, excluding East Jerusalem, comprising, as of 2015, almost four hundred thousand residents of these communities, enjoying the same system and network of public services as experienced by all residents of Israel inside the Green Line. This overview essay of the settlement network seeks to explain the dynamics behind the establishment and functioning of these communities over time and the extent to which they constitute a highly organized system, vastly different in character to the image often displayed of small hilltop communities, populated only by groups of settlers imbued with a radical ideology.

The chapter addresses and revisits the planning mechanisms and agencies through which this network came into being and underwent expansion and consolidation over a period of forty years. The central argument is that even the paradigmatic, ideological settlers, those who inspired the Gush Emunim movement and their settlement organization, Amana (which remains a legal development agency until today), were successful because they strategically positioned themselves in relation to the trends of suburbanization. The earliest settler leaders were always conscious of the fact that in order to succeed, they had to seek a balance between their ideological and political objectives on the one hand, while working with the state system of planning and development on the other (Newman 1986). To this end, they successfully latched on to the processes of suburbanization that were beginning to emerge in Israel during the 1970s and 1980s, understanding that the West Bank was in a prime geographic location, in relatively close proximity to the major metropolitan centers of both Tel Aviv and Jerusalem, and that the demands of the changing employment market could be put to use in such a way as to encourage many potential settlers to come and reside in these new exurban communities, even if they were not part of the ideological hard core of Gush Emunim national religious activists.

It is important to note at the outset that the planning agencies were by no means the sole facilitator of settlements—at the end of the day, colonization remains a political process aimed at expanding Jewish control over a region that, the settlers desire, should eventually be annexed to the State of Israel rather than ceded as part of any peace agreement. But the vast literature of the past forty years has tended to focus on the ideological and the political, while largely ignoring the technical and planning mechanisms that enabled the settlements to be physically constructed and which provided the necessary functional frameworks through which they could be administered. It is the purpose of this chapter to focus on these agencies as means of supplementing much of the political analysis that appears in previous research.

By latching on to the changing socioeconomic trends in Israeli society and the progressive shift in planning paradigms, which rejected the previous models of rigid centralized planning and the binary distinction between urban and rural in favor of a functional continuum that filled the gaps in between, Gush Emunim were therefore able to attract many other potential settlers who, while less turned on by a religious and ideological perspective, were nevertheless prepared to settle beyond the Green Line if it was seen also to be advantageous to them in economic and quality of life terms.

This chapter also shows that the establishment of a strong municipal hierarchy, parallel to the system of regional and local councils that operate inside Israel proper, enabled the settlement system to become an integral part of the national system of local government, even if normal civilian law does not formally apply to the West Bank, which, with the exception of East Jerusalem, has never been formally annexed by the State of Israel. The heads of the local and regional councils are no different in terms of their functions, salaries, access to government resources (especially the Ministry of Interior, which is responsible for local government) than any other municipal authority in the country. But, unlike the rest of the country, they are also represented by a nonformal political lobby, in the shape of the Settlement Council for Judea and Samaria, continuing their dual strategy of formal co-optation on the one hand, along with extragovernmental political lobbying on the other.

Revisiting the colonization through suburbanization thesis (which first emerged during the 1980s in the studies by Portugali and Newman 1986, and Reichmann 1986) with a perspective of forty years, a time period within which there are three generations of settler families, many of whom have lived in the Occupied Territories for their entire lives, allows us to deconstruct a series of myths that populate the discourse on settlements—some of which have also been used by the settler movement to portray the growth and expansion of settlements as part and parcel of an altruistic and ideological project. These include:

- The notion of *pioneering* and the idea that West Bank settlement is the true continuer of the earliest pioneering of the Zionist movement fifty years earlier.
- National planning aimed at widespread *population dispersal* and the idea that settling the West Bank contributes to the decentralization of the country's population away from the densely populated metropolitan center of the country.
- The *political argument* that the West Bank settlements have been a political and ideological movement that has constantly challenged government and has had to work beyond the frameworks of governmental and municipal support.
- The myth of *settlement freezing* and the idea that some Israeli governments have frozen all new settlement expansion as part of peace negotiations when in fact the partial slowdown in settlement expansion (when that has happened) has resulted in settlement consolidation and strengthening.
- The often-heard argument that all of the settlers who came for economic, rather than ideological, reasons could be *relocated back into Israel* as part of a peace agreement and would therefore be prepared to experience settlement evacuation for appropriate compensation, while enabling the ideologically motivated to remain in situ.

This chapter will argue that much of the settlement process can be understood through an analysis of the banality of colonization, through which the political settlement project has been translated into the terminology of house prices, employment, and mortgages on the one hand, and municipal and local government services on the other. This played a major factor in attracting tens of thousands of settlers to the West Bank, including many people who, while not ideologically opposed to settling beyond the Green Line, would not necessarily have moved to isolated, remote locations in the interior of the region. The geographic proximity factor, which explains the process of suburbanization, is the main reason why over 60 percent of the settlers residing outside East Jerusalem live in relatively close proximity to the Green Line, in concentrated settlement clusters. It is these concentrated "clusters" that have become the focus for much of the border negotiation discourse that attempts to redraw the boundary as part of a future peace agreement, taking into account potential land swaps between Israel and a future Palestinian state. During this period, transportation infrastructure has undergone significant improvement, thus bringing even larger areas of the West Bank into closer proximity to the central metropolitan region (proximity being measured by time and cost of access, which erodes the obstacles of physical distance), enabling the suburbanization process to extend over a greater geographical area.

The Geographical Factor in Settlement: Location, Location, Location

Since the onset of the West Bank settlement project, and especially through the first two decades, the settlement leaders and ideologues have attempted to portray their actions as constituting the "true" continuation of the Zionist settlement activities of the early part of the twentieth century. During this period, many remote rural communities were established throughout the area of mandate in Palestine as a means of gaining control of the land.

The early kibbutzim and moshavim served a double purpose. On the one hand they were part of the socialist and cooperative Zionist experiment of creating communal communities that experienced a "return to the land" based on agricultural self-productive labor. But equally their dispersed locations were aimed at expanding the territorial control on behalf of the Zionist project, later to be transformed into an independent state. The ideological hegemony of the rural cooperative settlements extended through to the post-State period for the first two to three decades of statehood. Despite the fact that the rural agricultural cooperatives never contained more than 5–6 percent of the total population at its peak, this was in sharp contrast with the political power enjoyed by this community within the leadership of the Zionist community and its governmental frameworks, especially through the hegemony of the Labor-Mapai political elites.

The settler movement always portrayed itself as the continuer of the pre-State pioneering activities around which there was, at the time, consensus. It was important for them to be seen as constituting part of the Zionist enterprise, an enterprise that, Gush Emunim argued, was now bereft of idealism and the torch of which would now be taken up by the ideologically motivated generation of national religious settlers in the West Bank. Thus, despite the fact that the West Bank, especially those areas settled by Gush Emunim (as contrasted with the unsuccessful attempt to settle the Jordan Valley with traditional rural agricultural cooperatives within the framework of the Allon Plan), was located in the geographical center of Israel/Palestine and that roads and technology enabled ease of access and communication, the settlers always portrayed the region as remote, isolated, and "unsettled" (by Jews) and themselves as the modern day pioneers who were taking up the challenge of the pre-State settler pioneers.

The long-term success of establishing new settlement networks is dependent on their locations relative to employment opportunities, accessibility, and the price of land. The use of the suburbanization model to attract new and potential settlers to the settlements, using slogans such as "five minutes from Kfar Sava" expressed the geographical reality whereby the settlements were located within the exurban belt of the two major metropolitan centers of Israel: Tel Aviv and Jerusalem. The West Bank was not a remote isolated region, such as the Galilee or the Negev of the 1920s and 1930s and, as such, settlers could relocate their place of residence from a crowded expensive three room apartment in Kfar Sava to a spacious detached housing unit in one of the new settlements, without having to worry about alternative employment opportunities. The notion of commuting communities had, until the 1970s, been perceived as anti-ideological within the hegemonic Zionist settlement ideology—you were either an urbanite who lived and worked inside a town, or a pioneering agricultural laborer who lived and worked within one of the rural communities. In this respect, the idea of "rurban" or "exurban" communities (such as *yishuv kehilati*) deviated from the traditional, rigidly centralized planning framework—emphasizing instead the inherent locational advantages of the West Bank.

The Gush Emunim ideologues of the 1970s and early 1980s were aware that the mountainous and densely populated West Bank did not lend itself to the sort of agricultural communities that were typified by the kibbutzim (and a lesser extent by the moshavim). They were equally aware that third-generation Israelis were no longer interested in the "pioneering" challenge of cooperative and communal communities and were seeking alternative, less rigid, less centralized forms of living in an Israel of social and generational change.

The earliest Gush Emunim challenge focused as much on the nature of the settlement communities that would be appropriate for the political objectives to be met as on the goals of colonization per se. They latched on to a societal demand for changing the nature of the planning hierarchy and the authorization of alternative modes of settlement planning as a means through which their colonization objectives could be met. The location of much of the West Bank, within relatively close proximity to the Israeli metropolitan centers of Tel Aviv and Jerusalem, lent itself to the establishment of both rurban communities (which partially adopted the community models of earlier settlements, but without any form of economic collectivism) and suburban communities numbering thousands of inhabitants as an alternative to the crowded and expensive housing market in Tel Aviv or Jerusalem.

The younger, proactive generation of settler leaders demonstrated its ability to acknowledge the changing social and economic patterns that were transforming the Israeli society: the definition of a new model of settlement, the *yishuv kehilati*, was the product of this awareness. From the West Bank, the Gush

Emunim–inspired model of rurban communities quickly slipped back into Israel itself. The *mitzpim* (hilltop small Jewish settlements) project in the Galilee in the late 1970s and early 1980s latched on to some of these new settlement ideas, thus legitimizing concepts of rurbanization within the formal planning frameworks— the *yishuv kehilati* was formally recognized by Israeli planning authorities in 1981. During the subsequent two decades, the loosening of the rigid planning dichotomy was further reflected in the construction of low density, detached housing neighborhoods within the towns, as well as the gradual transformation of many of the rural communities (especially the moshavim) into suburban commuting communities where fewer and fewer of the residents were engaged in either agriculture or cooperative modes of communal living. Today, the "rural" landscape is unrecognizable from that which existed in the late 1970s when Gush Emunim presented their first regional settlement plans. It has undergone an ex-urban transformation of a type that could not have been imagined at the time but which, in retrospect, is no more than could have been expected from a society undergoing rapid internal social and economic change along the classic Western patterns of evolving human landscapes and settlement patterns.

A crucial factor in the consolidation of the settlements over a period of forty years has been the ability of the settler leaders to harness the pragmatic realities of these changing social and economic aspirations of the Israeli population with the ability to play the ideological card in portraying the West Bank as a "remote" area when in reality it was never anything but a natural geographical extension to the suburban expansion of the metropolitan core of the country. This "natural" suburban extension had, to all effects, been prevented from taking place prior to 1967 because of the existence of the border separating Israel from the West Bank. This explains the historical growth of the Israeli metropolitan core in a linear north-south strip along the coastal plain, rather than the normalized model of exurban concentric rings that would have expanded in an easterly direction into what was the West Bank, but was prevented from doing so by the existence of the border separating Israel from this neighboring region.

The policies put into practice by right-wing governments to promote West Bank settlement have also dispelled another myth of the Israeli planning objectives, namely the dispersal of the country's population away from an overcrowded metropolitan center into the remote and peripheral regions of the country, such as the Negev in the south and the Galilee in the north. Successive governments promoted the colonization of these areas through the provision of cheap land, low interest mortgages, and a range of other benefits to entice new settlers, directly competing with similar benefits that were offered to residents of the country's true peripheries in the Negev and the Galilee, in an attempt to strengthen existing communities and to prevent continued out-migration or to attract new residents to these regions. The result has been unfair competition between the "real" periphery within the national consensus, to the "new" periphery that was outside the political consensus and which is geographically located in the exurban regions of the metropolitan core.

Government policy favoring the exurban West Bank resulted in a situation termed "double centrality" in which a geographical center was strengthened even further by the package of economic benefits and conditions. Why would someone opt to relocate to a "real" periphery such as the Galilee or the Negev, when one could receive the same benefits by relocating just beyond the metropolitan core region within the suburban commuting belt? The notion of double centrality draws on notions of "double peripherality," which were first discussed by geographer John House back in the early 1980s in an attempt to explain the developmental problems experienced by settlements and communities in geographically peripheral and borderland regions, where the locational attributes were exacerbated by additional social, economic, and educational peripheralities. The promotion of suburban middle-class communities in the West Bank, a geographically central region, is the exact opposite of the double peripherality and explains why this region is so attractive to anyone who does not oppose relocating in the West Bank for political reasons—in which case, no amount of benefits and cheap land will induce them to move.

Tied in with this is the fact that land prices in the West Bank, especially in the earlier phases of the settlement project, were significantly lower than those in the metropolitan core. In a seminal article, Hebrew University geographer and planner, Shalom Reichman (1986), presented the first analysis of the impact of the "line of price discontinuity" on the expansion of the suburban belt beyond the Green Line. Under normalized forms of suburbanization, the price of land has gradually decreased from the inner city centers and the central business districts out toward the suburban and exurban areas. A family then decides to optimize its decision to reside in the inner city or suburb based on the price of land, expected quality of life, travelling distance, and cost of commuting to their workplace.

But in the case of the West Bank, the political impact of the Green Line resulted in a sharp price discontinuity in place of the normal gradual decrease in land prices. Moving eastward from suburban areas such as Kfar Sava (in the 1970s and 1980s), a price per acre of land would undergo a sharp fall rather than a gradual decline when crossing the Green Line. As such, the notion of five minutes from Kfar Sava, which was so strongly promoted by the Likud governments of the early 1980s, kicked in as soon as you crossed the line—a sharp binary discontinuity rather than a gradual decline in the land market. This artificiality of land prices was brought on by political factors and resulted in those areas within the West Bank, but in closest proximity to the Green line, as being the optimal place for residential relocation, based on the combination of cheap (very cheap) land and relatively short commuting distances.

The construction of houses is but a small part of the problem involved in the creation of new communities. The price of land varies from region to region, but the cost of bricks and mortar is the same everywhere. What is not the same is the access to employment opportunities. Governments throughout the world, not just in Israel, who have attempted to bolster or revitalize peripheral regions have never been successful at creating long-lasting employment opportunities and preventing out-migration and depopulation of remote communities, regardless of the housing conditions.

It is the inability of successive Israeli governments to invest in long-term employment opportunities in the periphery that partially explains the failure of the country's development towns, most of which were established in the country's periphery during the 1950s as a means of absorbing poor immigrants and of encouraging population dispersal away from the country's metropolitan center. But within a short period of time, the more able and ambitious migrants were moving away from these peripheral locations in search of economic opportunities in the metropolitan center.

In the small piece of real estate that is Israel and the West Bank, this has begun to change in recent years, as the substantial improvement in transportation infrastructure (road and rail connections) has eroded the friction of distance between the periphery and the center. This has transformed many of the development towns into a new form of suburbia, enabling some residents of the Negev and the Galilee to remain within their communities and commute to the main employment centers; indeed, the country has by and large become functionally integrated into a single-city state, where the Gush Dan (Tel Aviv) region provides the employment opportunities for the rest of the country, which, in turn, has become transformed into an extended suburb of the single central metropolitan core. Since land and housing prices are so significantly cheaper in the Negev and the Galilee (and the West Bank), greater accessibility to the center is beginning to have a new impact on the development of these regions, based on the commuter-exurbia model rather than a reliance on local employment opportunities.

Since the early 1980s, and the earliest Gush Emunim settlement plans, the West Bank has always enjoyed these locational advantages and this explains the ability of the settler leaders to attract tens of thousands of settlers who are not necessarily turned on by the ideological or political challenges of the West Bank, but have opted for the economic and residential advantages of improving their housing conditions while remaining within the suburban belt of commuting opportunities. The transportation and road infrastructure in the West Bank has also experienced significant improvement during the past two decades, so that those areas previously considered as too remote and too interior have now been drawn into the expanding exurban reach of the metropolitan center. Thus the opportunities of the suburban belt have become self-perpetuating as the friction of distance decreases, along the classic models of suburbanization and commuting zones.

Municipal and Organizational Structures: The Duality of Functional and Administrative Systems

Despite acting as an ideological opposition to successive governments, the settler leaders have successfully developed a parallel strategy through a process of co-optation within the formal planning and municipal agencies, without which new communities and settlements are unable to receive public resources, to obtain zoning and planning permits, or to provide such essential public services such as welfare, education, garbage disposal, infrastructural development, as well as formal representation within governmental and planning agencies and committees. All of these activities are essential civilian activities that, by international law, are forbidden from taking place in those areas categorized as "Occupied Territories." As such, many of the permits and transfer of resources formally take place through the additional agency of the Civilian Administration (an administrative body dependent on the Ministry of Defense) but, in reality, are no different in nature to those that take place inside Israel that are directly authorized by the regular governmental and civilian agencies.

The most important of these agencies has been the municipal and local governmental framework, which is part and parcel of the local government structure of Israel. This is based on a system of cities, local councils, and regional councils (depending on settlement threshold size and the ability to operate as an independent free-standing community) that is exactly the same as that which operates within Israel. The respective municipal authorities are not differentiated from those inside Israel and take part in the nationwide umbrella organization of municipal authorities when they lobby central government for additional resources. They are all equally subject to the same local government legislation, subsidiary to the Ministry of Interior.

In addition to the normal municipal functioning, the West Bank settlements are also organized through a political lobby, the Council for West Bank Settlements (*Yesha* council), which lobbies on their behalf to government and to other agencies, which municipal authorities are forbidden from doing. As such they operate with parallel governmental and extragovernmental agencies, enabling them to compete for resources over and beyond the normal governmental budgetary transfers.

This system of political duality operates within a number of spheres, not least the echelons of highest government. Over the past three decades, residents of

West Bank communities have become increasingly involved in national political life and are currently one of the most overrepresented sectors within the Knesset (the Israeli Parliament) through membership in a number of right-wing parties, but never in a settler party as such. The most significant of these is the Bayit Yehudi (formerly Mafdal) Party, whose leader Naftali Bennet (not a West Bank resident) is one of the most extreme prosettler ministers in the present government and has recently proposed formal annexation of some of the settlements to Israel, as well as the "Israel Our House" (Yisrael Beteinu) Party headed by the current Minister of Defense, Avigdor Lieberman, who is a resident of the West Bank. The former housing minister and current Minister of Agriculture and Rural Development (Uri Ariel)—who has influence over national construction policy including the issuing of building permits for West Bank settlements—and the speaker of the Knesset (Yuli Edelstein) are both West Bank settlers. The government set up in 2015 was even more right wing than its predecessor, with many key functionaries residing in the West Bank and acting as an informal lobby on behalf of their own communities. At the same time, the nongovernmental leadership has continued to promote the settlement project as a political and ideological project that challenges any government policy aimed at slowing down, or freezing, the construction and expansion process. It is hardly surprising that the immediate response to any terrorist attack on Israelis within the West Bank is an immediate demand by the settler leaders to a responsive government, to expand settlements, often named after a resident who has been killed in act of violence.

The freezing (forced cessation) of settlement activity is one of the myths that have been promoted by the political lobby. On numerous occasions during the past twenty years, successive governments have announced a "settlement freeze" as a price that has to be paid for entering into political negotiations with the Palestinians, usually after a period of pressure on the part of the third party—the United States of America. This is, as expected, opposed by the settlement leadership and is portrayed as a dangerous step on the way to future territorial concessions and enforced settlement evacuation. Regardless of occasional settlement freezes, however, the settlement population has continued to grow almost unchecked; indeed, settlement freezes have almost entirely applied to the establishment of new settlements, rarely to the expansion and consolidation of existing settlements, within which the major growth has taken place.

To a certain extent, settlement freezes have been part of a process of progressive consolidation of the settlements. The first years of rapid settlement growth in the late 1970s and 1980s were characterized by a rush to create as many small communities, dispersed throughout the region, as possible. This process reflected, to a certain extent, the preferences of individual settler groups, which aimed at creating their own small community within which they desired to express their own "unique" way of life without recourse to a larger body of residents telling them what to do. This, however, gave rise to functional and administrative problems: few small communities reached the minimum economic thresholds that were necessary for stand-alone economic sustainability—even allowing for relatively high levels of public subsidization. On the other side, it was important for the settlement planners to ensure the long-term sustainability of the settlements over and beyond the immediate short-term political objectives. They were also keen to show that settlements were self-sustainable and would not continue to be an excessive and disproportional burden on the public purse, even if they believed that this was justifiable in order to attain their political objectives. In addition, longer term political objectives, aimed at creating an irreversible territorial situation, required less artificiality and subsidization and more internal growth.

As a consequence, the so-called settlement freeze, while politically unpalatable to settlers, enabled the planners to focus on the expansion and consolidation of the existing communities into larger settlements with a minimum threshold size, which enabled their functioning as independent communities and the transformation of some of the smaller settlements into fully fledged townships and independent municipalities. The growth of the fully fledged townships enabled demographic growth on a relatively small area of territory, as contrasted with the widespread dispersal of smaller communities throughout the region. The former, such as Kiryat Arba, Emanuel, Beitar Illit, Efrat, and Ariel—contain the bulk of the settler population and are organized as independent standing local councils (along with the large suburban communities) while Ariel has also obtained full "city" status at the top of the local government hierarchy. Some of these towns, notably Emanuel and Beitar Illit, have been populated by ultraorthodox spillover from Jerusalem and Bnei Brak, as their populations grow exponentially and they are unable to afford the cost of housing in the major cities (see Cahaner, chapter 7).

The smaller, more dispersed communities are organized, as in the rest of Israel, through a system of regional councils. But they are structured differently in the West Bank in that, while they provide services to an aggregate of settlements located within their jurisdictional area, they are not responsible for the open land areas between the settlements. Nor do they deal with the Palestinian villages and townships that fall within their municipal area. These latter are catered for through the Palestinian Authority or the Israeli Military Administration. There is therefore a dual and parallel system of municipal administration in a single territory, whereby neighboring Israeli and Palestinian townships are organized through entirely separate systems of local government and do not share resources or size thresholds in their respective provision of public, welfare, or educational services. There is perhaps no other single characteristic of the settlement network that, at one and the same time, reflects the banality of colonization (the functioning of local government and the provision of public services) alongside the artificiality of a system that separates neighboring communities into a system of territorial and spatial duality.

Settlement and the Border Discourse: The Suburban Paradox

Settlements have had a major impact on the border discourse. "Facts on the ground" are of considerable importance, regardless of the moral, ethical, or legal dimensions of the argument. The relocation or forceful evacuation of over 350,000 settlers and their communities (a figure that does not include the residents of East Jerusalem) appears to be unachievable. It therefore requires a demarcation of a border in such a way as to maximize the number of settlers who could remain in situ and offers land swaps as compensation to the Palestinian State/Authority. These are not new ideas. The idea emerged as long ago as the early Track II discussions that took place in Rome, as far back as 1990 (pre-Madrid Conference) and were also considered as part of the Beilin–Abu Maazen negotiations, which took place in the immediate aftermath of the signing of the Oslo Accords in the mid-1990s. But since that time, the settler population has increased threefold, resulting in a spatial situation that no longer lends itself to a "clean" cut and minimal settlement evacuation.

It is often assumed that the settlers who have moved to the West Bank for economic and quality of life reasons will be more amenable to accepting economic compensation on the part of the Israeli government if and when there is a peace agreement that necessitates settlement evacuation and relocation back into Israel proper. They will be less inclined, the argument goes, to oppose a decision taken by the Government aimed at withdrawing from all, or a significant part, of the Occupied Territories. Nor will they wish to be perceived by the rest of Israel as being the obstacle in the way to the implementation of a peace agreement that challenges the democratic foundations, and reputation, of Israeli society.

While this argument has never really been put to the test (the Gaza precedent is an inappropriate frame for any comparison), it has a basic inbuilt geographic and structural contradiction that lies at the very heart of the suburbanization thesis posited in this chapter. It is the major settlement blocs, those in closest proximity to the Green Line, which have a higher preponderance of economic or quality of life settlers who have latched on to the suburbanization process and could therefore be more susceptible to relocating for adequate compensation when, in reality, under any redrawing of the lines they could remain in situ and be included inside Israel. Wherever the line is redrawn, there will always be a significant number of settlers, located in the interior of the region, who would have to be evacuated (assuming that the territorial solution does indeed require clearly delineated compact and contiguous territories without exclaves or bypass roads of any sort). It is these settlements, such as Elon Moreh, Kedumim, Shilo, Beit El, and Ofra, that constitute the heartland of the ideological and religious settlers who, by most assumptions, will refuse to evacuate under any conditions—with or without compensation.

This is the built-in structural paradox of the suburbanization thesis as it interfaces with the political objectives of settler colonization, namely that those who have been less impacted or influenced by the economic considerations will continue to constitute a major obstacle on the path to drawing future borders. In other words, while suburbanization has served to bolster the overall demographic numbers, it has created a reverse geography inside the West Bank—those who would relocate back to Israel in return for compensation may not need to under a redrawing of the border, while those who remain beyond the border will never agree to peaceful relocation—regardless of the amount of compensation offered to them.

Concluding Comments: On the Banality and Myths of Settlement Colonization in the West Bank

This chapter has revisited the West Bank settlement project with a retrospective of forty years and has placed the political objectives of the project within the framework of planning mechanisms and agencies. It has explained the relative "success" of the settler movement by showing how its leaders were able to latch on to the trends of suburbanization and exurbanization to promote settlement in a region that is geographically close to the metropolitan center of the country. At the same time, this chapter has shown how this process has taken place against a background of a series of myths that have been used to sell the political message of the settler movement—such as settling the periphery, the dispersal of population, pioneering under difficult conditions, settlement freeze, and the potential for settlement evacuation. For forty years, the settlement movement and its leaders have successfully employed a dual strategy, one operating within government and its formal agencies, the other operating as an extragovernmental political lobby, an argument that was made as early as the mid-1980s (Newman 1986). Almost fifty years of unceasing settlement activity has demonstrated the effectiveness of this dual strategy.

Colonization through suburbanization is the essential banalization of the settlement project, transforming settlement into a series of daily life activities, such as cheap housing, easy commuting distances, better quality of life conditions, such that for all those who are not opposed to the settlement project, the potential for relocation to the West Bank is not considered a dangerous or threatening political endeavor. It is for this reason that while the settlement movement has not achieved its ultimate objective of formal de jure annexation of the region, they have created enough realities on the ground to substantially prevent any move toward the first stages of conflict resolution and associated Israeli withdrawal from the West Bank through the demarcation of mutually acceptable borders.

References

Newman, David. 1986. "Gush Emunim between Fundamentalism and Pragmatism." *Jerusalem Quarterly* 39: 33–43.

———. 1996. "The Territorial Politics of Exurbanization: Reflections on 25 Years of the Jewish Settlement Process in the West Bank." *Israel Affairs* 3 (1): 61–85.

———. 2005. "From 'Hitnachalut' to 'Hitnatkut': The Impact of Gush Emunim and the Settlement Movement on Israeli Society." *Israel Studies* 10 (3): 192–224.

———. 2006. "Colonization as Suburbanization: The Politics of the Land Market at the Frontier." In *City of Collision*, edited by P. Misselwitz, 113–120. Basel, Switzerland: Birkhäuser.

Portugali, Juval, and Newman, David. 1986. *Spatial Interaction between Israelis and Palestinians of the West Bank and Gaza Strip*. Research report presented to the Ford Foundation, New York.

Reichmann, Shalom. 1986. "Policy Reduces the World to Essentials: A Reflection on the Jewish Settlement Process in the West Bank since 1967." In *Planning in Turbulence*, edited by D. Morley and A. Shachar, 83–96. Jerusalem: Magnes.

3 "Outside Jerusalem—Yet so Near"

Ma'ale Adumim, Jerusalem, and the Suburbanization of Israel's Settlement Policy

Marco Allegra

Oᴜᴛsɪᴅᴇ ᴊᴇʀᴜsᴀʟᴇᴍ—ʏᴇᴛ sᴏ Near—A 7 minute ride from Jerusalem and you'll find yourself at Ma'aleh Adumim, a new town which is already attracting lovers of Jerusalem and its surroundings" (reproduced in Thorpe 1984, 119). This is how an ad published in the Jerusalem Post in 1983 described the settlement of Ma'ale Adumim to prospective buyers. The ad introduces the key issue that we will discuss throughout this chapter, namely the relation between the development of Israel's settlement policy and the transformation of Jerusalem, as well as the case study that we will use to illustrate our argument—the community of Ma'ale Adumim.

The status of Jerusalem is almost universally regarded as the single most divisive issue in Israeli-Palestinian relations, while Israel's settlement policy—and its territorial and demographic implications—is widely considered as the most significant "fact on the ground" established by Israel since 1967. This chapter will describe how Israel's settlement policy in the area of metropolitan Jerusalem transformed the material, symbolic, and political landscape of Israeli-Palestinian relations. The underlying argument of the chapter is that the development of Israel's settlement policy should be viewed in connection with broader trends and phenomena characterizing Israeli society as a whole—and not only through the lens of the Israeli-Palestinian conflict. In this respect, we maintain that the main driver of the transformation of the conflict has been the "suburbanization" of Israeli settlement policy (i.e., the metropolitan expansion of Jerusalem, and, to a lesser extent, Tel Aviv, into the West Bank through the establishment of relatively large, suburban, and nonideological communities). These communities considerably widened the potential audience of prospective settlers, offering to tens of thousands of Israelis affordable housing at commuting distance from the main employment centers of the country, and constituted vehicles for upward mobility for the low middle class and the most vulnerable sectors of Israeli society.

This chapter will present a case study on the settlement of Ma'ale Adumim, a bedroom community of forty thousand residents located in the eastern periphery of Jerusalem. Ma'ale Adumim ("red ascent" or "red hill" in Hebrew) was founded in the late 1970s on a hill about seven kilometers from the Old City of Jerusalem and is presently an autonomous municipality whose boundaries touch Jerusalem's and include some forty-eight square kilometers of West Bank territory. Today the geopolitical implication of its existence and planned expansion (through the so-called E1 plan; see Allegra 2014) are widely discussed at both the local and international levels. At the same time, however, the settlement also represents the paradigmatic suburban, nonideological bedroom community, inhabited by middle-class Israeli commuters who moved there for economic factors (such as attractive state subsidies, economic incentives, and, of course, a large stock of affordable housing) and, ultimately, to fulfill their aspiration to upward social mobility and a greater quality of life. There are three main rationales for the choice of Ma'ale Adumim as case study: first, this community represents both a significant outcome of Israel's settlement policy (as one of the largest settlements in the West Bank) and a good example of its suburban character (today the vast majority of settlers live in large suburban communities around Jerusalem, see the appendix; Allegra 2013, forthcoming); second, it is a "success story" of Israeli settlement policy (because of its steady and so far uninterrupted growth, the quality of life and wide range of services available to residents, and its relatively uncontroversial status in Israeli public opinion); finally, Ma'ale Adumim is a good example of the inextricable bundle of geopolitical issues that characterize the metropolitan area of Jerusalem today.

The chapter is mainly based on contextual and historical data and in-depth interviews realized in Ma'ale Adumim with residents of the community between 2012 and 2013. In particular, the chapter will focus on the connection between the personal histories and daily lives of the residents, and the progressive transformation of the space of metropolitan Jerusalem in its material and symbolic dimensions—what the French social theorist Henri Lefebvre has called "the production of space." Our argument in this respect is twofold. First, we maintain that the "suburban experience" embodied in the lives of the residents of Ma'ale Adumim illustrates the manifestation of powerful drivers of the overall process of normalization of Jewish presence in the West Bank; in turn, this rendered the settlement policy relatively uncontroversial for large sectors of Israeli public opinion and, ultimately, brought about a fundamental shift of the very idea of what Jerusalem is. Second, without any pretense of dehistoricizing the analysis of Israel's settlement policy or to disconnect it from the wider issue of Israeli-Palestinian relations, we maintain that settlements such as Ma'ale Adumim are also the product of the mundane, relatively nonideological quest for a suburban "safe space"—an enclosed space designed to avoid contacts with "unpleasant otherness" that residents of the suburbs all over the world often associate to life in the inner city.

Jerusalem, or the Suburbanization of Israel's Settlement Policy

The dominant views among scholars tend to set the "Jerusalem problem" within the framework of the cultural and religious significance of the inner city (and, in particular, the so-called Holy Basin, the area of the medieval Old City and its immediate surroundings). The historical legacy of the city is therefore usually described as the ultimate source of Israeli-Palestinian tensions in a literature informed by a conflict-resolution perspective and largely devoted to measuring the distance between the parties' negotiating positions.

Paradoxically, however, the Holy Basin represents the area of Jerusalem where the status quo has proved more durable—indeed, in the Old City no major structural alteration of the urban fabric has taken place after the demolition of the Moroccan Quarter and the renovation of the Jewish Quarter immediately after the end of the hostilities in 1967. From a planning and urban development perspective, the main locus of conflict has instead been the metropolitan area of the city, both within and outside the large municipal borders established by Israel in 1967 (see Pullan and Yacobi, chapter 11). Today, when we discuss the reversibility of Israel's expansion into the West Bank (a central issue in the debate on the one-state/two-state alternative) we mainly refer to the facts on the ground imposed by Israel in the metropolitan area of Jerusalem rather than the status of the Temple Mount/Haram al Sharif.

At the same time, while there is a wide consensus over the fact that Israel's settlement policy has represented a major driver in the integration between pre-1967 Israel and the West Bank, scholarly research has so far overwhelmingly focused on the immediate humanitarian, territorial, and legal implications of the establishment of settlements and on the ideological drivers of Israeli policies—and in particular on the settlers' movement, its ideological worldviews and political influence vis-à-vis the Israeli establishment (Allegra et al., introduction). Such emphasis has contributed to obscure the role of other mechanisms and drivers behind the progressive proliferation and expansion of the settlements, and especially the crucial importance of the metropolitan component of Israel's settlement policy, and the role of state policies in responding to suburbanization trends operating in the Israeli society by opening the land reservoir of the West Bank to tens of thousands of settlers/consumers.

Our argument here is that the expansion of Israeli settlements has amounted largely to a process of expansion of metropolitan Jerusalem (and, to a lesser extent, Tel Aviv) into the West Bank—that is, that the settlement policy has undergone, simultaneously, a process of "suburbanization" and "Jerusalemization" that paralleled the expansion of the city of Jerusalem into a large metropolis. In other words, and contrary to the prevailing stereotype, the typical settlement is a relatively large community, with fully functioning municipal services, good infrastructures connecting it to the main employment centers of the region, and whose population is made up of commuters who moved to a Jewish settlement for economic and mundane reasons, namely to find good housing opportunities at reasonable prices and escape the overcrowding of Jerusalem and Tel Aviv. As we have argued elsewhere (Allegra 2013, forthcoming), the rapid growth of settlements such as Ma'ale Adumim—but the same argument could be made for a number of other suburban planned towns in the area, both inside (such as Gilo or Pisgat Ze'ev) and outside (such as Giv'at Ze'ev or Beitar Illit) the municipal boundaries of the city—has been due to their success in becoming a politico-territorial platform for the convergence for the preferences of a pluralistic set of Israeli actors. A crucial component of these "success stories" was the possibility of establishing a (infrastructural, strategic, and symbolic) connection between the development of these settlements and the city of Jerusalem.

The slogan "Ma'ale Adumim is Jerusalem"—found in planning documents, political leaflets, and real estate commercials, each dimension strengthening and legitimizing the other—laid the conditions for the rapid growth of the settlement as the territorial common denominator of the preferences of different sectors of the Israeli society. For politicians, Ma'ale Adumim's link to Jerusalem was essentially politico-strategic, as the fast-growing new town represented a permanent territorial and demographic fact on the ground in the political game for Jerusalem. Planners saw this link in terms of urban planning issues, as Ma'ale Adumim constituted the appropriate answer to the need for a rational expansion of the city—and an occasion to apply their professional skills to the creation of a new town from scratch. Finally, for the Jerusalemite Jewish middle class, hungry for housing opportunities, the quiet suburban community of Ma'ale Adumim offered affordable, modern housing, and a good quality of life at commuting distance from the inner city.

This process had two important consequences as far as metropolitan development is concerned. First, the idea that settlements such as Ma'ale Adumim were part of the metropolitan fabric of Jerusalem has considerably lessened the controversial character of settlement expansion in the area and provided a model of colonization that could be supported by a broad and pluralistic set of Israeli actors—many of which were relatively uninterested in the ideological and territorial implications of Israel's settlement policy. This in turn greatly facilitated the steady growth of the settler population and thereby laid the ground for the establishment of territorial and demographic facts on the ground on a large scale. Second, the development of a large belt of suburban localities at the outskirts of pre-1967 Jerusalem has helped over time to transform the spatial and social perception of the city itself. Whatever their knowledge of the details of post-1967 territorial reality and jurisdictional arrangements (e.g., the exact route of the Green Line, the Israeli-defined municipal boundaries of Jerusalem, the legal status of Jewish communities in the West Bank), few Israelis would recognize these communities as "settlements" and consider them instead an integral part of the urban fabric of the city (see Kratsman and Ginsburg, chapter 4).

The Social Production of Territory

How did these processes of transformation of the sociospatial landscape of Jerusalem unfold? As Lefebvre noted, space is at the same time a social product and a tool that individuals and groups use in framing their relations—as a mean of mobilization, production, and control. For him, "any 'social existence' aspiring or claiming to be 'real' but failing to produce its own space, would . . . fall to the level of folklore and sooner or later disappear altogether, thereby losing its identity, its denomination and its feeble degree of reality" (1991, 53).

Indeed, few statesmen and nationalists would disagree with Lefebvre—and certainly not the founding fathers of Zionism, whose main political achievement and most enduring legacy consisted of the creation of a national ethos of the redemption of the land and the territorialization of Jewish nationalism. Israel's settlement policy as a whole can be interpreted as a territorial strategy (Brenner and Elden 2009) for the creation of a new state space in the land occupied by Israel in 1967. This overall reconfiguration of the landscape of the West Bank has many facets. Following Lefebvre, the production of space takes place along three main components (the Lefebvrian triad of *perceived*, *conceived*, and *lived* space). Israel's settlement policy entailed a thorough reconceptualization of the spatioterritorial relation between Israel and the conquered territory (i.e., of conceived space) and a redefinition of the material and spatial structure of social relations (i.e., of perceived space). This chapter focuses on the third component of Lefebvre's tripartite scheme of production of territory—namely the spatial experience of space by individuals and groups through a complex lens made up of senses, symbols, and culture (i.e., the lived space).[1]

Our argument is that the transformation of the social perception of what is Jerusalem is a crucial component of the process of selective incorporation of the West Bank into Israel, and in particular onto the path of progressive fetishization of space—the creation of what Lefebvre (1991) called "the illusion of transparency" and John Agnew (1994) "the territorial trap"—which resulted in the progressive normalization of Jewish presence in the West Bank and in the creation of a new definition of Jerusalem. Through selected quotes from a number of in-depth interviews realized with residents of the Jewish settlement of Ma'ale Adumim (the names given in the text are fictitious), we will explore issues of place attachment, personal geographies, and the relation between the latter and the production of space. The following two sections of this chapter will discuss—by presenting some impressionistic sketches from our fieldwork in Ma'ale Adumim—how the day-by-day dimension of suburban life has been paramount in shaping the transformation of the human geography of the area and creating a new sociospatial definition of what Jerusalem is.

A New Jerusalem

The conventional wisdom describes Israel's settlement policy as a plan of conquest carried out by the Israeli state and the national-religious settlers—although interpretations vary with respect to the nature of their mutual relationship—under the long-standing impetus of an ethnonational imperative toward the redemption of the land. It would be impossible to negate the partisan nature of planning in the area of Jerusalem or the influence of ideological motivations behind Israel's settlement policy; however, our argument is that the development of Israel's settlement policy is intimately coherent with wider trends characterizing Israeli society as a whole, namely marketization; welfare retrenchment; and growing inequality, privatization, and suburbanization, which were reflected in the transformation of Israel's spatial and development policy between the 1970s and the 1980s (Filc 2009, 42–54; Kristal 2013; Ram 1999; Shalev 2000; Maggor 2015).

The traditional Israeli planning policy since the 1950s was based on the principles of balanced spatial distribution, socioeconomic regional integration, and dispersal of industry to the peripheral regions. Since the 1970s, however, this policy was gradually abandoned in favor of a metropolitan approach that emphasized the consolidation of the metropolitan regions of Tel Aviv and Jerusalem, market-driven economic development, and a more complex articulation of state intervention at different scales (Razin 1990; Shachar 1998). The West Bank offered vast resources for this reorientation of Israeli spatial and development policies. Much of the area constituted, from a planning point of view, an ideal reservoir of land for the expansion of Israel's two main metropolitan centers, namely Tel Aviv and Jerusalem. The case of Jerusalem, which between 1949 and 1967 had been a truncated urban system, with its northern, southern, and western periphery controlled by Jordan, is particularly instructive in this respect. A number of additional economic factors added to the appeal of the West Bank. In the aftermath of the 1967 War, the Green Line functioned as a line of "price discontinuity" beyond which land prices immediately dropped to a much lower level; at the same time, significant economic incentives offered by the government to the prospective Israeli residents of the West Bank (in the form of tax benefits, discounted mortgages, and so forth) contributed to further increase its appeal for a wide Israeli audience.

Starting from the early 1980s, Ma'ale Adumim began its fast (and so far un-interrupted) growth precisely because of the influx of settlers/consumers attracted by what the Israeli geographer David Newman defined as a condition of "double centrality" of the West Bank: located at the geographical center of the country, and an integral part of the main metropolitan areas of Jerusalem and Tel Aviv, the area was nevertheless treated as a peripheral "development zone," where Jewish residents and economic activities enjoyed a full package of financial and fiscal benefits. The motivation behind the choice of the residents of Ma'ale Adumim for moving beyond the Green Line had nothing to do with the desire of contributing to a politico-ideological project. The underlying logic for moving to Ma'ale Adu-mim was—and still is—essentially linked to economic and logistic needs of the prospective residents rather that to a conscious interest in crossing the Green Line. Since its establishment as a planned town in the early 1980s, the community became a popular destination for young couples looking for housing opportuni-ties outside the increasingly crowded and expensive inner city of Jerusalem. "It was a pretty random kind of decision. . . . We moved here because it was close and convenient and the rent was affordable at the time. . . . We went to a real es-tate agent, he took us I think . . . he took us to Gilo, I think he took us to some place in Jerusalem which I forgotten. . . . It was a question of the rent, and one guy wanted us to pay every three months, one guy wanted us to pay every month. It was very random" (Daniel, interview).

Significantly, the range of alternatives available to the future residents regu-larly included other Jewish locations in the West Bank, while the inner city and more expensive "West Side" localities (such as Mevasseret Zion) remained out of their reach because of financial reasons. "We were looking for a place to live. . . . And basically our criterion for living was, number one, we could afford it. . . . [We considered other options,] we saw things in Jerusalem that we could not afford . . . Giv'at Ze'ev . . . Ramot . . . and Ma'ale Adumim, those are the things basically that we could afford. But basically the main factor was the financial factor" (Ruth, interview).

In our conversations, some of the respondents have been especially clear in contrasting their experience with the more pioneering lifestyle of ideological settlements such as the ones founded by Gush Emunim, the national-religious settler movement active in the 1970s. For example, in our interview, Michael (who moved to Ma'ale Adumim during the 1990s) remembers his brief experi-ence as a volunteer in Ofra (a settlement established by Gush Emunim in 1975): "Many years ago I came to Israel and worked in Ofra, when it was first being built; it was a rough two–three weeks . . . I am not a pioneer . . . meaning: if Ma'ale Adumim didn't have the infrastructure it has and the services and like that, I may have thought twice in terms of the pioneering spirit, going out and live in a tent somewhere. . . . I moved into a city that was already a city, already established."

Daniel—who describes himself as an "extreme right-wing person"—goes further in voicing his frustration for living in a quiet suburban location such as Ma'ale Adumim: "I actually wanted something more . . . more pioneering than Ma'ale Adumim. . . . I feel in many ways ideologically unaccomplished by living in Ma'ale Adumim. If I talk to people from outside Israel, they may see me as a settler . . . especially Jewish people, . . . they have a lot of respect for what I have done, but you probably know already enough about the situation to understand that . . . it's a kind of a phony settler situation. I am not really a settler in that sense."

On the opposite side of the political spectrum, Sarah (who used to be active in a nongovernmental organization that organized interfaith encounters between Jews and Palestinians—some of which took place in the past in Ma'ale Adumim) seems to share Daniel's distinction about the "real" and the "phony" settlers when she declares: "I don't consider myself a settler, I feel I just live in the suburbs. . . . To me lines are invisible. . . . I don't consider myself a settler, I joke around a lot with Rebecca [another residents of Ma'ale Adumim who works for the Israeli nongovernmental organization Rabbis for Human Rights], I say 'you know, we are settlers for human rights.'"

Sarah and Daniel are not isolated cases: from various personal and political standpoints—and despite a generalized awareness of the controversial status of Ma'ale Adumim as a settlement built on land conquered in 1967—all the residents seem to differentiate between the various groups of Israelis living beyond the Green Line. As Abigail puts it, "I cannot understand people that go out and live on a hill, with like caravans, in the middle of nowhere. That's a settler: somebody that lives in this hellhole for no reasons. . . . [In Ma'ale Adumim] there's none of the fanatics. . . . There are degrees of settlers, apparently [laughs]. . . . We're light, light settlers [laughs]."

Other respondents pointed out to the moral and legal legitimacy of their presence in Ma'ale Adumim. The community was established lawfully (in contrast to other settlements whose status remain dubious in the Israeli law) as a part of a state-sanctioned official policy of urban development, and did not constitute in any case a direct infringement of Palestinian property rights.[2]

I did want to live in an area [where I felt] I was within the area of community. . . . I did not have a problem living over the Green Line, as long as it wasn't in the middle of an Arab community saying "here I am." (Ruth, interview)

We were taking advantage of what the government was offering . . . then the government changed its policy but this does not make me into a settler in a negative sense. . . . Ma'ale Adumim was established within the boundaries of the law, it was not a flag on the hill. (Hannah, interview)

Probably the most interesting thing emerging from quotes presented is the total disregard of the Green Line as a meaningful territorial artifact. Indeed, Sarah's words ("I don't consider myself a settler, I feel I just live in the suburbs") forcefully illuminate a central element in the experience of the residents of Ma'ale Adumim, namely, its intimate connection with the inner city of Jerusalem and the broader context of the metropolitan fabric. It is interesting to note that this feature of Ma'ale Adumim has been a marketing platform used by real estate agents since the founding of the city. In 1983 the ad in the *Jerusalem Post* that we have quoted in the opening lines of this chapter encouraged prospective buyers with the following description of Ma'ale Adumim: "OUTSIDE JERUSALEM—Yet so Near—A 7 minute ride from Jerusalem and you'll find yourself at Ma'aleh Adumim, a new town which is already attracting lovers of Jerusalem and its surroundings. The area has been planned as one of the northern suburbs of Jerusalem. From here you have a magnificent view over the eastern slopes of Jerusalem and the Dead Sea—RAMET LTD—YOUR BIG ADVANTAGE—Ramet Ltd. offers you beautifully-planned apartments facing the magnificent view of Jerusalem. Well-planned neighborhoods and the best location in town" (reproduced in Thorpe 1984, 119).

The advertisement uses the conventional mantra used to market planned suburbs worldwide, emphasizing suburban values—such as "order/efficiency, daily exposure to nature's beauty and goodness, use of technology to improve the residents' quality of life, aesthetic quality, and the values of individuality, family and community" (Modarres and Kirby 2010, 116)—that directly resonate with the experience of the residents. "We wanted to live close to Jerusalem but not in Jerusalem. . . . I'm a city girl, I grew up in London, I can't live in the middle of nowhere . . . so we settled in Ma'ale Adumim. . . . [And] Jerusalem did not really feel more advanced than living over here, plus here you have the luxury . . . it's cheaper . . . you have the luxury to have a community feeling" (Rachel, interview).

Indeed, it seems that in many ways it is difficult, sometimes, to understand where Ma'ale Adumim stops and Jerusalem begins in terms of the daily experience of the residents of Ma'ale Adumim.

> If somebody asks me where I'm from, I'd say Jerusalem, I won't say Ma'ale Adumim. I could say Ma'ale Adumim, it happens, Ma'ale Adumim or Jerusalem it's like the same to me. . . . For instance: everything is in Jerusalem. If you want to go to the mall—and now the mall is nice, but it wasn't, there was nothing—if you want to go shopping with your parents, you go to Jerusalem. . . . Your parents went to work every day; I went to scouts in Jerusalem. . . . So we came [to Jerusalem] a lot. We went out, we went out in Jerusalem. (Abigail, interview)

A Safe Space

As we have noted, the prevalent scholarly and academic discourse tends to view settlements exclusively in the context of Israeli-Palestinian relations. Within this dichotomy, Israelis and Palestinians in the West Bank could be compared to oil and water: each substance is a homogeneous fluid that simply does not mix with the other. The settlements' role is that of ethnoterritorial bridgeheads whose function is simply to facilitate the expansion of the Jewish population into Palestinian territory. This argument implies a number of corollaries: that the Palestinians constitute the ultimate "others" for the settlers; that settlements are internally homogeneous and that ethnoreligious identity is the sole criteria for defining their identity; that settlements are gated for security reasons; and so on. Once again, while it would be impossible to discuss the development of the settlements without considering the Israeli-Palestinian dichotomy, there are other powerful forces behind the proliferation of settlements. In particular, drawing on our research on Ma'ale Adumim, we will argue that suburban settlements represent for their residents a "safe space," a model community protected from the intrusion of various forms of perceived "unpleasant otherness" (but not necessarily from the "Palestinian other").

The last section explored the connection between suburbs such as Ma'ale Adumim and Jerusalem. As the *Jerusalem Post* ad ("OUTSIDE JERUSALEM—Yet so Near") and Rachel's quote ("We wanted to live close to Jerusalem but not in Jerusalem") remind us, however, life in the suburbs is premised on the separation from the inner city as much as it is on the connection to it. If it is difficult on the one side to separate Ma'ale Adumim from the inner city of Jerusalem—which remains in many ways the center of life of Ma'ale Adumim residents as far as work, education, leisure, and services are concerned—there is no doubt that the suburban lifestyle is premised on the secession from the core of the urban fabric, as well as on a process of self-segregation within the boundaries of a sanitized community, where the negative externalities of life in the inner city are reduced or absent. As Oren Yiftachel puts it, "beyond the powerful impact of the settling ethnocratic culture, there are some influential groups that gain from the establishment of settlements. . . . [U]pwardly mobile groups who seek 'quality of life' . . . often an euphemism for the rush of middle-class families into gated, or controlled, suburban localities, 'protected' from the proximity of 'undesirables'" (2003, 36).

In our conversations with the residents, many different forms of "unpleasant otherness" emerged beyond the issue of Israeli-Palestinian relations, namely the presence of other groups whose integration in the Israeli melting pot proves to be more difficult for cultural and social reasons, as well as in the form of bad environmental conditions marked by poverty, crime, abusive behavior, poor services delivery, and so forth. For the residents, moving to Ma'ale Adumim had represented a chance to improve their life by joining a community that provided the kind of quality of life—from modern housing and infrastructure and efficient municipal services, to more immaterial values such as a general sense of safety and of belonging to a caring community—that they could not find, or afford, in Jerusalem.[3]

Since our main focus was on intergroup relations, we started to ask our respondents about their views on the Palestinians—the most obvious case in point of exotic and potentially dangerous "other."[4] To this end, beyond a few general questions, we explicitly asked our respondents to comment on the perspective of having Palestinian neighbors in Ma'ale Adumim—citing the case of French Hill, where Palestinians with Israeli citizenship began to move in relatively large numbers years ago (Pullan and Yacobi, chapter 11). It was interesting to see how the residents reacted to this mental experiment and learn that their narrative about the Palestinians did not exactly reproduce the dichotomy inherent to the Israeli-Palestinian conflict. In other words, while the residents' opinions on possible future coexistence with the Palestinians ranged from skepticism to outright refusal, this perspective was consistently seen beyond the lens of the Israeli-Palestinian conflict. Asked whether he would be surprised to learn that there are Palestinian residents in Ma'ale Adumim, Michael replied:

> The "why" would be a question mark. . . . I am from New York, the big melting pot, but still you have Chinatown, you have Little Italy. . . . Everyone has their own niche, ok? And that goes for Israel also. . . . You have al-Eizariya and Ma'ale Adumim, you know. . . . Do I see Jews living in al-Eizariya? Probably not. Do I see Arabs living in Ma'ale Adumim? Probably not. . . . I don't know what kind of Arab would want to live in Ma'ale Adumim, [since] the services that he personally may want may not be available for him in Ma'ale Adumim: schooling, religion. . . . I know why I am here, meaning it is a nice Jewish community outside Jerusalem, less expensive than Jerusalem and I love the place. And I moved to Israel to be in a Jewish nation.

Significantly, Michael refers to his experience as a New Yorker: even in the absence of an entrenched, violent conflict between opposed ethnic groups, he does not see any incompatibility between "the melting pot" and maintaining a certain degree of segregation between different communities. Daniel makes the same argument in a more ethnoreligious fashion:

> To be honest, from a social and cultural point of view, there are little relations between the people here and the Arabs. . . . Why? . . . The truth is that if you would have asked me a similar question when I was living in England, when I was 14, the answer would have been pretty similar. I am a religious Jewish

person, I don't have much contact with non-Jews, I don't even have much contact with non-religious Jewish people. . . . I lived with non-Jews in the past: it's not something I want but it's not something I would fight. I do believe in people's right to live where they want, as long as they behave.

These quotes and the ones that follow do not frame Ma'ale Adumim as a Jewish settlement on occupied land, but rather as a place reserved for a community of peers that should be protected against the invasion of others—but, once again, not necessarily Palestinian others. One interesting test in this sense is the comparative judgment passed by the residents on two "difficult groups" in terms of their integration in the broader Israeli society, namely Palestinians and Haredim—the Jews belonging to Ultraorthodox communities. A judgment that, sometimes, is not necessarily favorable to the fellow Jews: partly due to the fact that a future Haredi invasion of Ma'ale Adumim could probably appear more plausible than a Palestinian one, many residents tend to see the Haredi presence as a more dangerous threat to their lifestyle and the integrity of the community.

> [I would rather have Arab neighbors]. Yeah [laughs]! They would probably be nicer people. I'll tell you why: the Haredi have an ambition, they want me to be more Haredi, the Arabs would not do that, they don't want to convert me, the ones that would come here, they would just live their life. (Hannah, interview)
>
> This is going to sound horrible. . . . Let's say that [a group of Haredim] would come to my neighborhood. . . . To me it would be the same thing, it would be taking the whole identity and change it. The Arab in my neighborhood would probably not change much of it, but the religious Jew . . . would insist that I should wear a long skirt. . . . (Rachel, interview)

Beyond the cultural traits and the sociopolitical agenda (or the absence thereof) of the two groups, the comparison between Palestinians and Haredim also relates to their socioeconomic status. In Rachel's words, the negative judgment passed on the two groups depends on the fact that, "[Arabs and Haredim] are on the same level and standards: they are both not working; they take money from the social security and services, they both have lots of kids and they are both a drain on society. [The Haredi] throw rocks at us, just like the Arabs. If I drive through al-Eizariya I might get stoned, but if I walk through Me'a She'arim [dressed] like this I would for sure get stoned." (Me'a She'arim is a predominantly Haredi neighborhood in Jerusalem.)

Hannah's argument follows the same path in equating the socioeconomic profile as a sort of guarantee for maintaining good neighborhood relations: "Would I be against [the idea of having Arab neighbors]? No. . . . The population that are moving to French Hill have a certain socioeconomic status, they would be doctors, lawyers, etc. It's not the uneducated. . . . That's what I feel; the ones that are upwardly mobile would choose to live in these areas. The ones [who are not] would not think about living here, and they could not afford it in the first place."

Conclusion

After the evacuation of the settlements in the Sinai, following the Israeli-Egyptian peace treaty in 1979, Rabbi Yoel Bin-Nun, then a leader of Gush Emunim, observed that the settler movement had been unable to "settle in the heart" of the nation—meaning that the settlement project remained controversial for the Israeli society as whole.[5] Indeed, the residents of Ma'ale Adumim seem to have succeeded in that purpose: albeit in ways that Bin-Nun would have probably considered too mundane, they did manage to "settle the heart" of Israel. The banality of life in Ma'ale Adumim (which was planned precisely to appeal to a vast audience of settler-commuters) has represented the most powerful driver for the growth of this suburb of Jerusalem into a community of thousands of residents, whose evacuation in the foreseeable future would seem politically impossible. In this respect, the process of normalization underlying Israel's settlement policy was the key condition for its success. At the same time, suburban life in Ma'ale Adumim was in itself an engine in the process of normalization: new senses of what Jerusalem and Israel are arose not simply by Zionist ethos of committed pioneers, but from Ma'ale Adumim's villas, shopping mall, and neat boulevards beautified by palms and olive trees; from seemingly mundane and banal daily activities as commuting to work or buying an apartment; and from the new sense of community feeling of a flourishing new town at the outskirts of the inner city.

The quotes in this chapter represent brief flashes into the process of place making underlying the process of banalization of Jewish life in the West Bank. Throughout this process, Jerusalem has represented both the key arena and the ultimate object of the protracted territorial struggle. In this sense, this chapter's emphasis on life histories, everyday practices, and discourses developed by individuals and groups does not strip Israel's settlement policy of its controversial and contested character. Indeed, our argument is that today the status of Jerusalem represents an intractable diplomatic problem precisely because of the consequences of the suburban, banal character of Israel's settlement policy. Better than many maps and reports, the words of the residents of Ma'ale Adumim indicate how the very definition of Jerusalem changed after almost five decades since 1967: the "old" Jerusalem ceased to exist for all purposes—except, maybe, for international law—following the dramatic changes of its urban fabric, which transformed it from a truncated border city, to a metropolitan region of about two million inhabitants.

Our analysis of Israel's settlement policy invites us to rethink the "exceptional" character of the conflict. By emphasizing the metropolitan dimension and the political economy of the proliferation of settlements, it challenges one-dimensional explanations exclusively based on the inherent ideological traits of Zionism and the settlers' movement and connects instead Israel's settlement policy to trends and patterns developing in the Israeli society as a whole, as well as at the global level. At the same time, the idea that settlements also constitute "safe spaces" (or gated communities) challenges the dichotomist understanding of Israeli-Palestinian relations by suggesting that these urban developments are also part of a process of stratification and spatial segregation within the boundaries of the Jewish community. Overall, the analysis of the normalization of Jewish presence in the West Bank—and especially from the vantage point of Jerusalem— suggests that the increasing interconnectedness between Israeli and Palestinian spaces, population, institutional settings, and economies is today the most strategic field of analysis for those interested in the future of Israel/Palestine.

Notes

This chapter is largely based on the author's previous work on Israel's settlement policy (Allegra 2013) and includes material from a paper coauthored with Erez Maggor (New York University), currently in an advanced stage of writing. It presents for the first time a selection of empirical material from the author's fieldwork in Ma'ale Adumim (2011–2015)—in large part in-depth interviews conducted with the residents of the settlement.

1. The three terms used by Lefebvre roughly correspond to spatial practices (i.e., the spatial structure of social relations), abstract representations of space (i.e., the formalized space of planners and social engineers), and spatial perceptions (i.e., the space as directly experienced by individuals through a complex lens made up of senses, symbols, culture), respectively.

2. Despite the arguments raised by our respondents, the legality of the establishment of Ma'ale Adumim—even not considering the provision of international law and the Fourth Geneva Convention—remains controversial on various accounts (Shalev 2009). While it would be impossible to discuss here the consequences of the building of Ma'ale Adumim on the Palestinian population of the area, it could be pointed out that, while the new town was planned on a green-field site, Palestinians from the surrounding localities repeatedly claimed ownership of the land, and small groups of Bedouins living in the area were displaced—in a process that still continues today—to make room for the expansion of the settlement. Apart of that, Ma'ale Adumim's location in a bottleneck between Jerusalem on the west, and the steep slopes of the Judean Desert falling toward the Dead Sea on the east, cuts the West Bank into two parts, and by doing so also affects the possibility of establishing a viable future Palestinian state.

3. It is not by chance, we argue, that the fastest growing settlements in the West Bank are Ultraorthodox communities at the outskirts of Jerusalem such as Beitar Illit, or Modi'in Illit (which recently surpassed Ma'ale Adumim as the most populous settlements). While the Haredi community has always been scarcely interested in the politics of Israeli-Palestinian conflict—and even less in the settlement enterprise—its tendencies to self-segregation, fast

demographic growth, and low socioeconomic status makes it a perfect candidate for settlement in suburban planned towns in the Jerusalem area (see Cahaner, chapter 7).

4. There are three main categories of encounters that take place between the residents and the Palestinians. First, the Palestinian locality of al-Eizariya sits just in front of the southwestern gate of Ma'ale Adumim beyond the traffic circles. Traditionally, the population of Ma'ale Adumim relied on al-Eizariya for a number of services and commercial facilities. The First Intifada and especially the Second Intifada, however, brought these interactions to the minimum, and the residents now rarely venture into the Palestinian town. Second, many Palestinians work in Ma'ale Adumim as janitors, gardeners, housekeepers, and in the construction sector. To the Palestinians working within the settlement we can add those employed in the nearby industrial area of Mishor Adumim, which represents a major employment center for the entire area of Jericho (see Paz-Fuchs and Ronen, chapter 10). Third, a limited number of commercial facilities (primarily the Rami Levy supermarket located in the industrial area, and, to a lesser extent, the mall of Ma'ale Adumim) are used by both communities.

5. The quote gives the title to Michael Feige's 2009 book, *Settling in the Hearts: Jewish Fundamentalism in the Occupied Territories.*

References

Agnew, John. 1994. "The Territorial Trap: The Geographical Assumptions of International Relations Theory." *Review of International Political Economy* 1 (1): 53–80.

Allegra, Marco. 2013. "The Politics of Suburbia: Israel's Settlement Policy and the Production of Space in the Metropolitan Area of Jerusalem." *Environment and Planning A* 45 (3): 497–516.

———. 2014. "E-1, or How I Learned to Stop Worrying about the Two-State Solution." *Open Democracy*, August 1, 2014. Accessed January 25, 2016. https://http://www.opendemocracy.net/arab-awakening/marco-allegra/e1-or-how-i-learned-to-stop-worrying-about-twostate-solution.

———. "The Politics of Suburbia: The Suburbanization of Israel's Settlement Policy and the Production of Space in the Metropolitan Area of Jerusalem." *Theory and Criticism.* [Hebrew.] Forthcoming.

Brenner, Neal, and Stuart Elden. 2009. "Henri Lefebvre on State, Space, Territory." *International Political Sociology* 3 (4): 353–377.

Feige, Michael. 2009. *Settling in the Hearts: Jewish Fundamentalism in the Occupied Territories.* Detroit: Wayne State University Press.

Filc, Dani. 2009. *The Political Right in Israel: Different Faces of Jewish Populism.* New York: Routledge.

Kristal, Tali. 2013. "Slicing the Pie: State Policy, Class Organization, Class Integration, and Labor's Share of Israeli National Income." *Social Problems* 60 (1): 100–127.

Lefebvre, Henri. 1991. *The Production of Space.* Oxford: Blackwell.

Maggor, Erez. 2015. "State, Market and the Israeli Settlements: The Ministry of Housing and the Shift from Messianic Outposts to Urban Settlements in the Early 1980s." *Israeli Sociology* 16 (2): 140–167. [Hebrew.]

Modarres, Ali, and Andrew Kirby. 2010. "The Suburban Question: Notes for a Research Program." *Cities* 27 (2): 114–121.

Ram, Uri. 1999. "Between Colonialism and Consumerism: Liberal Post-Zionism and the 'Glocal' Age." In *"Ethnocracy" and "Glocality": New Perspectives on Society and Space in Israel,* edited by Uri Ram and Oren Yiftachel, 41–100. Be'er Sheva: Be'er Sheva Center for Regional Development. [Hebrew.]

Razin, Eran. 1990. "Urban Economic Development in a Period of Local Initiative: Competition among Towns in Israel's Southern Coastal Plain." *Urban Studies* 27 (5): 685–703.

Shachar, Arie. 1998. "Reshaping the Map of Israel: A New National Planning Doctrine." *Annals of the American Academy of Political and Social Science* 555 (Jan. 1998): 209–218.

Shalev, Michael. 2000. "Liberalization and the Transformation of the Political Economy." In *New Israel: Peacemaking and Liberalization*, edited by Gershon Shafir and Yoav Peled, 129–159. Boulder, CO: Westview Press.

Shalev, Nir. 2009. "The Hidden Agenda: The Establishment and Expansion Plans of Ma'ale Adummim and Their Human Rights Ramifications." *Bimkom/BT'selem.* http://bimkom.org /eng/the-hidden-agenda/.

Thorpe, Merle. 1984. *Prescription for Conflict: Israel's West Bank Settlement Policy.* Washington, DC: Foundation for Middle East Peace.

Yiftachel, Oren. 2003. "Settlements as a Reflex Action." In *A Civilian Occupation: The Politics of Israeli Architecture*, edited by Rafi Segal and Eyal Weizman, 32–39. London: Verso.

4 Educating Architecture

Miki Kratsman and Ruthie Ginsburg

In recent years, many of the settlements have changed their appearance. They are not just small communities with red-tile roofs; they now also have multistory buildings. Instead of village roads suitable for riding bicycles and strolling with baby carriages, there are wide roads with condominiums. The small grocery store has been replaced with a shopping center and in some places even with a mall.

The series of photographs we call "Educating Architecture" deals with this alternate panorama that is being formed in the Occupied Territories. The conversation between Miki Kratsman and Ruthie Ginsburg following these photographs tries to understand the *raison d'etat* behind the planning, the construction, and the appearance of the settlements in the West Bank.

RG: Why did you decide to photograph what you photographed?

MK: I am interested in seeing how appearances shape the consciousness of a certain place and also in seeing how it is shaped throughout time. The move being made with the settlements is genius. Instead of "selling" the settlements as places with quality of life and detached homes, they have started to look like many other ordinary cities in the country, such as Modi'in, Rishon LeZion, Carmiel, Rosh HaAyin, Netanya, and others. The place really does not look like what we imagine a settlement would ordinarily look like.

On maps, they obscure the fact these are settlements by replacing the Arab name with a Jewish one. The Palestinian El-Carmel becomes Carmel and the Na'alin Palestinian village becomes Na'aleh. And there are many other examples. The change that is desired is being realized through mapping. The question is whether in the future we will be able to distinguish between the Palestinian Susya and the Susya settlement. It is unclear. These are strategies for camouflage. Decor that changes the place. The same with construction. I think that whoever is going to live there will feel that it is not a settlement. The way it looks blurs the boundaries; it blurs the Green Line. You cannot identify the places in the photographs. Even when you are driving within them they are difficult to identify. If I were to be parachuted into one of these settlements, I would not know where I was.

Already toward the end of the 1970s there were suburban settlements, such as Ariel (and the Jewish neighborhoods in East Jerusalem), but the pace in which these types of settlements are being constructed in recent years has increased so much that it is changing the settlement panorama.

I went looking for the ways in which the settlements do not belong to where they are located. It is true that the outskirts immediately disclose the place, certainly for whoever is looking at a settlement or visiting it. But this change in appearance is different from the settlements that we knew in the past.

RG: Why did you choose to take panoramic shots of the settlements?

MK: The choice of a panoramic view is meant to demonstrate that it is still possible to encompass the entire place in one glance. It is impossible, for example, to shoot a panorama of Tel Aviv, and yet Modi'in can be shot in panorama. Today I am photographing places that do not yet have territorial continuity between them, but clearly that will come. I am photographing them in a certain state of matter. In the future it will no longer be possible to encompass everything in one glance. This strategy, from the government's point of view, is correct. There will one day be a bus, say, from Tel Aviv, with many stops on the way to the settlement, and we will never know when it crosses the Green Line. When I look at Route 446, which travels from within the Green Line to the settlement Modi'in Illit, there is no reason why there will not be territorial continuity. The barrier will move north and be relocated between the chain of settlements that will be created and the other Palestinian villages. The border will be the border of the Palestinian village.

RG: Will the Palestinian villages become exceptions in the landscape?

MK: Yes. Every settlement is already a bloc. The government is building in such a way so that it is impossible to think of evacuation. It is naturalizing the settlements through this type of construction. The strategy on the ground is that with every day that passes more is being built. These things are not hidden from sight. A consensus is being created that it is bizarre to talk about evacuation. It is a result of education, or indoctrination. You can see this conception everywhere. Everything is being harnessed for this purpose, including what can be viewed as a type of educating architecture. They show you that if X looks like Y, then it is Y. In other words, if a settlement looks like the city of Rishon LeZion, then apparently it really is like Rishon LeZion. For instance, if you want to boycott a soccer team that plays for a town located beyond the Green Line, I am not even sure that everyone in the settlement of Ma'ale Adumim will understand that this means them. The roads are like that too. The road that begins before the

Settlement: Modi'in Illit. Photo by Miki Kratsman.

Settlement: Giv'at Ze'ev Illit. Photo by Miki Kratsman.

Green Line is the same road that leads to the settlement. Today, the settlements look much more like a suburb of Tel Aviv and much less like places such as Savion or Herzliya Pituah (upper-middle class localities within Israel proper). It makes more sense to create blocs not only because of population density, but also because of the visual effect that I discussed earlier. Modi'in helped usher in a trend of urban construction near the Green Line border. The settlement Modi'in Illit is right next to Modi'in except it is located beyond the Green Line in the Occupied Territories. This is similar to blurring the distinction between the names of Palestinian and Jewish communities that I mentioned earlier.

At the end of the 1970s it was possible to distinguish between a settlement and a Palestinian village by the lights of the community's bypassing road. The spacing between the lights of the settlement's bypass road was the same, like the same beat. Today when you look at Modi'in Illit, you see the lights of a city.

The separation wall was built because there are still places in which roads permit access to Palestinian communities. In the future, instead of a barrier there will be continuity, and I do not know whether there will be access to the Palestinian villages. They are being cut off. The villages are being suffocated. For instance, in the village of Na'alin, a barrier is being built so its residents will not be able to reach the fence. That is the trend—a barrier that will stop the Palestinians before the wall. The visual and physical continuity cuts off the Palestinians; it changes the condition of the place.

RG: What is the relationship between the appearance of the settlements and their—at least in theory—temporary status?

MK: The first time I arrived at a settlement near the Palestinian city of Nablus—I think it was Elon Moreh—I saw that most of the red-tiled roofs were actually asbestos roofs painted red. There was a simulation there too; to appear "as if." Everything is "as if," but the difference between "real" and

Settlement: Har Homa. Photo by Miki Kratsman.

Settlement: Hashmonaim. Photo by Miki Kratsman.

"as if" is small. It is important to have a mall in the settlement, because the mall is an urban phenomenon, so all of a sudden there is a mall. Today the shopping mall is more important than the pedestrian malls of the 1980s. The character of the thing, of the settlements, has changed. It is obvious that they are aiming for urban construction, not rural. Urban construction guarantees a quality of life similar to that which exists within the Green Line. The similarity between localities within the Green Line and the Occupied Territories will not necessarily attract people, but it will enable them to live there. Because it is no longer about evacuating a detached house but an apartment building, a multistory building. How do you evacuate such a building? How do you destroy it? In Gush Katif (the settlements bloc in the Gaza Strip that was evacuated in August 2005 as part of Israel's Disengagement Plan), I saw bulldozers practically erasing homes. How will they destroy a fifteen-story building as in Har Homa? I am sure that whoever lives in those buildings feels much less temporary. I remember how Har Homa looked in the beginning, with a Palestinian

protest tent that included Faisal Husseini, who spent a few weeks there.[1] I was there again in the middle of 2015 and it is unbelievable—if you are talking about a construction drive, then that is it.

RG: Is the change in visible landscape also a change in the social-political character of the settlements?

MK: I followed the establishment of the settlements in the 1980s and 1990s. Often they were initiated by very homogenous groups. Now it is a city, with neighborhoods and diverse populations. A city that is open to anyone. You can even claim that living there is not ideological. Today they are interested in numbers, not ideology. I am not saying that ideology has disappeared from the settlements, just that the situation is no longer monochromatic. In the past there were entire settlements that were painted the same color. Today it is different. A while ago I met someone who lives in Oranit, which is a settlement that straddles the Green Line, half here and half there, and I asked her where she lives, within or outside the Green Line; she did not know. Is the community half inside and half outside by mistake? This blurring is on purpose.

RG: You used panoramic photography in the photography project of the Bedouins' unrecognized villages in the Negev.[2] Is there a connection between the two projects?

MK: There is no link. It is true that I took panoramic shots with a GPS, which enables reshooting from the same place. GPS is metadata that marks the exact location of the camera, so you can relocate the camera in exactly the same spot and see the changes in the panoramic view. The difference is that the Bedouin villages are under a real and imminent threat—I am photographing them out fear of their disappearance. Here the situation is reversed: While in the settlements the outskirts will disappear, in the Bedouin villages they will continue to grow. Every photograph is a historical documentation, especially in regard to the panoramic view. You can also think about what is happening to the panorama itself. The Jewish communities, within the Green Line and outside of it, level the ground. In other words, they level the tops of the hills, especially when they are built on dominating terrain. The Palestinian villages and communities are built with the hills. I am not saying that the hills must be preserved, but what is happening is a complete change in the landscape. Entire areas that used to be rural are now urban. The topography is being leveled and they are building high-rises. Taking over land is also taking over the panoramic view and as a result—the essence of the place as well.

RG: What about Palestinian construction?

MK: The interesting part is that the Palestinians are now building a city not far from Ramallah—Rawabi. It looks like the Israeli city of Modi'in on steroids: more crowded and taller. It is confusing too. When you go from Ramallah toward the villages, toward Nabi Salah, after a curve in the road you suddenly see this intimidating city, and you are sure that it is another settlement. The Palestinians are also trying to blur the differences. Soon the Occupied Territories will cease from looking like the Occupied Territories. The villages, whose economy is mainly agriculturally based, will not have any land left, their space is being constricted. In the future, the Palestinian villages will be surrounded by high-rises. Although I am a totally urban type, it is incredibly sad to see this.

In 1982, after I got married, my father-in-law offered to help me enter a lottery for purchasing an apartment in Ma'ale Adumim. Although he opposed construction in the Occupied Territories, he said that Ma'ale Adumim will be part of Jerusalem. At about the same time I went with friends to see an apartment up for sale in Ariel. They were afraid to go there and asked that I accompany them. On the way I tried to convince them not to buy. Today no one would ask me to accompany them to Ariel. The road no longer travels through Palestinian communities. You barely realize that you are in the Occupied Territories. It is the Israeli political dream.

Notes

1. The Palestinian protest against construction in Har Homa was held in 1997. See, for example, *The Independent*, March 19, 1997, accessed January 29, 2016, http://www.independent.co.uk/news/world/bulldozers-blast-trail-for-new-settlement-1273719.html.

2. See Negev Coexistence Forum for Civic Equality website, accessed January 31, 2016, http://www.dukium.org/wpcontent/uploads/2015/03/IDARD_2015_Eng_Web2.pdf.

PART II

Between Cities and Outposts: The Heterogeneity of the Settlements and the Settlers

5   Embedded Politics in a West Bank Settlement

Hadas Weiss

SETTLING PALESTINE/ISRAEL HAS always been an immigrants' enterprise. The Zionist ideal of the ingathering of exiles has traditionally served as voiceover for Jews from the Russian Pale of Settlement, the Middle East, North Africa, and to a lesser extent the Americas and other parts of Europe, Asia, and Africa, inhabiting newly acquired lands of the emerging polity. Israeli discourse frames contemporary immigration patterns in the spirit of their predecessors, as a manifestation of political deliberation. This deliberation is alternately represented as self-motivated, as among pre-State pioneers with exceptional ideological commitment to nation building, or as superimposed, as among the 1950s immigrants from Muslim countries dispersed in peripheries for state-sponsored development projects. Either way, immigrants feature publically as either the zealous agents or the mobilized victims of well-defined political projects. This holds true also for the immigrants inhabiting the West Bank. Received wisdom has them realizing colonial agendas, whether their own or those of the Israeli state.

The assignment of political determination to immigrants parallels common perceptions of West Bank settlers at large, and, by extension, of the Israeli-Palestinian conflict. It is part and parcel of a salient view that exaggerates the regional role of politics in its narrowest sense, as an actualization of some explicit set of beliefs. This view runs counter to a more grounded understanding of politics as the powers congealed through and anchored in social and economic forces that transcend actors and deliberations on the ground. Yet it is this latter form of politics that characterizes the Israeli-Palestinian conflict today, including the practices of some of its most notorious actors: West Bank settlers. For them, I would like to argue here, politics is socially embedded, a factor of the local and global dynamic of normalization that they are caught up in.

An important goal of this volume, the editors explain in the introduction, is to consider the landscape of Israel/Palestine as an ongoing normalization of Jewish presence in the West Bank. My contribution to this goal is through the lens of one settlement and its sizable immigrant population. Drawing on ethnographic fieldwork in Ariel—a West Bank settlement of some eighteen thousand residents, about half of whom are immigrants from the Former Soviet Union (FSU)—I make the case for a different kind of political agency among immigrant-settlers of the 1990s and beyond than the one most often attributed to immigrants and settlers. I show that the immigrants in Ariel figure into larger colonial processes by dint of their pursuit of private interests. The Israeli state, vulnerable as it is to the pressures of the global market, strives to economize on social reproduction with a view toward maximizing national market growth, and it shapes settlement policies accordingly. The pursuits of the state and immigrant-settlers coalesce therefore on an ideological plane that might best be described as pragmatism. This alliance is a key feature of normalization. It creates a socially embedded politics that renders immigrants the quintessential neoliberal settlers, amenable to market-adjusted fluctuations in settlement patterns that include opportune expansion, depreciation, and dismantlement.

Normalization takes on special features in recent decades. Immigration to Israel has always been attuned to socioeconomic constraints and possibilities.[1] Yet it is primarily since the 1990s that immigrants and nonimmigrants alike have been activated by the Israeli state as the optimizing private agents of economic growth. With welfare and well-being linked to global market pressures on profitability, and with policies shaped to keep costs low and productivity high, citizens are put in charge of their investment decisions and bear sole responsibility over their outcomes. Their pragmatic adaptation to constraints aligns their practices with whatever policies are imposed on them. Forced to choose prudently among pregiven alternatives in order to provide optimally for their households' present and future needs, they are optimally responsive to flexible changes in the social and economic variables that define their environments (Foucault 2008; Brown 2003; Lemke 2001).

Operating within the boundaries of economic pressures beyond their control, these actors charge their strategic operations with moral value. It usually appears in the form of care and devotion in the domestic and communal sphere, combined with hard-boiled pragmatism regarding social and political issues, along with dismissal of agendas beyond practical reach as naïve or utopian. This attitude makes its bearers complicit in the normal state of affairs, which they help reproduce (Hacking 1990, 160). Normalization is put into relief with respect to West Bank settlement processes. Widely considered a collective undertaking for the politically committed, the act of settlement is rather a calculated choice for struggling or socially aspiring individuals who manage to leverage public resources for the attainment of private ends. The state provides these resources in response to market incentives and limitations. Far from settlement dynamics manifesting the rivaling agendas of agents wielding respective powers, West Bank politics responds to global and local pressures that transcend individual deliberations.

These, in turn, figure into politics indirectly through the private strategizing that normalization encourages.

There has been a surge in academic interest in immigration since the early 1990s, driven by the vast increase in the volume and salience of migration in its various forms (Suárez-Orozco 1998). Scholars explore the normalization of immigration through its implication in neoliberalism, globalization, and multiculturalism. They study how immigrants challenge national identities and the integrity of nation-states (Appadurai 1996; Gupta and Ferguson 1992; Ong 1999) and change relationships between global and local communities (Hollifield, Martin, and Cornelius 2014; Kearney 1995; Maurer 2000). Immigration policy is transferred from state to market and nonstate agencies (Sassen 2004), while immigrants' civic engagement is mediated by local government, nonprofits, and nongovernmental organizations (McDonald 2000; Miranda and Rich 2005). Social inequalities are thereby reproduced, and migration policies depoliticized (Fassin 2005; Fuglerud 2004). Regulation of immigration is increasingly driven by economic advantage in an environment of flexible production and global finance, rendering resettlement of immigrants less selective (Papastergiadis 2000).

In what follows, I discuss how immigration to the West Bank settlement of Ariel drove this settlement's expansion, and now how its current normalization renders immigrant-settlers amenable to socioeconomic decline or threat of dismantlement. I describe settlement processes and the ways in which FSU immigrants figure into them, as background for an ethnographic account of Ariel. Revisiting ethnographic fieldwork I conducted there a decade ago, I establish that it is precisely through their pragmatism that immigrant-settlers become political agents despite themselves. This has serious consequences for the Israeli-Palestinian conflict in general, which I refer to in the final part of this chapter.

Background

Although Israel has ruled over the West Bank since 1967, most of the Jewish settlements constructed in the first decade of the Occupation were remote and rural. Promoted as security assets and opportunities for latter-day pioneering, they held little appeal to Israel's growing urban and consumerist populace. Only with the state's mid-1980s neoliberal turn did the incentive for settlement transform from pioneering pull to economic push, fueling a settler population hike in the West Bank. More intensively integrated in the global market, Israel had undergone changes akin to those reshaping economies worldwide, including deregulation, privatization, withdrawal of state services, and restructuring of institutional frameworks to support strong private property rights, free markets, and free trade

(Harvey 2005). Scholars studying the specificity of these processes in Israel—such as Filc (2004) and Ram (1999, 2005)—describe a steady rise in the private sector's role in production and consumption, and in its share of the gross domestic product and employment, along with government withdrawal from the financial market and selling of its assets to private investors. Occupation and settlement have come to rely on bureaucratic and expert management at the expense of political leadership, even as political parties retained their symbolic appeal to a divided electorate (Grinberg 2001).

Around this time, increasing pressure on space and services in the coastal plain precipitated a drive toward suburbanization (Gonen 1995). City planners drafted remedial blueprints for satellite residences in the West Bank, subsisting on the services and employment opportunities in the metropoles (Benvenisti 1986b; Zohar 2002). Government agencies capitalized on rising demand for suburban life by denationalizing settlement activity and facilitating private land purchases in the West Bank and the Gaza Strip. They granted mortgages and incentives to encourage private investment by realtors, developers, and homebuyers. The West Bank became a popular residential destination for a growing urban workforce, offering private homes with a reasonable commute to Jerusalem and Tel-Aviv (Benvenisti 1986a; Lein and Weizman 2002; Peled and Shafir 2002; Swirski 2005). Settlements closer to the Green Line attracted a white collar workforce, while distant ones relied more heavily on government assistance. Settlements were advertised in the same way as outlying towns in Israel proper. People relocated to them in pursuit of well-being and upward mobility, like suburbanites anywhere (Applebaum and Newman 2002; Krein 2002).

The Israeli government initially wrested many advantages out of settlements in the form of revenue from settlers, cementing and legitimizing the occupation of land and resources, and easing housing pressures in the metropoles. The cost of social reproduction was lowered as settlers were given previously untapped residential resources in proximity to existing urban infrastructure, while being encouraged to invest privately in improving their living conditions. Their ability to work in Israel's urban centers and increase their spending on construction projects, goods, and services was a boon to the sluggish market. But the politicization of Palestinians since the 1987 uprising drove up the economic and political costs of maintaining settlements in the Occupied Territories far beyond initial expectations. Settlements were restructured in response to changing circumstances. To maximize the value of public investment in settlements, zoning laws and incentives were changed in ways that intensified settlements' infrastructure and services.[2]

Many settlements were subsequently thrust over the precipice of material and social decline. Forced to forgo selection committees, they absorbed needy populations and confronted compromised welfare, not to mention evacuation of the most costly settlements (Ben 2008). Settlers who had dug deep into their pockets for the prospects of realizing their social and economic aspirations came to shoulder hefty mortgage debts over devalued homes in settlements that have become impoverished and marginalized and are teaming with radicals and facing the threat of dismantlement.

One of the most striking features in these settlement dynamics is how smoothly they have unfolded, without the benefit of public discourse, and with near total compliance on the part of the settlers (a hopeless resistance by religious nationalists to their evacuation from the Gaza Strip notwithstanding). Settler acquiescence is even more remarkable with respect to the immigrants among them, insofar as misfortune had already driven them to relocate and transform their lives for the sake of their future prospects. Against the precarity and economic pressures that now plague them, the normalization that has come to define their existence in the West Bank calls for explanation.

Immigration to Ariel

Israel's mass immigration wave of the early 1990s comprised Jews and claimants to legally defined Jewish identity, who were escaping socioeconomic and political decline in the FSU. Many migrated to the United States, while those who immigrated to Israel increased its population by about 12 percent by 1996.[3] Housing prices in Israel skyrocketed, further fueled by inflation, driving growing demand for affordable housing. Immigrants received income support and rental subsidies amounting to approximately US$10,000 per family for their first year in Israel, subsidized mortgages of about 50 percent off the purchase price of an apartment, and the freedom to find housing and employment wherever they could. Their residential choices followed availability and cost-effectiveness. Most opted for the core regions while some were drawn to the peripheries (Hasson 1996; Lipshitz 1998; Peled and Shafir 2002). Others still set their sights on the West Bank, for the very same reasons. A former immigrant recounts, "I was told of a tour of the settlements . . . that the Peace Now movement organized for the newly arrived Soviet immigrants. The immigrants were supposed to see the fancy villas settlers were living in and respond with class resentment. Much to the chagrin of the tour organizers, immigrants stepped off the buses in each settlement and inquired how much the houses cost" (Slivaniak 2002, 52).

Ariel is among the largest settlements in the West Bank, located due south of Nablus and surrounded by smaller Palestinian towns like Salfit, which it overlooks from atop a mountain ridge. Approximately five kilometers long and seven hundred meters wide (three miles long and 0.4 miles wide), its municipal boundaries are convoluted to circumvent Palestinian-owned lands. A highway connects it to the greater Tel Aviv area, where many of its residents earn their living.

Initiated in 1978 by a small group of employees in the Israeli aircraft and military industries seeking suburban quality of life, its construction was aided by government ministries, and it was advertised as a bourgeoning city for other young families. For many years, it failed to grow enough to realize its founders' vision. It was only after the influx of FSU immigrants in the 1990s that its population of approximately eight thousand multiplied, changing its status in 1998 from local council to municipality.[4] In recent years, however, Ariel has been suffering from stagnant growth. Its grand villas stand adjacent to slum districts, schools are losing their best students, and children grow up and leave.

Immigration to Ariel had auspicious beginnings. Ariel's councilpersons, eager to attract highly educated middle-class taxpayers, had encouraged immigrants' arrival by campaigning for Ariel in prospective immigrants' hometowns and even at Ben-Gurion Airport. As immigrants started trickling in, residents volunteered all manner of furniture and appliances, helping immigrants through the ins and outs of bureaucratic red tape. The vacant modular houses of Ariel's old-timers, who had since upgraded to permanent homes, were converted to temporary housing for immigrants. Hebrew classes were provided for adults, schools took in children, and employment opportunities were available in the nearby Barkan Industrial Park and in the greater Tel Aviv area. Word of mouth accomplished the rest as immigrants, pleased with their absorption in Ariel, encouraged friends and relatives to follow in their footsteps.

A veritable media frenzy broke out over the arrival of the first two hundred or so immigrants to Ariel. It had all the trappings of a grand political recruitment, inflamed by then-Prime Minister Yishak Shamir's notorious pronouncement that "a great immigration requires a great Israel." "Ariel—in the Eye of the Storm" proclaimed one headline, describing how "on Wednesday alone [Ariel's Mayor Ron] Nachman received journalists from *Time, The Toronto Star, Al Hamishmar* and *The Jerusalem Post* in his office." Yet the immigrants interviewed for these news outlets knew next to nothing about Ariel prior to arrival and were uninterested in politics (*Jerusalem Post*, February 2, 1990). Asked whether they recognized how controversial their decision was, one immigrant replied, "I didn't think so in Russia, but I realize now it is a political action" (*Independent Sunday Star Review*, February 18, 1990). As far as the immigrants were concerned, disputes over settlements were inconsequential. They insisted on making Ariel their home for its affordable housing, freshness of climate, comfortable lifestyle, local friends and relatives, and welcoming attitude (Sharlin, Arzi, and Moin 2002, 8). "We told them where we were located, showed it to them on the map, explained that these were occupied territories," said a municipal representative who had marketed Ariel in the FSU to prospective immigrants, "but they didn't care one bit. Even if you talk to those who have been here for fifteen years already, you see that they have no qualms" (interview, January 15, 2006).

Ariel's fundraising periodical reported that immigrants had been referred to Ariel by real estate agents. "We had no idea we were coming to the [occupied] territories," explained one, marveling that "it is very peaceful here" (*Washington Post*, January 29, 1990). I found this former immigrant living in a sizable villa in Ariel, gainfully employed in its local high school and college. She recounted her early encounters with the press: "I didn't understand what the West Bank meant, it took me a while to figure out what was going on here . . . correspondents from NBC and other foreign media were here all the time. They asked me, 'Don't you understand that you're an obstacle to the peace process?' I never did understand why I would be. I replied, 'No, I don't think I am'" (interview, November 10, 2005).

Relative latecomers in the settlement boom, immigrants exhibited the pragmatism that defined their most recent Israeli predecessors. Nonimmigrant settlers of the 1980s had flocked to Ariel against the backdrop of stagflation and declining profitability in Israel. The purchase of homes through long-term installments had then seemed like the safest place to invest one's capital. A settler of the 1983 inrush recalls spending what little cash he and his wife had on purchasing a house in Ariel that "cost $37,000, of which $36,000 we took out in mortgage and loans that we're still paying off 32 years later" (interview, December 4, 2005). Nor was the escalating violence in the West Bank much of a deterrent: insecurity barely factored into assessments about quality of life, while economic concerns bore far more heavily on the decision to stay or leave (Moin and Sharlin 2005).[5]

Shortly after the immigrants' arrival, the 1993 Oslo Accords between Israel and the Palestinian Authority heralded rising foreign trade and capital investment in the region, yet their fruits were only felt by those in privileged positions (Ram 1999; Yiftachel 1999). Despite rhetoric about Palestinian sovereignty, Israel wished to avoid the cost of evacuating the larger settlements, and the guiding principle for drafting future borders was retention of settlement blocks (Eldar and Zertal 2004). Retention did not, however, portend prosperity for the settlements, as residents were left to fend for themselves in the open market. Israel's economic downturn, declining living standards, and swelling unemployment made these settlements attractive to a cohort of young families who could no longer afford living in the metropoles. The expansion of roads bypassing Palestinian towns shortened the commute to places such as Ariel, and the settler population grew by over 40 percent from 1992 to 1996 (Peled and Shafir 2002). The coexistence of a population hike in settlements with a socioeconomic downturn is a trend that has persisted well into the twenty-first century. An Ariel realtor describes its effects on immigrants like herself:

No one wants to buy second hand anymore when contractors build new apartments here at the same price, so people can't leave, they can't sell their old apartments . . . when there was a buying spree in Ariel, banks wanted to make a profit and gave out loans with up to 7 per cent interest rates. People stretched beyond their means and now they're making higher and higher mortgage payments. When they hear what the market value for their apartment is, they're shocked. They still owe the bank more money than they stand to gain by renting or selling it. They're stuck here, they can't even afford to move into a smaller apartment. (Interview, November 20, 2005)

Normalization

Ariel, according to early real estate ads, was to realize the vision of "a sector that would give room for private initiative and enable people to attain self-realization" (1983 real estate supplement, private collection of Uzi Amir). What is today among the larger and better known settlements in the West Bank was never considered a political project in the traditional expansionist sense, neither by the Israeli state nor by its settlers. As an early settler asserted of his fellow Arielites: "[They] are not Messianic, nor are they mystics, rather they believe it will improve their own lot, here and now. What, then, do these Jews need in order for their vision, the full significance of which they are not even aware of, to be realized? ... A government that will not interfere" (Ben-Ami 1981).

A magazine report from as early as 1982 had already pronounced Ariel an allegory of normalcy. It contrasted Ariel to surrounding settlements "of the extreme right" (Eylon 1982), where walls were presumably plastered with slogans and residents spoke of religion and politics. Ariel's media advertised commerce, banks, and contractors, while its residents voiced pedestrian concerns for comfort, consumerism, and quality of life. Over three decades later, Ariel remains virtually unmarked as a settlement, its physical and human terrain akin to towns of similar size and social makeup in Israel proper. Its local college has students dressing and talking like students anywhere, and ads referencing neighboring settlements— rental rooms in Ma'ale Levona or babysitting gigs in Elkana—identical to those referencing Israeli towns. Ariel's local papers feature local business, niche market ads for Russian-speaking consumers, segments on petty theft or vandalism, news on sporting or recreation events, and columns devoted to astrology, health, and child rearing. The town's physical normalcy resounds with its residents' patent disinterest in issues that transcend routine household concerns. The given state of affairs is the framework within which they pursue immediate advantages and communal sociability.

Even the monthly council meetings I attended exhibited nothing so much as pragmatism; if security issues could procure government funds or foreign donations, councilpersons played them up, but insofar as incidents of violence threatened to agitate settlers or deter visitors, they repressed them. Attitudes regarding the security wall were a case in point. Ariel's late Mayor Ron Nachman had early on opposed the wall in principle but later revised his view in order to save what was salvageable (interview, April 26, 2006).[6] Councilpersons would try to ensure that the wall's course be conducive to the preservation of Ariel, maintaining the appearance of a security fence rather than a political border. In a council meeting held on February 11, 2006, a plan was discussed to move the wall beyond mountain ridges and out of sight. Also discussed was a decision to close Ariel's eastern gate, blocking access to settlements further east, because state budgets for its protection were not provided. Maintenance of West Bank roads was fine and good so long as it would not be funded by Ariel's taxpayers.

The values one hears voiced in Ariel are intersubjective rather than traditionally political. Local papers boost businesses that offer good service, advocate competition and fair play, and condone cheating. Nearly everyone touts moderation and the leading of a simple life devoted to work and family while avoiding ostentation and radicalism. The virtues everyone extolls are those of honest, hardworking folk who eschew big city excesses, nurture community warmth, and look out for one another in need. Arielites model their public image as moderate, law-abiding citizens. Heightened attention by the national media to illegal outposts, hilltop squatters, and religious radicals in the West Bank underscores Ariel's normalcy; just as Palestinian acts of violence provide a stark contrast to their own professed peacefulness.

The salience of immigrants in Ariel reinstates these patterns and serves as a magnet for soliciting public and private aid for their absorption. The fact that aid to immigrant settlers is indirectly supporting settlement is no hindrance to its providers, who manifest the same narrow concerns that undergird Ariel's normalcy. This applies to private donors as well as to government officials who publically oppose the settlement movement. Financial assistance for welfare and immigrant absorption has been channeled to the West Bank by left-leaning governments with antisettlement platforms, just as it has by right-leaning governments with expansionist leanings. Ariel's local paper, *Mabat L'Ariel*, gleefully reported on visits by dovish politicians as evidence of its consensual status. It told, for example, of Labor Party's Yuli Tamir's visit to Ariel to oversee the absorption of immigrants (Editorial 1999) and of Meretz Party's Shulamit Aloni's visit to support the Russian-speaking members of Ariel's active choir, greeted by the mayor's pronouncement that "Arts and sciences have no borders" (Editorial 1993).

Immigrant settlers' preoccupation with private affairs holds true even when a struggle for settlements might bear more significantly on their fate. They are collectively disenfranchised insofar as their investments depreciate and opportunities for self-betterment diminish. Still, their attitudes are thoroughly self-serving. Like fellow immigrants in the settlement of Hebron, they deconstruct metanarratives in their concern with individual gain (Neuman 2002).[7] They are happy to deliver the public sphere to officials, so long as their private affairs are not meddled with. "Could anyone imagine Mayor Giuliani consorting with blacks in the Bronx?" One immigrant asked: "It's not his job. A modern city doesn't run that way" (interview, November 16, 2005). Councilmen are likewise emphatic about residents keeping out of public affairs: "People naturally concentrate on themselves, their daily struggles, on making a living, on educating their children, on their health, their parents, their kids. Why get involved in politics? They understand they can't do much and don't have much influence" (interview, November 14, 2005).

One advantage of living in a place like Ariel is that residents can claim idealism without straining to back it up in practice, merely by residing in a political frontier. One immigrant initially consumed only Israeli-made products, the biggest sacrifice of which was smoking local cigarettes. She has since come to deem her residence in Ariel loyalty enough, saying, "Now if there are better cigarettes, I smoke them. But if there's a better place to live in, I won't live there" (interview, September 27, 2005). Ariel's late mayor would approve: "Anyone who lives [in the West Bank] is an idealist because he performs thereby a Zionist act, and it makes no difference what his original feelings were" (Nachman 1996).

Yet with the pendulum of public opinion swinging against settlers, mere residence in Ariel also suffices for them to stand accused of the injustices implicated in the settlement movement. Arielites resent such accusations. They consider themselves unfairly stigmatized both socially, as undeserving recipients of government handouts, and politically, as obstacles to peace. Still, far from drawing them together in a sense of shared fate, they experience their turning fortunes individually and grant them significance according to their personal stakes in their place of residence. The more tentative their bonds to Ariel, the less concerned they are over its public image. Economic concerns absorb much of their attention. An immigrant-settler recounted being approached by councilpersons to draw on his European connections for a local tourism campaign: "It's not like I'm the Baron Rothschild, lounging about and engaging in public affairs. It's all nice and well, but if I don't even have the 30,000 shekels I need to fix my teeth, I also can't volunteer for the sake of Ariel" (interview, October 31, 2005).

FSU immigrants are generally the most indifferent to Ariel's political status and the least troubled over its larger ramifications. Less integrated in local networks, they define themselves according to individual attachments. The life they had experienced under a totalitarian regime has left them distrustful of public institutions, particularly government-sponsored ones (Leshem and Sicron 2004). They are often inclined to question the national ethos and embody an individualist orientation that contributes to their separateness (Kimmerling 2001; Rapoport and Lomsky-Feder 2001). Having arrived at Ariel provisionally, they keep an eye out for alternatives. Over half of them conveyed uncertainty as to whether they would continue living in Ariel if better options presented themselves (Sharlin, Arzi, and Moin 2002).

Their indifference is mirrored by attitudes of old-timers toward them. Immigrants' conspicuousness in Ariel, expressed in distinct consumption habits that include specialty shops and recreational activities, makes them appear to many Israeli-born Arielites as a "Russian bubble." Some old-timers see it as evidence of Ariel's normalcy, while others are less accepting. "What kind of people are they?" vituperates an Israeli-born Arielite. "Opportunists, uncaring, wanting the state to give them money and fund them" (interview, October 27, 2005). Religious nationalists considering relocation to Ariel have been particularly bothered by its Russian speakers. "I heard that there are 30 percent non-Jews in Ariel. What is this, a city of all its citizens?" demanded one, to which the mayor replied, "Of the 9,000 Russians living in this city, several are interreligious couples; so what?" (*Maariv*, September 9, 2005).

An Arielite depicts Ariel's fragmentation in a short story. Set in Chanukah, a large menorah erected in Ariel's commercial center stands adjacent to a Christmas tree placed by the Russian bookstore keeper. Reprimanded by an outraged Orthodox Jew, an immigrant shopper calls attention to the call to prayer sounding from a neighboring mosque. "That doesn't bother you?" he asks. "Only a Christmas tree bothers you?" (Vitkon n.d., 29). Others chime in, either complaining about immigrants selling pork in Ariel, or commending their service in the military. Unresolved, the argument recedes into the background as the narrator concludes, "When I arrived here 20 years ago, I could scarcely imagine such a scene, but I could also not fathom how, despite all of its contradictions, friction and abrasiveness, I would love my city" (Vitkon n.d., 32). Beyond the facility with which immigrants invoke Palestinians to deflect from their own otherness, the story reflects the relegation of Ariel's multiple voices to politically irrelevant background noise. A quintessential narrative of normalcy, the politics that all of these actors are implicated in collectively does not figure into their private lives.

Immigrant and nonimmigrant Arielites alike are often marginalized and even vilified among the Israeli public. They see falling returns on their economic and social investments, and they are helpless to alter their circumstances. Throughout, they strategize individually among given alternatives in a variety of exchanges and disinvestments, with the future of only their own households in view. I end this section with these sentiments as they infuse the ruminations of one FSU immigrant. She recalls that during the second Palestinian uprising,

> I was so frightened that I wanted to take the kids and run. I was willing to go to outer space even. Do you know what it's like to hear weekly gunshots from Salfit? And the terror attacks, we felt like we were in a war zone. So why didn't I leave? When you'll be married with two children and mortgage payments, you'll understand. . . . But I just bought a cottage, I enjoy my life here, I don't worry about what will happen next. I have a garden that I love. Every meter of it will be remunerated so I am not afraid. (Interview, October 16, 2005)

Conclusion

This ethnography of Ariel's immigrant-settlers demonstrates their incorporation in colonial processes as private investors, rather than as the political agents or victims they are perceived to be. Immigrants follow a political course charted within market perimeters, by dint of their concern for their own households. They respond strategically to constraints and opportunities determined by forces outside their reach. Their investments, which have generated value in the West Bank, have also bolstered their successful absorption in their new homeland. But increasingly they become entrapped by their choices, with deteriorating welfare and security devaluating their prior investments. They advocate pragmatism, which provides them some room for private maneuver. They do not realize that their efforts to protect their savings contribute to the current they must all peddle against. Having been compelled to migrate once, they anticipate a retreat to the next line of defense against material and social decline.

Their predicament forces us to rethink the nature of Middle East politics in the neoliberal era. Discourse on the West Bank has long been expressed in terms of the conflicting agendas of its main actors and the political powers they wield. But insofar as settlements are key to the future status of the West Bank, politics is assuming a different role, one far more amenable to pressures by global market and the local constraints of social reproduction. No attempt to understand the current situation in the Middle East, let alone to think through solutions to the Israeli-Palestinian conflict, can afford to ignore the socially embedded nature of its politics. If normalization grounds settlement practices, it is necessary to question its effects on other coordinates of occupation.

Great strides in this direction have been made by scholars such as Neve Gordon (2008), who describes Israel's occupation as a process of normalization that shifted in the 1990s from direct intervention in the lives and practices of Palestinians to indirect governing through control over infrastructure and resources, without assuming responsibility over Palestinians' lives and livelihoods. Parallels can also be drawn between Ariel and the new Palestinian town of Rawabi, which depoliticizes the occupation by erasing its rhetorical and visual reminders from the discursive and the spatial aspects of life within it (Grandinetti 2015). While it would be inconceivable to compare the fortunes of occupied Palestinians to those of occupying settlers, they nonetheless undergo an analogous transition to indirect forms of governance and a politics more closely interwined with socioeconomic dynamics.

Settlers intuit this correlation insofar as the Israeli government's disdain for the well-being of the Palestinians makes them question their own status. In a conference by the One Home movement promoting willful evacuation of settlements for equitable compensation, convened not long after the unilateral disengagement from the Gaza Strip and dismantlement of its settlements, settlers expressed these concerns openly. Pleaded one settler, "If the state has pilot plans for further evacuation, I call on it to do so now. . . . We are not negotiation chips, we are not cannon fodder . . . a settlement like Ariel is a veritable city. [Prime Minister] Olmert promised it will be retained, and still 60 per cent want to leave. We've had enough of the poor security, the price, the deterioration in quality of life . . . we cannot live with the uncertainty" (public speech at the One Home Conference, Tel Aviv, February 8, 2006). Even if the state withdraws from the West Bank, insisted another, "It has to take into account the human beings crushed under the wheels of the bulldozer. We're not pawns in a game of checkmate. The state may have already decided that the Palestinians are no partner for negotiation, but it must negotiate with us" (public speech at the One Home Conference, Tel Aviv, February 8, 2006).

Not only does the Israeli state disregard the desires of Palestinians, it makes scant efforts to seek legitimacy for settlement policies from its own citizens, who begrudgingly accept them as authoritative, as was most blatantly demonstrated during the forceful evacuation of Gaza Strip settlements. The transparent subjugation of Palestinians becomes instrumental in obfuscating settlers' lot, making it seem as though their civic rights and duties grant them far more control over their fate in the West Bank than their less fortunate neighbors have. This account of immigrant-settlers suggests otherwise. As settlers are encouraged to pragmatically follow their interest in the confines of what is socially, economically, and politically given, the settlement dynamic falls prey to global and local forces superimposed upon them. True justice in the Middle East is unlikely without a better understanding of its socially embedded politics.

Notes

This chapter is based on work reproduced by permission of the American Anthropological Association from *PoLAR: Political and Legal Anthropology Review* 34 (1): 112–130, May 2011. Not for sale or further reproduction.

1. Even the most ideologically committed pioneers of early Zionism gained collectively from nationalized production; just as the state's directing of impoverished immigrants to underdeveloped peripheries followed economic reliance on streamlined industrial production (Gonen 1995; Grinberg 2001; Lissak and Horowitz 1978; Kimmerling 1983a, 1983b; Shafir 1996; Sternhell 1995; Smooha 2004).

2. Studies by the West Bank database project have shown average operating costs decreasing the larger the settlement (Dehter 1987).

3. In the 1990s, approximately 1.3 million left the FSU, of which some 800,000 immigrated to Israel (Leshem and Sicron 2004, 81).

4. For more on Ariel, see Lein and Weizman (2002), Levin (1988), Shalit (2003), Shvut (2002), Amizur et al. (2004), Eldar and Zertal (2004), and Ariel's municipal website: http://www.ariel.muni.il.

5. Ariel's information center reported a rise in housing prices in Ariel between 1987 and 1990 "despite the intifada [Palestinian uprising], and perhaps as an answer to it" (1990 advertisement, private collection of Uzi Amir).

6. It had been decreed that the portion of the wall built around Ariel be independent of the main separation barrier with the hopes of it being perceived as a security wall rather than as a political border (*Ynet*, September 14, 2004). An Ariel councilman warned that "with the completion of the barrier wall, the small citizen will understand he has nothing going for him in settlements east of the wall, including Ariel. We will all feel the effects in the prices of homes and assets" (Rot 2005). Housing prices west of the wall have indeed risen higher than those east of it (*Yedioth Ahronoth*, December 16, 2005).

7. Tamara Neuman's (2002) ethnography of FSU immigrants in Hebron confirms many of my own findings, though I would qualify her claim that this immigration served to sustain right-wing agendas. That FSU immigrants are often hawkish in no way translates into a commitment to settlement, and it is irrespective of which side of the Green Line they happen to live on (Arian, Knafelman, and Philippov 2009; Sheleg 2003).

References

Amizur, Liron, Yaakov Eshel, David Solomonika, and Chaim Tsaban. 2004. *Ariel and Rosh Ha'ayin: Comparison by Urban Development Factors*. Ariel: Research Institute. [Hebrew.]

Anonymous. 2006. Public speech at the One Home Conference, Tel Aviv, February 8, 2006.

Appadurai, Arjun. 1996. "Sovereignty without Territoriality: Notes for a Postnational Geography." In *The Geography of Identity*, edited by Patricia Yaeger, 40–58. Ann Arbor: University of Michigan Press.

Applebaum, Levia, and David Newman. 2002. "Features of the Community Settlement in Judea and Samaria." In *Ascent to the Mountains: Renewal of the Jewish Settlement in Judea and Samaria*, edited by Avraham Shvut, 167–174. Beit El: Beit El Books. [Hebrew.]

Arian, Asher, Anna Knafelman, and Michael Philippov. 2009. *The 2009 Israeli Democracy Index: Auditing Israeli Democracy: Twenty Years of Immigration from the Former Soviet Union*. Jerusalem: Israel Democracy Institute.

Ben, Aluf. 2008. "A Different Perspective on Settlements." *Idkun Astrategi* 11 (2): 39–49. [Hebrew.]

Ben-Ami, Aharon. 1981. "An Idea Seeking a City." *Ha'ir Ariel*, Succoth [October 12–19]. [Hebrew.]

Benvenisti, Meron. 1986a. *1986 Report: Demographic, Economic, Legal, Social and Political Developments in the West Bank*. Boulder: Westview Press.

———. 1986b. Conflicts and Contradictions. New York: Villard Books.

Bredenstein, Eli. 2005. "Netzarim against the Christians." *Maariv*, September 9. [Hebrew.]

Brown, Wendy. 2003. "Neo-Liberalism and the End of Liberal Democracy." *Theory and Event* 7 (1): 1–29.

Dehter, Aaron. 1987. *How Expensive Are West Bank Settlements? A Comparative Analysis of the Financing of Social Services*. Boulder: Westview Press.

Diehl, Jackson. 1990. "Soviet Refugees Get a Warm Welcome." *Washington Post*, January 29.

Editorial. 1993. Ariel Ensemble—A Festive Opening Concert. *Mabat L'Ariel*, November. [Hebrew.]

———. 1999. Ariel—A Very High Quality Immigrant Absorbing City. *Mabat L'Ariel*, November. [Hebrew.]

Eldar, Akiva, and Idith Zertal. 2004. *Lords of the Land: The Settlers and the State of Israel 1967–2004*. Or-Yehuda: Kinneret. [Hebrew.]

Eylon, Amos. 1982. "Ariel as Metaphor." *Haaretz*, November 12. [Hebrew.]

Fassin, Didier. 2005. "Compassion and Repression: The Moral Economy of Immigration Policies in France." *Cultural Anthropology* 20 (3): 362–387.

Filc, Dani. 2004. "Israel Model 2000: Neoliberal Post Fordism." In *The Power of Property: Israeli Society in the Global Age*, edited by Dani Filc and Uri Ram, 34–56. Jerusalem: Van Leer Institute. [Hebrew.]

Firsh, Felix, and Efrat Weiss. 2004. "The PM Determined: Ariel Is outside the Fence." *Ynet*, September 14. [Hebrew.]

Foucault, Michel. 2008. *The Birth of Biopolitics: Lectures at the Collège de France, 1978–1979*. Translated by Graham Burchell. New York: Palgrave Macmillan.

Fuglerud, Oivind. 2004. "Constructing Exclusion: The Micro-Sociology of an Immigration Department." *Social Anthropology* 12 (1): 25–40.

Gonen, Amiram. 1995. *Between City and Suburb*. Aldershot: Avebury.

Gordon, Neve. 2008. *Israel's Occupation*. Berkeley: University of California Press.

Grandinetti, Tina. 2015. "The Palestinian Middle Class in Rawabi Depoliticizing the Occupation." *Alternatives: Global, Local, Political* 40 (1): 63–78.

Grinberg, Lev. 2001. "Social and Political Economy." In *Trends in Israeli Society*, edited by Efraim Yaar and Zeev Shavit, 585–697. Tel Aviv: Open University. [Hebrew.]

Gupta, Akhil, and James Ferguson. 1992. "Beyond 'Culture': Space, Identity, and the Politics of Difference." *Cultural Anthropology* 7 (1): 6–23.

Hacking, Ian. 1990. *The Taming of Chance*. Vol. 17. Cambridge: Cambridge University Press.

Harvey, David. 2005. *A Brief History of Neoliberalism*. Oxford: Oxford University Press.

Hasson, Shlomo. 1996. "From International Immigration to Internal Migration: The Settlement Process of Immigrants from the Former Soviet Union in Israel." In *Immigration and Integration in Post-Industrial Societies: Theoretical Analysis and Policy-Related Research*, edited by Naomi Carmon, 166–184. London: Macmillan/St. Martin.

Hollifield, James, Philip Martin, and Wayne A. Cornelius. 2014. *Controlling Immigration: A Global Perspective*. Stanford, CA: Stanford University Press.

Horovitz, David, and Michael Shridan. 1990. "Fears of a New Holocaust." *Independent Sunday Star Review*, February 18.

Kearney, Michael. 1995. "The Local and the Global: The Anthropology of Globalization and Transnationalism." *Annual Review of Anthropology* 24: 547–565.

Keinon, Herb. 1990. "Ariel—In the Eye of the Storm." *Jerusalem Post*, February 2.

Kimmerling, Baruch. 1983a. *Zionism and Economy*. Cambridge, MA: Schenkman.

———. 1983b. *Zionism and Territory: The Socio-Territorial Dimensions of Zionist Politics*. Research Series. Berkeley: Institute of International Studies, University of California.

———. 2001. *The Invention and Decline of Israeliness: State, Society, and the Military*. Berkeley: University of California Press.

Krein, Gideon. 2002. "The Physical Planning of the Community Settlement." In *Ascent to the Mountain: Renewal of Jewish Settlement in Judea and Samaria*, edited by Avraham Shvut, 101–106. Beit El: Beit El Books. [Hebrew.]

Lein, Yehezkel, and Eyal Weizman. 2002. Land Grab: Israel's Settlement Policy in the West Bank. Tel Aviv: B'Tselem. Accessed January 31, 2016. http://www.btselem.org/publications /summaries/200205_land_grab.

Lemke, Thomas. 2001. "'The Birth of Bio-Politics': Michel Foucault's Lecture at the Collège de France on Neo-Liberal Governmentality." *Economy and Society* 30 (2): 190–207.

Leshem, Elazar, and Moshe Sicron. 2004. "The Soviet Immigrant Community in Israel." In *Jews in Israel: Contemporary Social and Cultural Patterns*, edited by Uzi Rubhun and Chaim Waxman, 81–117. Hanover, MA: Brandeis University Press.

Levin, Esther. 1988. *Ariel—Capital of Samaria*. Philadelphia: Publishing House of Peace. [Hebrew.]

Lipshitz, Gabriel. 1998. *Country on the Move: Migration to and within Israel, 1948–1995*. Dordrecht: Kluwer Academic Publishers, in cooperation with the Jerusalem Institute for Israel Studies.

Lissak, Moshe, and Daniel Horowitz. 1978. *The Origins of the Israeli Policy: Palestine under the Mandate*. Chicago: University of Chicago Press.

Maurer, Bill. 2000. *Recharting the Caribbean: Land, Law, and Citizenship in the British Virgin Islands*. Ann Arbor: University of Michigan Press.

McDonald, David A. 2000. "We Have Contact: Foreign Migration and Civic Participation in Marconi Beam, Cape Town." *Canadian Journal of African Studies/La Revue canadienne des études africaines* 34 (1): 101–123.

Miranda, Marta, and Brian L. Rich. 2005. "The Sociopolitical Dynamics of Mexican Immigration in Lexington, Kentucky, 1997–2002: An Ambivalent Community Responds." In *New Destinations: Mexican Immigration in the United States*, edited by Victor Zúñiga and Rubén Hernández-León, 187–219. New York: Russel Sage Foundation.

Moin, Victor, and Shlomo Sharlin. 2005. "Reactions of Shomron Inhabitants to Political Uncertainty and Insecurity: Opinions and Attitudes of Veterans, Immigrants from the Former Soviet Union, and 'Experts.'" In *Judea and Samaria Research Studies*, edited by Yaakov Eshel, 275–294. Ariel: Research Institute, College of Judea and Samaria. [Hebrew.]

Nachman, Ron. 1996. Ray of Light, a New Government. *Mabat L'Ariel*, Cheshvan. [Hebrew.]

Neuman, Tamara. 2002. "Alienations of Exilic Return: Russian Immigration and 'Ingathering' in Hebron." In *Realms of Exile: Nomadism, Diasporas, and Eastern European Voices*, edited by Domnica Radulescu, 125–148. Boston: Lexington Books.

Ong, Aihwa. 1999. *Flexible Citizenship: The Cultural Logics of Transnationality*. Durham, NC: Duke University Press.

Papastergiadis, Nikos. 2000. *Mapping Global Migration: The Turbulence of Migration, Globalization, Deterritorialization, and Hybridity*. Cambridge: Polity Press.

Peled, Yoav, and Gershon Shafir. 2002. *Being Israeli: The Dynamics of Multiple Citizenship*. Cambridge Middle East Studies. Cambridge: Cambridge University Press.

Ram, Uri. 1999. "Between Colonialism and Consumerism: Liberal Post-Zionism in the Glocal Age." In *"Ethnocracy" and "Glocality": New Perspectives on Society and Space in Israel*, edited by Uri Ram and Oren Yiftachel, 43–100. Be'er Sheva: Negev Center for Regional Development. [Hebrew.]

———. 2005. *The Globalization of Israel: McWorld in Tel Aviv, Jihad in Jerusalem*. Tel Aviv: Resling. [Hebrew.]

Rapoport, Tamar, and Edna Lomsky-Feder. 2001. "Homecoming, Immigration, and the National Ethos: Russian-Jewish Homecomers Reading Zionism." *Anthropological Quarterly* 74 (1): 1–14.

Rot, Yehuda Meir. 2005. "Ariel Is Worth More." http://www.arielplus.il (site no longer available).

Sassen, Saskia. 2004. "Beyond Sovereignty: De-Facto Transnationalism in Immigration Policy." In *In Worlds on the Move: Globalization, Migration and Cultural Security*, edited by Jonathan Friedman and Shalini Randeria, 229–249. London: I. B. Tauris.

Shafir, Gershon. 1996. "Zionism and Colonialism: A Comparative Approach." In *Israel in Comparative Perspective*, edited by Michael N. Barnett. New York: State University of New York Press.

Shalit, Dina. 2003. "Interview with the Mayor." *Shalom Ariel*, October. [Hebrew.]

Shalita, Chen. 2005. "Right of Return." *Yedioth Ahronoth*, December 16.

Sharlin, Shlomo, Lilach Arzi, and Victor Moin. 2002. *Adjustment of New Immigrants from the Former Soviet Union to Ariel*. Ariel: Haifa University/College of Judea and Samaria. [Hebrew.]

Sheleg, Yair. 2003. *The Political and Social Significance of Evacuating Settlements in Judea, Samaria and Gaza*. Jerusalem: The Israel Democracy Institute [Hebrew].

Shvut, Avraham. 2002. "Stages in the Renewal of Jewish Settlement in Judea, Binyamin and Samaria." In *Ascent to the Mountain: Renewal of Jewish Settlement in Judea and Samaria*, edited by Avraham Shvut, 75–92. Beit El: Beit El Books. [Hebrew.]

Slivaniak, Dmitri. 2002. "Neither a sign of courage nor a sign of disgrace." *Eretz Acheret* 10: 50–52. [Hebrew.]

Smooha, Sammy. 2004. "Jewish Ethnicity in Israel: Symbolic or Real." In *Jews in Israel: Contemporary Social and Cultural Patterns*, edited by Uzi Rebhun and Chaim Waxman, 47–80. Hanover, MA: Brandeis University Press.

Sternhell, Zeev. 1995. *Nation Building or a New Society?: The Zionist Labor Movement (1904–1940) and the Origins of Israel*. Tel Aviv: Am Oved. [Hebrew.]

Suárez-Orozco, Marcelo. 1998. "Epilogue." In *Crossings: Mexican Immigration in Interdisciplinary Perspectives*, edited by Marcelo Suárez-Orozco, 413–419. Cambridge: Harvard University Press.

Swirski, Shlomo. 2005. "The Price of Occupation and the Cost of the Occupation to Civil Society." *Civil Society* 12 (1). Accessed July 14, 2016. http://www.pij.org/details.php?id=335.

Vitkon, Esther. n.d. *Cross-Samaria: From the Diary of a Settler 1985–2005*. Ariel: Da'at. [Hebrew.])

Yiftachel, Oren. 1999. "Israeli Society and Jewish Palestinian Reconciliation: 'Ethnocracy' and Its Territorial Contradictions." In *"Ethnocracy" and "Glocality": New Perspectives on Society and Space in Israel*, edited by Uri Ram and Oren Yiftachel, 11–40. Be'er Sheva: Negev Center for Regional Development. [Hebrew.]

Zohar, Ezra. 2002. "The Settlement of Judea and Samaria by Means of Satellite Towns." In *Ascent to the Mountain: Renewal of Jewish Settlement in Judea and Samaria*, edited by Avraham Shvut, 93–99. Bei El: Beit El Books. [Hebrew.]

6 Informal Outposts in the West Bank
Normality in Gray Space

Erez Tzfadia

THE DOZENS OF new Jewish settlements that have been established in the West Bank (WB) since the Oslo Accords in 1993 are typically known as "informal outposts" (outposts). Several researchers, politicians, human rights organizations, journalists, and even settlers' organizations consider these outposts as exceptions to Israel's settlement policy and to Jewish life in the West Bank: an exception to the legal order (Sasson 2005), an exception to the trend in the settlement project (Billig 2015), an exception in the composition of residents (Feige 2009; Friedman 2015), an exception in locations (Billig 2015), and an exception in the intensity of violence against Palestinians ("price tag" strategy) (UNHRC 2014; Ghanim, chapter 9).

Against this consideration, and based on the assumption that politics of space expresses ideologies, interests, and attempts to design social relations accordingly, I argue (1) that the outposts are in conformity with the standard and pattern of the colonization of Israel/Palestine and are "normal" as a result of "gray spacing" (a set of technologies designed to inhabit and control a territory) (Yiftachel 2009; Tzfadia and Yiftachel 2014), and (2) that the outposts are relatively normal localities for ordinary people. In this case, "normal" suggests that the outposts are informal, but at the same time they are heterogeneous, affordable, and have conventional activities. But more importantly, this normality rather suggests that everyday life in the outposts (or perhaps the banality of life there) does not differ from life in authorized settlements or in any other place in Israel that has been built as part of the colonization of Israel/Palestine.

The two parts of the argument are interlinked because both parts depend on the assumption that the production of space in Israel/Palestine through acts of colonization has blurred the border between formality and informality. Informality, as a technology of controlling space and society, is not an exception to colonization. Together with legal and formal decision making and spatial planning, informality is a normal way of spatial production that results in normal localities for living. Formality and informality are also symbiotically interdependent. As I will show, the colonization is fueled by "ordinary" people who seek to improve their standards of living, thus the colonization must benefit its settlers. In most cases, benefiting particular groups—settlers in this case—works against the principle of equity in law. Informal spaces have the ability to upgrade the rights of a particular group beyond the limits of law, as the spaces are not subject to law. After a while informal settlements are legalized, to insure the rights of the settlers. This is exactly what makes these places attractive for ordinary people, and these people promote the colonization by their ordinary geographical behavior.

Though I maintain that the two parts of the argument are interlinked and symbiotically interdependent, I will analyze each part separately. The analysis of the first part focuses on the legal and political processes that guided the making of the outposts, the political support that the outposts gained, and their relation to ethnonational ideology of territorial control. The analysis of the second part of the argument undermines the stereotypical image of radical, ideology-driven, messianic youth typically associated with these communities (Mendelsohn 2014), by describing the heterogeneity of the residents, and the marketing method of the outposts and tourism there. Both parts are based on analysis of legal and official documents, protocols of the government and parliament, statements by politicians, and interviews with officials, plus "softer" materials that indicate the mode of life in the outposts, such as newspaper articles (mainly newspapers published in the Occupied Territories, hereafter OT), interviews with residents, documentaries, advertisements of activities in the outposts, representation on internet sites, and the marketing methods of houses in the outposts. I should emphasize that the chapter does not rely on ethnographic research, though several interviews were conducted.

We shall start with elaborating and linking several key concepts: gray space/spacing, informality, and normality. "Gray spacing" refers to various "technologies" of developments and land possessions, not necessarily legal and formal, aimed at contributing to territorial control and social hierarchies. The result, "gray space," refers to a mixture of legal statuses of developments that define the scope of rights of different groups there: from "upgraded grayness," which refers to groups who enjoy more rights than the law permits, to "survived grayness," which refers to groups who are denied the rights and privileges that the law should guarantee.

Schematically, one can refer to four technologies of gray spacing that together produce and reproduce gray spaces: (1) *Formal planning and policy*, usually conceived as a tool for reform, justice, and individual dignity, derives its power from the rule of law. But, it can also be used for the opposite purpose of oppressing minorities and controlling territory (Harvey 1973; Yiftachel and Huxley 2000; Watson 2014) and specifically to occupation and colonization (King 1990; Weizman 2007). (2) *Patchwork* of laws and regulations obtained by "juggling" between a variety of legal systems—the law of empire, colonial law, customary law, and local law and regulations. Such a patching process aims at presenting legal façade to oppression and territorial control (Hussain 2003; Comaroff 2001). (3) *State of emergency* refers to a sovereign's decision to suspend the law and to declare a "state of emergency," which enables space's reconstruction in favor of dominant interests and privileged groups—see Graham (2004) on the American cities and the War on Terror, and Tarlo (2003) on the reorganization of Delhi during the Indian Emergency in 1975–1977. And (4) *Informality* usually is about the agency of the poor and the disenfranchised in the slums, but gray spacing considers it as one of its technologies of territorial control, by focusing on the role played by the authorities. For example, informal development might exist partially outside "the gaze" of state authorities, sometimes as a means to deny services and rights, and sometimes as a way to enable an extension of rights—beyond the limits of law. Informal spaces include various informal activities, which due to political, social, and ideological reasons, continue existing as apparently temporal, and de facto permanent spatial phenomena (Yiftachel 2009; Avni and Yiftachel 2014).

The four technologies of gray spacing are interlinked: what might begin as informal development from below, if serving ethnonational interests, might be legalized by patching process and afterward by formal planning. The same goes with state of emergency; when development is justified and approved in an emergency context, it might be embedded in the formal planning when the state of emergency ends. All of these acts might be deemed upgraded grayness because the informal development expanded the rights beyond the limits of law, and the process of legalization accepted and affixed these rights. An apposite example, as I discuss elsewhere (Tzfadia 2013) and elaborate hereinafter, was the building of "authorized" settlements in the OT in the 1970s. Some had been built informally, justified within the context of emergency and security needs, and were then legalized afterward by a patching process. In this context, the rights of the settlers were extended beyond the limits of law, as they enjoyed land for free that they were inhabiting illegally. They had the ability to dispossess the landlords, to enjoy public investments and funds, to be recognized as pioneers, and finally, to be the legal beneficiaries of the land and its property rights (ibid.).

Are gray spacing and gray spaces normal or an exception? The answer to this question is crucial to my argument that the outposts are normal, that is, they conform to the standard and pattern of the colonization of Israel/Palestine. Apparently, gray spacing as a bureaucratic-political technology of designing space and social relations is an exception to the technical or scientific understanding of planned space. Public policy and administration, for example, do not question whether formality is the norm. Formality is simply taken as obvious and rational (Di Maggio and Powell 1983). Within the field of urban informality, the main question is how to "tame" informality or how to "solve" the problem of informal development (Chiodelli et al. 2013; Davis 2006).

More critical analyses of informality, state of exception, and patching processes indicate that gray spaces are normal, mainly in a colonial context. State of exception is not only the norm, but is the definition of the juridical (Agamben 2005) and the political orders (Schmitt 1985), mainly in a colonial context (Hussain 2003), which is so relevant to this case study. AlSayyad (2004, 7) famously described: "urban informality as a 'new' way of life," meaning that informality is a contemporary and normal mode of life, which is linked to the physical setting of unplanned development, informal economy, and unauthorized settlements. And as Roy (2011, 211) adds: "urban informality . . . is a mode of the production of space . . . an idiom of urbanization, a logic through which differential spatial value is produced and managed." Upon this suggestion, Yiftachel (2009) and Tzfadia and Yiftachel (2014) theorize gray spacing and gray space as a set of political technologies that design space and places, resulting in a social hierarchy of rights and citizenship.

The Outposts: Background

Since the mid-1990s, some settlers organized themselves into groups called "hilltop youth" and began to establish outposts, without statutory plans and sometimes on land that was privately owned by Palestinians (Sasson 2005; Etkes and Ofran 2006; Friedman 2015). The number of outposts is unclear. The nongovernmental organization Peace Now (2012) counts ninety-nine outposts, inhabited by 9,689 residents, who lived in 2,454 mobile houses, and 615 permanent houses (in 2011). The outposts cover approximately 4,000 acres of land, of which 1,700 acres consist of private, Palestinian-owned land. Many outposts are neighboring "formal" settlements, whereas others are located near the main roads that serve the Jewish settlers. Currently, this is the most detailed available data on the outposts.

Various methods have been used to establish outposts: a communication transmitter was planted and built formally on a hill, with a "watchman" assigned to guard it, who would then bring along friends and family; an educational institution was established, requiring quarters for staff and students; new houses were designated as a neighborhood in an existing settlement, even if located many miles distant from the authorized settlement; farming new areas and building adjacent "workers' quarters," etc. All of these methods were mentioned by Feige (2009) and Friedman (2015), wherein they were described as, quoting Sasson (2005, 24), "circumventing procedures and suspension of law, displaying a false picture to some authorities, while cooperating with other authorities."

Most of these outposts, eighty-three in total, were established during Prime Minister Barak's government (1999–2001). During the first Netanyahu government (1996–1999), nineteen outposts were established; thirteen more were established during Sharon's government (2001–2006); and two outposts were established during Olmert's government (2006–2009). Another two outposts have been established during Netanyahu's governments (2009–).[1]

Israel's legal authorities had identified the outposts as illegal or unauthorized settlements, because they did not correspond with four conditions that are needed in order to be a legal settlement in the OT: (1) governmental approval, (2) available state land, (3) a statutory plan approved by the planning authority of the military governor, and (4) approved jurisdiction by the commander-in-chief (Sasson 2005). The High Court of Justice (HCJ) ruled that the outposts should be evacuated and issued restraining orders regarding any construction or other physical presence by settlers.[2]

Yet, the illegality of the outposts did not prevent politicians and officers from supporting the outposts, as was explored by Sasson (2005). Land, infrastructure, and budgets were allocated for this purpose, as Shaul Goldstein, head of Gush Etzion Regional Council, explains: "Every single outpost was coordinated with the Civil Administration[3] and the army. But, all the instructions were delivered by phone. Nothing was official" (interview, June 30, 2008, and see more in interviews with Jewish mayors in the WB in [Tzfadia 2013, 2016]). Moreover, Segula and Boaz Melt, the founders of Adi-El outpost, add that: "It is ridiculous to think that we build the outposts alone. We were sent by the government and the army that regards the outposts as a strategic goal. . . . The government does not build the outposts officially . . . government officers tell us: 'Settle! And we will take care of all your needs.' Public authorities financed the roads. They paved the roads when the supervisors were absent. The state plays a game: its right hand says 'Build! Do! Settle!' And its left hand stops the construction. We are willing to play this game" (Yavin 2005).

While few outposts have been demolished, in recent years the Israeli government has attempted to legalize outposts.[4] It began in court, on October 19, 2010, with the state prosecutor's brief: "State policy . . . is considered vis-à-vis broad national interests, which include security considerations. It is obvious that the national logic has an influence on the priorities of law enforcement in the area. . . . As the issue of the West Bank construction is a core issue in the negotiations between Israel and the Palestinians, political considerations must be taken into account when deciding on enforcement and the state is currently re-evaluating the issue of outposts."

Prime Minister Benjamin Netanyahu supported the state prosecutor and said that the government needed more time to decide when and how to dismantle outposts, due to the "political implications" involved. The government, he added, "needs time to consider its priorities" with regard to these outposts (*Ynet*, October 19, 2010). A few months later, he stated that "we are trying to maintain the construction, but have to understand that we are facing a difficult international reality" (Lis and Mualem 2011). From this point onward, the government adopted a policy of legalizing outposts. Accordingly, any outpost that was built over land which is not formally recognized as privately owned by a Palestinian landlord will be legalized. Houses, and not necessarily the entire outpost, built over private Palestinian land will be demolished.[5] On May 2011, the Attorney's Office announced this new policy to the court (HCJ 9060/08). The judicial branch acknowledged this modus operandi. By 2015, thirteen outposts had retroactively been planned by the authorities, and twelve others were in the planning process (YeshDin 2015), which is the legalization of outposts.

This new policy has been criticized by the Greater Israel Lobby in the parliament. In a letter to Prime Minister Netanyahu, the lobby argued that "the officials should be instructed to utilize all possibilities to ensure that there will be no more demolishing of houses in settlements in Judea and Samaria . . . wherever construction has innocently been made over private land, there is a way out by compensation" (*Walla News*, October 11, 2011). In a parliamentary debate on the legalization of outposts built on private Palestinian land, National Religious Party Member of Parliament Zevulun Orlev, and also a member of the Greater Israel Lobby, asked: "Are we dealing with property rights? Are you concerned by the dilemma of how to prevent damage to Palestinian real estate? The actual dilemma is policy . . . what is the settlement policy in Judea and Samaria of this government?" (Israel Parliament protocol, June 6, 2012). In July 2015, Minister of Justice Ayelet Shaked, a right-wing politician herself, announced that the ministry is working to find a legal way to legalize houses built on private Palestinian land. It seems that it is only a matter of time until all the outposts will be legalized, which conforms to the standard and pattern of colonization of Israel/Palestine.

Outposts as a "Normal" Pattern of Jewish Colonization in Israel/Palestine

The impression that the outposts are an exception is related to their informal nature and retroactive legalization, which is part of the creation of a gray space. However, Zionism enjoys a rich history of informality, patching process, state of exception, and retroactive legalization of unauthorized settlements, including in the OT (Sprinzak 1986). It seems that respecting the law in the arena of Zionist settlement has not been a fundamental value; rather it has been a matter of choice, depending on instrumental considerations of expediency. Legalization usually comes afterward. Examples include the mythical *Homa u'migdal* (Tower and Stockade) settlements which were built in the 1930s (Rotbard 2003), the new villages constructed during the 1948 War (Tzfadia 2010), and more recently the wine-route farms developed in the Negev (McKee 2015). Some settlement projects did not have all the necessary permissions at the time of building. But retrospectively they were legalized.

Not surprisingly, many of the new settlements built in the OT after the 1967 War were informal, too. Internationally, Israel presented the new settlements as temporal, as military bases, as archeological camps, etc., and not as formal and planned localities (Gorenberg 2006). Each settlement needed emergency orders from the army commander, and violations of Palestinian landlords' property rights were justified by claiming that the settlements were an emergency act. Later, predominantly after 1973, Gush Emunim assumed that a weak Israeli leadership had delayed the territorial acts necessary to revive the ancient Jewish Kingdom. Accordingly, Gush Emunim eagerly and illegally stepped into the field of building new settlements, sometimes on Palestinian privately owned land (ibid.). The settlers were not evacuated from the informal settlements. Rather, these settlements were legalized, justified by security needs, and the court permitted violation of property rights of Palestinian landlords to build these settlements, based on security reasoning (Kretzmer 2002).

Indeed, frontiers have been marked as targets for Jewish settlements, as part of internal and external colonization, because Jewish settlements have been perceived as a means to control territory and its contents, both within the pre-1967 state borders (Tzfadia and Yacobi 2011; Yiftachel 2006) and within the post-1967 borders. In this sense, the Jewish colonization in the OT has continued this trend, thereby adding another dimension of erasing the differences between pre-1967 Israeli territory and the OT[6] and, of course, between the "authorized" settlements in the WB and the outposts.

Nationalism, territory, power, and frontier practices are obviously connected to gray spacing and its technologies of territorial control. Gray spacing is a means of accumulating property and land—sometimes against the rule of law—stimulating national spirit through a mythos of settlement and frontier heroism and demarcating the border between "us" and "them" as part of the nation-building project (for Turner's frontier thesis, see Turner [1962]; for more contemporary writing, see Anderson [2013]). Settlement in Zionism history, particularly the informal one, has had an essential role in shaping national spirit, leadership, Israel's borders, citizenship, resource allocation, culture, and ethnoclass relations (Kimmerling 1983; Lustick 1993; Zerubavel 1995; Yiftachel 2006; Tzfadia and Yacobi 2011; Jabareen 2015). Beyond the vague political terms, settlements by gray spacing affect the rights and spatial rights of people, according to whether they belong to the "upgraded gray" (beyond the limit of law) category, or "survived gray" (below the minimum set by law) category (Tzfadia and Yiftachel 2014).

Throughout the post-1948 Zionist colonization, dilemmas regarding the rule of law obligated Israel's governments to create a patchwork legal solution to be approved by a court. In my previous work on this issue, I referred to the Beit El

(1978) petition and the Elon Moreh petition (1979) to point toward the special rule that the court plays in legitimizing the act of Jewish colonization of the OT (Tzfadia 2010, 2013). As I already mentioned, in the early years of Jewish settlement in the OT, the violation of Palestinian landlords' property rights was justified in court by claiming that the settlements were an emergency act against Palestinian terror attacks (Tzfadia 2013). In 1979, the Israeli HCJ forbade the expropriation of Palestinian land for Jewish settlements, arguing that civil localities do not contribute to security, and that the expropriation violates property rights of Palestinian landlords (HCJ 390/79, Elon Moreh petition). Prime Minister Begin declared that the government would comply with the court's ruling, but that a legal way to continue the colonization project must be found (Gordon 2008). The legal bureaucracy created patchwork regulations and laws from a variety of legal systems that were applicable in the WB, with the aim of ensuring the approval of the judicial branch in the "legality" of land expropriation from Palestinian landlords for the purpose of building new settlements (Weizman 2007).[7]

Less familiar is the role played by the court in denying property rights of Palestinians after 1948—refugees and those who remained in Israel and became Israeli citizens (Kedar 2001; and in relation to the Bedouins in the Negev: Shamir 1996). De facto expropriation of Palestinian property during the war and shortly thereafter was essential for establishing new Jewish settlements on Palestinian farmland in territories that were occupied by the Israeli Army during the war, near borders, and in regions where Palestinians composed the majority. This expropriation also functioned by housing Jewish immigrants in absentees' homes. Kedar's words depict the informal way land was seized, and the role of the court in legitimizing and legalizing it: "Land was seized either on the basis of temporary emergency regulations or with no legal justification whatsoever. After a short period, the Israeli legal system began to legalize this land transfer. Until the mid-1950s, this legal ordering was effected mainly through the Absentee Property Law (1950), the Land Acquisition Law (1953), administrative actions taken in conjunction with these statutes, and court decisions interpreting and implementing them" (2001, 948).

In all cases, both within Israel's 1949 borders and within the OT, the court had a crucial duty in legalizing informal settlements; when the court agrees on a method of legalization, it actually legitimizes and depoliticizes the act of settlement (Tzfadia 2016; Shamir 1990).

And the strategy was successful. After 1948, the State of Israel expropriated five thousand square kilometers of land owned by Palestinians. Part of this land was allocated to establishing part of the 465 Jewish settlements that were built from 1946 to 1967 (Kedar 2001). From 1967 onward, 40 percent of the land in the WB has been annexed to Jewish settlements, with 32 percent of this area having been owned by Palestinian landlords (Peace Now 2012). In 2014, 356,000 Jews lived there, not including the 200,000 residents in East Jerusalem neighborhoods (CBS 2014). However, about 10 percent of the houses in the authorized settlements have been built without permission, sometimes over land owned by Palestinians (Spiegel 2006).

What is the logic of retrospective legalization, and when and under what circumstances would an informal locality enjoy legalization? These questions are meaningful, beyond the Israeli context, as they link informality to law and power (Chiodelli and Moroni 2014). One answer is grounded in arguments set forth by De Soto (2000). Accordingly, legalizing informalities should be based on market logic and capital development, which can be achieved through property rights and titling. The research on gray space does not reject the logic of capital, but it also emphasizes the logic of ethnonationalism and territorial control in legalizing informalities. Accordingly, informalities that serve the goals of demographic engineering (McGarry 1998) or territorial control (Yiftachel 2006) in "frontiers" are likely to be legalized.

In Israel, two discourses that aim at legitimizing and legalizing informal settlements manifest the logic of ethnonationalism: security and theology. By security, I refer both to tactics of defense (Shiran 1998), and to the more abstract notion of national survival, which is inspired by the bonds among nation, territory, and state. For example, security considerations have determined where and when to establish Jewish settlements in the pre-State period (ibid.), during the war in 1948, after in the OT (Tzfadia 2010), and now in the outposts, sometimes without considering questions of law and legality. Zvi Bar-Chai, head of the Mount Hebron Regional Council, explains how the outposts serve security needs and strategic interests: "There is an attempt to create settlement blocs, ensuring the security of communities . . . build an outpost in between two remote settlements that face terrorist attacks—and that allows control. . . . If I build an outpost in the middle of the road then I control the road, and it contributes to security. This is how the army thinks, but the officers do not say so" (interview, May 22, 2008).

Shaul Goldstein, head of Gush Etzion Regional Council, links security and informality and describes the outposts as a strategy in a war over land. "A settlement should be legal . . . but the outposts are not. In a war, you do things that you are not allowed to do normally. . . . Our war against the Arabs is over the land . . . they take our land . . . and if the state is too weak to stop it, then we do so. It is true, it is not always legal. But in a time of war you have to act in a different way" (interview, June 30, 2008).

Beyond the security reasoning, theology is also encapsulated in the ethnonational logic of territorial control, and occasionally it prevails over the law. Indeed, theology has served many colonial movements (Smith 2003) aimed at justifying the colonialists' moral rights. In the Zionist context, religion marks the boundaries of the nation and its promised land (ibid.). Therefore, despite the secular nature of the Zionist project, religion adds moral legitimacy to the claim for exclusive territorial rights (Roded 2005).

However, the theological discourse did not really become prominent until after 1967, through the activism of Gush Emunim in colonizing the OT, inspired by Rabbi Zvi Yehuda Kook, one of the Zionist-religious leaders. Shortly after the Occupation in 1967, Kook argued that building Jewish settlements in "the land of God," as allotted to the Jewish people in the Bible, was an important step in the process of redemption (Newman 2005). Accordingly, the secular Zionist state is a holy entity, because its territorial goals are in accord with the biblical commandments (Inbari 2012). Bar-Chai illustrates these ideas in relation to the outposts: "The Jewish people came into being in Judea and Samaria. Here in Hebron our fathers lived, King David—the founders of my nation. After 2,000 years we returned. Our mission is to rebuild the ruins. The land of Israel is the vigor of the Jewish people. Thus we have to tighten our grasp on the land and to settle it. This is what we do and will do" (interview, May 22, 2008).

But what happens if building Jewish settlements in "the land of God" contradicts the law? Itai Harel, one of the prominent leaders in the outposts, answers: "If the law contradicts the Holy Bible, the Bible takes precedence. You are obligated [to fulfill] the law as part of your conscience. . . . . We are acting morally. This is the well-being of Israel. One who doesn't agree to live here has nothing to do in Israel. This is the land of the Jewish people—here in Judea and Samaria" (interview, July 1, 2008).

We should be aware that theology plays a role in justifying the settlements, including the outposts. This theology is espoused by the Zionist-religious settlers' leadership, Gush Emunim, as well as some segments of outposts' settlers that have been nicknamed "hilltop youth." But, theology is not what necessarily motivates most settlers to settle in the WB, as I will show. What I claim here is that theological reasoning behind the outposts is more prominent in relation to past and present Zionist settlement acts. Yet, it is clear that the outposts are another link in a chain of settlements that can be described as a technology of territorial control that does not obligate itself to norms of legality. Informality in the arena of Zionist settlement is the norm, and that includes many of the characteristics of gray space: land expropriation; employing technologies of territorial control such as patchwork, emergency, and informality; legitimizing violation of property rights through court; legalizing the informal; violating the concept of equal citizenship and rights; and finally justifying the settlement project through discourses of security and theology. This is not typical to outposts only. In fact, this is the normal pattern of colonization of Israel/Palestine.

Yet, one should ask: Why do people take part in it? Who are the people that settle these places? In the following section I will show that the outposts, as many other localities in Israel created in past Judaization programs, are for or-dinary people.

Outposts as Localities Are for Ordinary People

An easy way to find how people are stereotyped is by looking at Google images (Baker and Potts 2013). Searching under the term "Jewish settlers" leads to the fol-lowing results: bearded Orthodox men with big yarmulkes covering their heads, wearing old-fashion military coats (*dubon*), rifles hanging on their backs, guns in their hands; women wearing scarves over their heads, long skirts, athletic shoes or sandals, and usually holding either babies or guns. This stereotype projects the belief that all the Jewish settlers not only look the same, but are all messianic right-wing religious radicals (Ellis 2014).

Stereotyping the settlers as messianic right-wing religious radicals becomes more prominent in relation to the outpost settlers. These settlers, the hilltop youth, are conceived to be the engine behind the building of the outposts. They are described as "young, violent, extremist settlers, who rejected the Israeli estab-lishment and Israel's mainstream culture, and who rebelled against the settler elders' alliance with the Israeli establishment" (Nir 2011, 282). They are conceived of as the second generation of Gush Emunim settlers that radicalized their par-ents' ideology and actions as a response to the crises in the settlements movement after the 2005 withdrawal from Gaza. In this sense, the "new settlers" take for granted the colonization, which is based on a simplistic understanding of the commandment to settle the "sacred land" (Kaniel 2004; Feige 2009).

In opposition to this stereotyping, Friedman (2015) suggests that the outposts' settlers are far from being a homogenous group: some of them are the second generation of settlers, whereas others arrived from families and places that are disconnected to the settlements in the OT. Some have religious or ultraorthodox backgrounds, while others have secular roots. Moreover, because of their youth, Friedman argues, the frontier shapes their identity and communality.

Yet beyond the hilltop youth, the composition of the outposts' settlers is much more varied. Some of the settlers are indeed the second and third genera-tions of the 1970s and 1980s settlers, but the reason behind their living in outposts is rooted in their search for affordable housing. Shira, a young settler, lives in the Abigail outpost. Abigail is in South Hebron Mountain and is inhabited by one hundred residents, who live in five permanent houses and twenty-five mo-bile houses (as estimated by Peace Now [2012]). Abigail, according to Amana's website, "was set up in coordination with the regional council on a hill watching the Susya-Maon road, in front of Biblical Maon. The goal was completing settle-ment continuity . . . settling location that controls the road and answering the terror attacks."[8] Shira presents alternative reasoning why people like her live in an outpost, beyond the security rationale: "It's really inexpensive to live here. Along with property tax and water it comes to about 1,000 NIS [approx. $280 USD monthly]. . . . Some of the residents have created their own organic, environmental and suburban middle-class communities, and they are far from the image of the 'hilltop youth.' . . . In Abigail there are people looking for an alternative, sane life, and connected to the land and nature . . . rather than running after rent and mortgage and other materials. Just to live simply and calmly" (interview, October 2009).

It seems that the logic of ethnonationalism met the logic of capital in the outposts. The housing prices in Israel have increased dramatically since the early 1990s, including in authorized Jewish settlements in OT. From 2008 to 2013, housing prices in Israel have increased by 55 percent, and in authorized Jewish settlements in the OT by 68 percent (State Comptroller 2015). The construction freeze policy of the 1990s (a result of international pressure) exacerbated the housing problem there. But when this policy ended in 2010 with a construction boom policy, the prices continued to rise. In recent years, the housing prices in the OT are similar to the Israeli average and higher than in the northern, southern, and Haifa districts (ibid.). Indeed, many young families have moved to the outposts from old settlements, but also from other localities in Israel, in search for affordable housing. As a result, between 2008 and 2011, the number of residents in the outposts has grown from 5,945 to 9,689 (Peace Now 2012).

Beyond affordable housing, some outposts serve ultraorthodox communities for studying. Other outposts attract "new age" communities: environmentalists, spiritualists, organic-loving, and bourgeoisie—all of which are far from the messianic stereotype of the hilltop youth. These communities search for undeveloped lands, far from civilization, to create a place wherein people naturally connect, regardless of whether this entails expropriating Palestinian land and resources, breaking the law, or stymieing efforts to end the occupation. Noam Cohen details such ideas about the outpost at which he lives: "We build a road, no problem; but that harms how the ground absorbs water. Our house damages nature, but you have to try not to do harm. In our region there is too much Bedouin grazing; this kills many types of flora and animal life. On our hilltop, we are repairing what we can. Grazing is done in a measured way here. We don't view ecological commitment as a form of self-denial. Instead, we do it for our own benefit, here and now" (Levinson 2010).

For many of the new age environmentalists, the ethnonational ideology does not matter, as Amihai, a settler in Mitzpeh Lakhish, explains: "I didn't say 'this is an illegal outpost so I should live here.' People live here because they love the place and the environment. Everyone has their own reasons. Some have less ideological motivations. . . . I assume that our neighbors are idealists, but I didn't stick an ideological barometer in them" (Blau 2008).

Some of the outposts' settlers might be confused by questions of legality, as Shira relates: "Usually, I hope, I am a law-abiding citizen, with the exception of this minor issue of living in an illegal settlement. Truly, it is not easy for me, because I educate my son, and he pays attention to all and asks many questions. . . . I face an educational dilemma because I am a lawbreaker. So what if I believe that it is justified [to live in Abigail, ET]? . . . I respect the authority of the state, its law, and the authority of IDF. These are the values that we were raised on" (interview, October 2009).

It seems, therefore, that the classic, yet imprecise, division between "national-religious settlers" and "quality of life settlers" is applicable to the outposts as well. The heterogeneity of the residents in the "legal" settlements and in the outposts thus adds another tier to the "normalization" of the outposts.

The social heterogeneity of the outposts' residents and their quest for affordable housing is expressed in the marketing of houses in the outposts. Marketing is an integral part of consumerism, which emphasizes the normality of the outposts. De Soto (2000), in his research on informality in South American favelas, pays particular attention to real estate marketing, as if this marketing is integral part of capitalism. If real estate marketing is normal commercial activity, then marketing informalities indicates their "normality."

The marketing of houses in Jewish settlements in the OT, mainly in newly established settlements or small ones, is carried out by Amana: "the settlement movement of Gush Emunim, was established in 1978 with the primary goal of developing communities in Judea, Samaria. . . . This goal includes not only the establishment of communities and their supportive industries and social services but their continued maintenance and development."[9] On its website, Amana advertises the possibilities of living in twenty-three outposts in the West Bank. In these twenty-three outposts live approximately four thousand residents. These outposts are integrated in the same list with "authorized" settlements and thus cannot be identified as outposts.

El Matan is marketed as a community that "provides a natural environment of peace and serenity." Mevo'ot Jericho, an outpost near the Palestinian city of Jericho, is advertised as a community with a "mixture of backgrounds and life-styles . . . interesting human mosaic . . . [that is] one big family" with excellent educational facilities and nice weather. Givat Harel offers the residents a cool and natural swimming pool, and a great location—thirty-five minutes from Jerusalem and Tel-Aviv. Its "residents thrive on the pristine air and surrounding beauty." Kedah enjoys cool weather and an awesome view thanks to its altitude. Migron has a "gas station, vegetable market, shoe store and children's clothing store adjacent to it." According to Amanda, many outposts have a multicultural community, great schooling, scenic views, and are close to Jerusalem, Tel Aviv, Ariel, or Be'er Sheva.[10]

Besides the marketing of houses, the outposts are promoted as tourist attractions. Tourism masks political dilemmas of contested places: Mount Hermon's skiing and wineries all over the OT normalize the Jewish colonization (Handel, Rand, and Allegra 2015; Ram 2014). Handel et al. (2015) reveal the slogan "YESHA is fun"[11] as the title of a guidebook that offers its readers to taste the good life at the Jewish settlements in the OT (Eldad and Bashan 2011). The outposts enjoy some benefits that make them ideal sites for recreation, such as locations in beautiful, calm, and relatively isolated hilltops, with breathtaking views in all directions. Tamari's Guesthouse at Havat Yair outpost serves Mehadrin kosher brunch on Friday mornings, "because of the food, because of the serenity and the view" (Eldad and Bashan 2011). Pesto Pizza Café in Abigail delivers its food to settlements on Mount Hebron. The artist Aaron Bons invites you to visit his home in the Bat Ayin West outpost. Zimmers and guest suites are spread all over the outposts: Kedah suites offer "luxurious guest cottages and wake up to a spectacular view of the Jordan Valley and the Gilad Mountains." The Esh Kodesh outpost offers suites in a vineyard. In all the tourist sites of the regional councils, the dichotomy between tourist sites in outposts and "authorized" settlements does not exist.[12]

Final Remarks

It is now essential to interweave the two parts of argument and analysis: (1) the part that argues for the normality of the outposts as being in the gray space of Israel's colonization, in particular integrated in Zionist and Israeli settlement activism with a clear goal of promoting spatial Judaization and territorial control; and (2) the part that argues for the normality of the outposts, as these are relatively ordinary places for relatively ordinary people and heterogeneous communities, who are seeking affordable houses, in a friendly and relaxing environment that welcomes tourism and commercialism.

What I want to stress here is that these two parts are symbiotically interdependent. Why? The colonization of Israel/Palestine has represented itself as one that is performed by brave pioneers. But the sustainability of this project cannot be based on a few heroes. It should be attractive to many residents, which means it should offer attractive conditions to potential residents. Indeed, critical inquiry into the making of Israeli society reveals the ways in which Jewish communities have been compelled to live in frontier localities and regions, as part of Judaization: for example, the exploitation of Jewish immigrants from Muslim countries in making Israel's borders in the 1950s (Kemp 1998; Yiftachel 2006; Tzfadia and Yacobi 2011; Shohat 1997); and the housing shortage that pushes ultraorthodox families (Algazi 2006; Cahaner, chapter 7) and lower-middle class Jews (Newman

1996) into settlements in OT, where they find affordable housing and government assistance that do not exist within Israel (Gutwein 2004, chapter 1).

However, usually, at the level of a family's microeconomy, Jews who moved to localities in frontier regions improved their standard of living. This was exactly the idea behind the Judaization of the Galilee in the 1970s and 1980s that aimed at bringing middle-class Jews to newly established suburbs, by offering them communal life, better infrastructure, and land for free, while the goal of the project was to change the demographic balance in the Galilee in favor of the Jews. The same can be said for the Jewish immigrants from Muslim countries in the 1950s, who had been offered public houses in newly established towns in frontier regions instead of remaining in transit camps.

Gray spaces are capable of ensuring attractive conditions in newly established settlements and ensuring the implementation of colonial goals. This capability is a result of the following: (1) Gray spaces create possibilities to allocate newly established settlements to particular groups, without being subject to demands of equity in law. While formally planned localities are open by law to all citizens, informal localities are not. (2) Gray spaces enable allocation of resources beyond the limit of law. This is what I term "upgraded gray" (Tzfadia and Yiftachel 2014), meaning that the settlers of the outposts, for example, can get more rights than the law permits—land for free, security services, houses, etc.—just as it was with many other settlement projects (Tzfadia and Yacobi 2011). (3) Gray spaces have the potential to be legalized, yet the legalization does not fix the deprivations or preferences that had been utilized in the creation of gray space. To ensure the attractiveness of colonization, and to be able to sustain upgraded rights for the settlers, legalization should be achieved. In other words, state institutions attempt to maintain a "good credit rating" for colonization projects by allocating rights beyond the limits of law and making sure that the status of "unauthorized" or "informal" is transitory, until legalization to ensure the cooperation of Jews in future colonization projects. It seems that the future projects will be done in the gray, yet normal spaces, just as with the outposts.

Notes

This chapter was written while I was an Israel Institute Visiting Scholar at Rutgers University's Bildner Center for the Study of Jewish Life and Department of Jewish Studies. I have benefited from the opportunity to present and discuss my work on "Normality in Gray Space" at the Settlements in the West Bank (1967–2014): New Perspectives workshop, organized by the volume editors, at Tel Aviv University (June 2014). Comments addressed by Ian Lustick and Ronen Shamir were very helpful. I thank my student Yasmin Boaz who collected part of the data and conducted the interviews. This chapter comprises part of the research on Grey Urbanism. I am grateful to the Israel Science Foundation for funding the project (ISF 612/07) and to my core-searcher Oren Yiftachel.

1. More details on each outpost are available at the interactive map of Americans for Peace Now, accessed January 20, 2016, http://archive.peacenow.org/map.php.

2. See for example: HCJ 7891/07 Peace Now v. Ministry of Defense; HCJ 1019/06 Regional Council Mateh Asher v. the Government of Israel; HCJ 8255/08 Ali Mahmed Issa Musa v. Ministry of Defense.

3. The Civil Administration is a unit in the Ministry of Defense of Israel that operates as a governing body in the WB.

4. An attempt that has not been finally implemented by October 2016.

5. By 2012, the search for a legal solution resulted in appointing Edmond Levy to head a committee with the aim of finding a legal solution to informal construction in the Jewish settlements. The committee put in question the legal status of the WB as occupied area, arguing that it is not an occupied area, thus any construction and legalization is possible (Levy 2012).

6. I definitely affiliate with the school that argues for uniformity between the two sides of the Green Line (Shenhav 2012).

7. This recognition does not indicate that the settlements are legal according to international law. But they are recognized as legal by the Israeli legal authorities.

8. Amana website, accessed January 20, 2016, http://www.amana.co.il/?CategoryID=100 &ArticleID=168.

9. Amana website, accessed January 20, 2016, http://www.amana.co.il/?CategoryID=101 &ArticleID=166.

10. Amana website, accessed January 20, 2016, http://www.amana.co.il/?CategoryID=100.

11. YESHA is the Hebrew acronym for "Judea, Samaria, Gaza." Judea and Samaria are the biblical names for WB. The use of this acronym suggests that this region historically and theologically belongs to Jews.

12. The information and quotations, and more information on tourism in outposts, can be found on the regional councils' websites, accessed January 20, 2016, http://www.gobinyamin .org.il/?CategoryID=1196&ArticleID=4964#.VfsjjNVViko; http://goyatir.co.il/; http://etziontour .org.il/en/; http://www.tourshomron.org.il/.

References

Agamben, Giorgio. 2005. *State of Exception.* Translated by Kevin Attel. Chicago: University of Chicago Press.

Algazi, Gadi. 2006. "Offshore Zionism." *New Left Review* 40: 27–37.

AlSayyad, Nezar. 2004. "Urban Informality as a New Way of Life." In *Urban Informality: Transnational Perspectives from the Middle East, Latin America, and South Asia,* edited by Ananya Roy and Nezar AlSayyad, 7–30. Oxford: Lexington Books.

Anderson, Malcolm. 2013. *Frontiers: Territory and State Formation in the Modern World.* Cambridge, UK: Polity Press. [Original edition, 1996.]

Avni, Nufar, and Oren Yiftachel. 2014. "The New Divided City? Planning and 'Gray Space' between Global North-West and South-East." In *The Routledge Handbook on Cities of the Global South,* edited by Susan Parnell and Sophie Oldfield, 487–505. Abingdon, UK: Routledge.

Baker, Paul, and Amanda Potts. 2013. "'Why Do White People Have Thin Lips?' Google and the Perpetuation of Stereotypes via Auto-Complete Search Forms." *Critical Discourse Studies* 10 (2): 187–204.

Billig, Miriam. 2015. "The Jewish Settlements in Judea and Samaria (1967–2008): Historical Overview." *Israel Affairs* 21 (3): 331–347. doi: 10.1080/13537121.2015.1036552.

Blau, Uri. 2008. "Hilltop Youth Wedded." *Haaretz*, February 19. Accessed January 27, 2016. http://www.haaretz.co.il/misc/1.1306373. [Hebrew.]

CBS. 2014. Statistical Abstract of Israel 2014. Jerusalem: Central Bureau of Statistics. http://www.cbs.gov.il/reader/shnaton/shnatone_new.htm?CYear=2014&Vol=65&CSubject=2.

Chiodelli, Francesco, Beatrice De Carli, Maddalena Falletti, and Lina Scavuzzo, eds. 2013. *Cities to Be Tamed? Spatial Investigations across the Urban South.* Newcastle upon Tyne: Cambridge Scholar Publishing.

Chiodelli, Francesco, and Stefano Moroni. 2014. "The Complex Nexus between Informality and the Law: Reconsidering Unauthorised Settlements in Light of the Concept of Nomotropism." *Geoforum* 51: 161–168.

Comaroff, John L. 2001. "Colonialism, Culture, and the Law: A Foreword." *Law and Social Inquiry* 26 (2): 305–314.

Davis, Mike. 2006. *Planet of Slums.* London: Verso.

De Soto, Hernando. 2000. *The Mystery of Capital: Why Capitalism Triumphs in the West and Fails Everywhere Else.* New York: Basic Books.

Di Maggio, Paul, and Walter W. Powell. 1983. "The Iron Cage Revisited: Collective Rationality and Institutional Isomorphism in Organizational Fields." *American Sociological Review* 48 (2): 147–160.

Eldad, Karni, and Shlomo Bashan. 2011. *YESHA Is Fun: The Good Life Guide to Judea and Samaria.* Tekoa, Israel: Self-published.

Ellis, Donald. 2014. "Three Discursive Dilemmas for Israeli Religious Settlers." *Discourse Studies* 16 (4): 473–487.

Etkes, Dror, and Hagit Ofran. 2006. *Breaking the Law in the West Bank—The Private Land Report.* Tel Aviv: Peace Now.

Feige, Michael. 2009. *Settling in the Hearts: Jewish Fundamentalism in the Occupied Territories.* Raphael Patai Series in Jewish Folklore and Anthropology. Detroit: Wayne State University Press.

Friedman, Shimi. 2015. "Hilltop Youth: Political-Anthropological Research in the Hills of Judea and Samaria." *Israel Affairs* 21 (3): 391–407. doi: 10.1080/13537121.2015.1036554.

Glickman, Aviad. 2010. "Court Chides State over West Bank Outposts." *Ynet*, October 19. http://www.ynetnews.com/articles/0,7340,L-3971965,00.html.

Gordon, Neve. 2008. *Israel's Occupation.* Berkeley: University of California Press.

Gorenberg, Gershom. 2006. *The Accidental Empire: Israel and the Birth of Settlements, 1967–1977.* New York: Times Books.

Graham, Stephen. 2004. *Cities, War, and Terrorism: Towards an Urban Geopolitics.* Malden, MA: Blackwell.

Gutwein, Danny. 2004. "Some Comments on the Class Foundations of the Occupation." *Theory and Criticism* 24: 202–211. [Hebrew.]

Handel, Ariel, Galit Rand, and Marco Allegra. 2015. "Wine-Washing: Normalization and the Geopolitics of Terror in the West Bank's Settlements." *Environment and Planning A* 47 (6): 1351–1367.

Harvey, David. 1973. *Social Justice and the City*. Baltimore: Johns Hopkins University Press.

Hussain, Nasser. 2003. *The Jurisprudence of Emergency: Colonialism and the Rule of Law*. Ann Arbor: University of Michigan Press.

Inbari, Motti. 2012. *Messianic Religious Zionism Confronts Israeli Territorial Compromises*. Cambridge: Cambridge University Press.

Jabareen, Yosef. 2015. "Territoriality of Negation: Co-production of 'Creative Destruction' in Israel." *Geoforum* 66: 11–25.

Kaniel, Shlomo. 2004. "Settlers of the Hills—Is It a Biblical Sabra?" In *Religious Zionism: An Era of Changes*, edited by Asher Coehn, 533–558. Jerusalem: Bialik Institute. [Hebrew.]

Kedar, Alexandre. 2001. "The Legal Transformation of Ethnic Geography: Israeli Law and the Palestinian Landholder 1948–1967." *NYU Journal of International Law and Politics* 33 (4): 923–1000.

Kemp, Adriana. 1998. "From Politics of Location to Politics of Signification: The Construction of Political Territory in Israel's First Years." *Journal of Area Studies* 6 (12): 74–101.

Kimmerling, Baruch. 1983. *Zionism and Territory: The Socio-Territorial Dimensions of Zionist Politics*. Research Series. Berkeley: Institute of International Studies, University of California.

King, Anthony D. 1990. *Urbanism, Colonialism and the World Economy: Culture and Spatial Foundations of the Urban World System*. London: Routledge.

Kretzmer, David. 2002. *The Occupation of Justice: The Supreme Court of Israel and the Occupied Territories*. SUNY Series in Israeli Studies. Albany: State University of New York Press.

Levinson, Chaim. 2010. "An Outpost of Earthy Environmentalism." *Haaretz*, September 24. Accessed July 21, 2016. http://www.haaretz.com/weekend/week-s-end/an-outpost-of-earthy-environmentalism-1.315443.

Levy, Edmond. 2012. *The Commission to Examine the Status of Building in Judea and Samaria*. Jerusalem: Prime Minister Office. http://www.pmo.gov.il/Documents/doch090712.pdf. [Hebrew.]

Lis, Jonathan, and Mualem Muazal. 2011. "PM Netanyahu: We Are in a Difficult International Reality." *Haaretz*, February 28. http://www.haaretz.co.il/news/politics/1.1164429.

Lustick, Ian. 1993. *Unsettled States, Disputed Lands: Britain and Ireland, France and Algeria, Israel and the West Bank-Gaza*. The Wilder House Series in Politics, History, and Culture. Ithaca: Cornell University Press.

McGarry, John. 1998. "'Demographic Engineering': The State-Directed Movement of Ethnic Groups as a Technique of Conflict Regulation." *Ethnic and Racial Studies* 21 (4): 613–638.

McKee, Emily. 2015. "Demolitions and Amendments: Coping with Cultural Recognition and Its Denial in Southern Israel." *Nomadic Peoples* 19 (1): 95–119.

Mendelsohn, Barak. 2014. "State Authority in the Balance: The Israeli State and the Messianic Settler Movement." *International Studies Review* 16 (4): 499–521.

Newman, David. 1996. "The Territorial Politics of Exurbanization: Reflections on 25 Years of Jewish Settlement in the West Bank." *Israel Affairs* 3 (1): 61–85. doi:10.1080/13537129608719408.

———. 2005. "From Hitnachalut to Hitnatkut: The Impact of Gush Emunim and the Settlement Movement on Israeli Politics and Society." *Israel Studies* 10 (3): 192–224.

Nir, Ori. 2011. "Price Tag: West Bank Settlers' Terrorizing of Palestinians to Deter Israeli Government Law Enforcement." *Case Western Reserve Journal of International Law* 44 (1): 277–289.

Peace Now. 2012. "Settlements and Outposts Numbers and Data." Accessed December 25, 2014. http://peacenow.org.il/eng/sites/default/files/settlements database for publication_0.xls.

Ram, Mori. 2014. "White but Not Quite: Normalizing Colonial Conquests through Spatial Mimicry." *Antipode* 46 (3): 736–753.

Roded, Batya. 2005. "Spatial Expansion in an Ethnic Homeland." PhD diss., Ben-Gurion University of the Negev, Be'er Sheva. [Hebrew.]

Rotbard, Sharon. 2003. "Wall and Tower." In *A Civilian Occupation: The Politics of Israeli Architecture*, edited by Rafi Segal and Eyal Weizman, 39–56. London: Verso.

Roy, Ananya. 2011. "Slumdog Cities: Rethinking Subaltern Urbanism." *International Journal of Urban and Regional Research* 35 (2): 223–238.

Sasson, Talya. 2005. *Unauthorized Outposts: Report for the Prime Minister.* Jerusalem: Ministry of Justice. http://www.pmo.gov.il/SiteCollectionDocuments/PMO/Communication /Spokesman/sason2.pdf. [Hebrew.]

Schmitt, Carl. 1985. *Political Theology: Four Chapters on the Concept of Sovereignty.* Translated by George Schwab. Cambridge: MIT Press.

Shamir, Ronen. 1990. "'Landmark Cases' and the Reproduction of Legitimacy: The Case of Israel's High Court of Justice." *Law and Society Review* 24 (3): 781–805.

———. 1996. "Suspended in Space: Bedouins under the Law of Israel." *Law and Society Review* 30 (2): 231–257.

Shenhav, Yehouda A. 2012. *Beyond the Two-State Solution: A Jewish Political Essay.* Cambridge: Polity Press.

Shiran, Osnat. 1998. *Strongholds of Settlements.* Edited by Ministry of Defense. Tel Aviv: Ministry of Defense. [Hebrew.]

Shohat, Ella. 1997. "The Narrative of the Nation and the Discourse of Modernization: The Case of the Mizrahim", *Critique: Critical Middle Eastern Studes* 6 (10): 3–19.

Smith, Anthony D. 2003. *Peoples, Chosen: Sacred Sources of National Identity.* Oxford: Oxford University Press.

Spiegel, Baruch. 2006. *Spiegel Report.* Jerusalem: Ministry of Defense. http://peacenow.org.il/sites /default/files/SpigleReport.pdf. [Hebrew.]

Sprinzak, Ehud. 1986. *Illegalism in the Israeli Political Culture.* Jerusalem: Jerusalem Institute for Israel Studies. [Hebrew.]

State Comptroller. 2015. *Housing Crises: Special Report.* Edited by State Comptroller. Jerusalem: State Comptroller. [Hebrew.]

Tarlo, Emma. 2003. *Unsettling Memories: Narratives of the Emergency in Delhi.* Berkeley: University of California Press.

Turner, Frederick Jackson. 1962. *The Frontier in American History.* New York: Holt, Rinehart and Winston.

Tzfadia, Erez. 2010. "Militarism and Space in Israel." *Israeli Sociology* 11 (2): 337–361. [Hebrew.]

———. 2013. "Informality as Control: The Legal Geography of Colonization of the West Bank." In Chiodelli et al., *Cities to Be Tamed?*, 192–214.

———. 2016. "The Grey Space of Colonization: A Legal-Geography Analysis of the Outposts." *Theory and Criticism* 47, n.p. [Hebrew.]

Tzfadia, Erez, and Oren Yiftachel. 2014. "The Gray City of Tomorrow." In *Cities of Tomorrow: Planning, Justice and Sustainability Today?*, edited by Tovi Fenster and Shlomo Oren, 176–192. Tel Aviv: Hakibbutz Hameuchad. [Hebrew.]

UNHRC. 2014. *Israeli Settlements in the Occupied Palestinian Territory, including East Jerusalem, and the Occupied Syrian Golan.* New York: U.N. Human Rights Council.

Watson, Vanessa. 2014. "The Case for a Southern Perspective in Planning Theory." *International Journal of E-Planning Research* 3 (1): 23–37.

Weizman, Eyal. 2007. *Hollow Land: Israel's Architecture of Occupation.* London: Verso.

Wolf, Pinhas. 2011. "Netanyahu Re-Evaluates Legalizing Outposts." *Walla News,* October 11. Accessed January 27, 2016. http://news.walla.co.il/item/1867554. [Hebrew]

Yavin, Haim. 2005. *The Settlers' Land.* Jerusalem: Telad. Documentary. [Hebrew.]

YeshDin. 2015. "Under the Radar: Israel's Silent Policy of Transforming Unauthorized Outposts into Official Settlements." Accessed January 26, 2016. http://files.yesh-din.org/userfiles /Yesh%20Din_Under%20The%20Radar%20-%20English_WEB(3).pdf.

Yiftachel, Oren. 2006. *Ethnocracy: Land and Identity Politics in Israel/Palestine.* Philadelphia: University of Pennsylvania Press.

———. 2009. "Theoretical Notes on Gray Cities': The Coming of Urban Apartheid?" *Planning Theory* 8 (1): 88–100.

Yiftachel, Oren, and Margo Huxley. 2000. "New Paradigm or Old Myopia? Unsettling the Communicative Turn in Planning Theory." *Journal of Planning Education and Research* 19 (4): 333–342.

Zerubavel, Yael. 1995. *Recovered Roots: Collective Memory and the Making of Israeli National Tradition.* Chicago: University of Chicago Press.

7 Between Ghetto-Politics and Geopolitics

Ultraorthodox Settlements in the West Bank

Lee Cahaner

Over 120,000 residents live in the ultraorthodox communities located in the West Bank outside East Jerusalem, constituting over 30 percent of the settlers currently living in that area and 15 percent of the entire ultraorthodox population in Israel and the Occupied Territories (OT) (CBS 2014). In contrast to common belief, the new ultraorthodox communities beyond the Green Line are not a product of religious ideological commitment regarding the future of the OT; rather, they are a result of the growing demand for affordable housing among the ultraorthodox population coupled with their limited ability to compete in the "free" housing market. About two-and-a-half decades ago, with perfect timing, the urgent ultraorthodox need for housing—preferably as close as possible to Jerusalem and Bnei Brak[1]—coincided with the state's interest in expanding Jewish settlement beyond the Green Line, thereby marking the beginning of intensive ultraorthodox settlement in the West Bank (Shilhav 1993; Cahaner and Shilhav 2012b, 2013).

This chapter will focus three main issues. First, it will examine the motivations that drive the ultraorthodox population to settle in the OT. It will demonstrate that despite conventional wisdom—i.e. that settlers reside beyond the Green Line either because of their adherence to a national-religions ideology, or because they are looking for opportunities to improve their quality of life—the ultraorthodox were driven to the settlements due to a lack of better alternatives. It will then propose to view them first and foremost as "out of necessity" settlements. Second, it will highlight the ways in which settling in the OT has caused the ultraorthodox society to adopt a more right-wing political agenda, at least as far as it pertains to their stance regarding the future of the OT, as well as a different geopolitical orientation than in the past. Third, it will delve into the changing geography of the ultraorthodox society in order to probe whether ultraorthodox settlements have proved able to recreate and maintain the structure of "complementary segregation" (Shilhav 1991) and relative insulation that has previously characterized the relation of the ultraorthodox communities to the wider Israeli society.

Ultra-Orthodox Population beyond the Green Line: Between Ideology and Necessity

The ultraorthodox population residing beyond the Green Line is concentrated within eight distinctive ultraorthodox settlements. The large majority reside within four large urban settlements: Beitar Illit, Modi'in Illit, Tel Zion, and Emanuel. The rest can be found in four smaller settlements, all of which are considered to be outside the mainstream of the ultraorthodox community (Ma'ale Amos, Nahliel, Metzad, and Matityahu). In 2013 these eight communities together comprised over 120,000 ultraorthodox residents, making up over 30 percent of all Jewish settlers currently living in the West Bank and about 15 percent of the entire ultraorthodox population of Israel.

Ma'ale Amos, Nahliel, Metzad, and Matityahu were established in the 1980s. They are populated primarily by what are called "NUOs" (the national-ultraorthodox, a group representing mainly national-religious people who have adopted ultraorthodox customs), "outsider" communities comprised mostly of communities of Anglo-Saxons and French Jews, and Hassidic communities such as Breslov and Chabad, which include communities of repentant Jews, whose way of life is considered to be doubtful among the core ultraorthodox. Contrary to the large, urban ultraorthodox settlements that were established at a later stage by the "core" ultraorthodox groups, which will serve as the main focus of this analysis, these ideological settlements were similar to the religious-national community living in the OT (Cahaner and Shilhav 2013), and therefore located at the outer limits of ultraorthodox society; indeed, most ultraorthodox do not view them as part of their community at all. Although they represent the oldest ultraorthodox settlements, these four "ideological" ultraorthodox settlements have failed to grow and develop. This is due to the fact that some of them are located within secluded regions of the West Bank and to the marginal character of their residents (Cahaner and Shilhav 2013; Shoshana and Samimian-Darash 2014). As a result, their small size matches their limited status and influence in ultraorthodox society in general.

This chapter will focus on the four, large ultraorthodox settlements that are more distinctly considered a part of the geographical-social continuum of ultraorthodox society in Israel, and were established beyond the Green Line first and foremost out of material necessity determined by more structural considerations and constraints. Two main parameters in particular determine the ultraorthodox choice of where to live. The first are pure market constraints of the housing market, which in recent decades has suffered from a systematic crisis which has proved even more consequential for the ultraorthodox population. The second derives from the necessity of the ultraorthodox population to reside as close as possible to the central ultraorthodox cities—Bnei Brak and Jerusalem—where the core of their communal, cultural, and social functions are concentrated (Cahaner 2009; MoH 2015).

The housing crisis that the ultraorthodox community is facing is a direct result of a combination of their demographic characteristics and a social norm that poses a (nearly impossible) demand from ultraorthodox parents to purchase an apartment for their soon-to-be-married children (Ministry of Construction data from 2015 speak of annual housing required for five thousand ultraorthodox couples). The annual growth of the ultraorthodox population is 5 percent (compared to 1.8 percent in the general population) and its relative share of the state's population is constantly rising. The high fertility rates (close to seven births), a low age at marriage, particularly for women (twenty years of age), and social pressure to deliver the first-born child in the first year of marriage create a short intergenerational gap between parents and their children (Cahaner and Shilhav 2012a). This sociocultural characteristic of the community further exacerbates the already high demand for housing. For most parents with large families, the burden of marrying off their children is almost too much to bear, yet nevertheless this norm is almost always fulfilled. The ongoing expansion of the ultraorthodox settlements in the West Bank is a direct result of this reality.

The "Out of Necessity" Ultraorthodox Settlements

The process of venturing out of the protective ultraorthodox space of Bnei Brak and Jerusalem as a response to the housing crisis began in the 1960s. The first wave, fifty years ago, consisted of ultraorthodox families leaving for small, established cities at the periphery of the ultraorthodox center. However, the swift growth of these cities and the rise in the price of housing reduced their affordability and attractiveness in the eyes of the ultraorthodox population. The second stage, in the 1960s and 1970s, consisted of migration to Israel's "development towns," which are cities of low socioeconomic status located at the periphery of the state. Currently, there are ultraorthodox communities in nearly every development town in the country. The third stage was ultraorthodox settlement in new, suburban ultraorthodox cities, some of which are located in the OT (Cahaner and Shilhav 2012b, 2013; Shilhav 1993).

The planning of ultraorthodox communities beyond the Green Line was accompanied by internal disagreements among Israeli policymakers. These stemmed from a host of reasons, including doubts regarding the settlements' long-term viability, their location within a politically disputed area, and particularly the opposition within the ultraorthodox community to political Zionism and to the idea of people seizing control of their destiny while generating conflict and risk. Nonetheless, the ultraorthodox population seemed to be particularly suitable for the nature of the settlements, since its demographic and religious-cultural attributes impel them to prefer segregated residential areas within a homogenous, gated community, which frequently includes low-cost residential units and designated infrastructure appropriate for their large families and religious needs (Cahaner 2009; Stern and Canaan 2006; Sadan, Gonen, and Plessner 2011; MoH 2015). The decision to establish an ultraorthodox community beyond the Green Line marked therefore a meaningful shift in the attitude of the state toward the spatial segregation of the ultraorthodox. For the first time, this segregation was viewed as legitimate, at least in practical terms, and received significant financial and administrative assistance from state authorities. Instead of being excluded and its geographical concentration considered illegitimate, the ultraorthodox population served as a vehicle for the realization of the state's territorial and political goals (Shilhav 1997).

From the ultraorthodox perspective, settlements provided, on the one hand, a conservative-religious way of life within segregated and selective communities, and a viable solution to the economic problems that originated from the structural shortage of suitable housing solutions; on the other hand, it required a massive departure from "the walls" of the established communities and the main ultraorthodox concentrations in Jerusalem and Bnei Brak, as well as from the boundaries of the Green Line. Such a departure was no small matter, as it occurred within a closed religious community, which lacks the ideological, "pioneering" motivations that characterized other Zionist settlement movements in Israel's history.

This partnership between the state and the ultraorthodox sector was therefore not founded on the basis of an ideological overlap or even an identical strategic conception, but on partial correspondence between different interests. Cooperation between the two parties, however, was not without its costs. Successfully inhabiting these localities and achieving a sustainable municipal system required massive investment in public resources. The financial limitations of the ultraorthodox community meant that the state, and particularly state agencies responsible for the planning and implementation of housing and development policies, such as the Ministry of Housing, had to commit to large financial investments, far beyond the standard costs of public construction. The extent of the state's involvement in funding and subsidizing life in these settlements included subsidizing housing costs, providing tax benefits, funding construction of educational institutions and community infrastructure which included a separate transportation system. In return, the ultraorthodox community had to conform to settling in a geographic location that did not necessarily coincide with its proclivities and desires and that at times caused internal conflicts within the community that are still very much ongoing (Cahaner and Shilhav 2012b; Shilhav 1997; Cahaner 2009; MoH 2015).

Natural demographic growth and the growing demand for housing among the ultraorthodox population turned Beitar Illit (located between Gush Etzion and Jerusalem) and Mod'in Illit (near the Israeli city of Modi'in-Maccabim-Re'ut)—the two largest ultraorthodox cities beyond the Green Line—into the two main contributors to the growth of the settler population. Together with the ultraorthodox community of Emanuel, and the ultraorthodox neighborhood Tel Zion, located in the Kochav Ya'akov community, the ultraorthodox population in the OT makes up almost one-third of the number of settlers (Rotem 2003; Shragi 2003a, 2007; Cahaner 2009; Cahaner and Shilhav 2013). The growth rate of Beitar Illit and Modi'in Illit is one of the highest in Israel. The former is growing at an annual rate of 12.5 percent and the latter at an annual rate of 10 percent; five and even six times the growth rate of the population in Jerusalem and Tel Aviv and twice the average rate of growth in many other settlements (CBS 2014). According to the Israel Central Bureau of Statistics, without the outstanding rate of growth of these two settlements, the total Jewish population in the West Bank would have diminished considerably while the rate of migration would have been negative, with more settlers returning to reside within the Green Line than vice versa. In addition to natural population growth, the significant increase in the number of ultraorthodox settlers was also a result of the continued migration from within Israel; the ultraorthodox population frequently requires new housing units and a large part of new available units was and remains in the settlements (CBS 2008, 2013; Cahaner and Shilhav 2013).

The settlements are usually divided into "ideological settlements" and "quality of life settlements." Neither of these categories, however, seems to accurately represent the ultraorthodox settlements. Understanding the growing presence of large numbers of ultraorthodox settlers therefore requires an additional category, that of "out of necessity" settlements. Far from offering a typical quality of life, these settlements represent relatively poor cities which are repeatedly ranked in the lowest cluster of Israel's municipalities' socioeconomic index as they lack employment opportunities, suffer from low participation in the labor force, have difficulty collecting municipal taxes, and face various other social problems that turn them into "socially suffocating cities" (Cahaner 2009; Cahaner and Shilhav 2013).

From Ghetto-Politics to Geopolitics: Between Ideology and Exigency

If necessity has pushed ultraorthodox communities into the OT, what is the political fallout of this mass movement for the ultraorthodox society as a whole?

Since the 1880s, settling in the "Land of Israel" was considered one of the most important means of realizing Zionism, and, after 1967, the Israeli state and its institutions—with very little difference between the various Israeli governments—have always been the main agent behind settling beyond the Green Line (Rosen and Shlay 2010; Weizman 2007).

On the other hand, ultraorthodoxy inherently, fundamentally, and decisively opposes any change in the Jewish way of life, particularly as it pertains to changes initiated by the Zionist movement. This resistance has extended to settlements in the OT. The ultraorthodox attitude toward Israel does not read any meaning of redemption into the existence of the Jewish state and sovereignty, even though Israeli control of the West Bank allows everyone, including the ultraorthodox, free access to the holy places (Shilhav 2001). The fierce opposition to the settlements in the OT derives not only from the fundamental principles mentioned here, but also from practical considerations, primarily the uncertainty of the future of the settlement project, the degree of danger inherent in travelling to them, and their distance from the established ultraorthodox centers in Bnei Brak and Jerusalem. These factors are significant not only because of the geographical distance, but also because of the possibility of the physical distance translating into a moral distance—a distance from moral influence and religious supervision.

Throughout the years, it was the Lithuanian-born leader Rabbi Elazar Menachem Shach who led the fierce opposition to the establishment of the first ultraorthodox settlements. On the other hand, among Hassidic groups there was less opposition and some even cooperated with the settlement project (Cahaner and Shilhav 2013). The Hassidic rabbis were joined by Rabbi Ovadia Yosef, the patron of the Oriental-ultraorthodox party Shas, which originally held a rather dovish outlook regarding the Israeli-Palestinian conflict and was open to negotiating "land for peace." Leon (2015a) argues that the ability to implement the "tense political pragmatism" of Ovadia Yosef and Shas, which opposed settlements beyond the Green Line, became ever more restricted in the political conditions of the past decade. As he argues, the deterioration of the relations between Israel and the Palestinians, the housing crisis of the ultraorthodox public, and the issue of dividing Jerusalem led Rabbi Ovadia Yosef to reverse his party's previous opposition to settling beyond the Green Line (ibid.).

The first waves of migration to the large ultraorthodox settlements were driven by a search for affordable housing close to a suitable ultraorthodox community. A typical ultraorthodox individual did not feel as if he or she was living in a settlement, but rather as a person who came to live in a place that was marketed as any other housing project would be. A Yeshiva student living in Modi'in Illit has no interest in seeing the political significance of his private act of settlement. He reached this Lithuanian stronghold because of a supply of cheap housing, Talmud Torah schools, his colleagues at the Yeshiva who settled in before him, and his parents, who sent him to live in a housing project that happened to be located beyond the Green Line. In his personal conception, he is not a settler. The demonstrative lack of identification on the part of this anonymous ultraorthodox individual reliably reflects the majority of the residents of the ultraorthodox cities beyond the Green Line. Besides low-cost housing, the ultraorthodox found additional advantages in the communities built beyond the Green Line, including quality of life and comfort. Indeed, in these communities, the "build your own home" projects with the red roofs that characterize the religious-Zionist settlements have yet to appear, but a four-bedroom apartment with optional expansion, new playgrounds, spacious roads, sophisticated public services, and a young, burgeoning ultraorthodox society—all of these were a source of attraction to go beyond the Green Line, especially for those that had been raised in the crowded neighborhoods of the established ultraorthodox cities (Rotem 2003; Shilhav 1997, 2001; Cahaner 2009).

Nonetheless, despite the adversarial ultraorthodox ideology and the refusal of the ultraorthodox to view themselves as settlers, in recent years there has been a growing tendency to adopt political positions that can be seen as "hawkish" (Shilhav 2001, 2007). The right-wing positions of the ultraorthodox public, and particularly the younger generation, represent a dramatic change within ultraorthodox society. Shilhav (2001) pointed out three developments whose accumulated effects are leading the ultraorthodox in this direction.

The first is the introduction of mainstream Israeli discourse into ultraorthodox society through various media outlets. The background of this shift is constituted by several transformations that have been observed by Shilav in the ultraorthodox communities since the beginning of the previous decade, namely a growing presence in higher education, more massive participation in the workforce, exposure to different voices and opinions through the internet, and a spiritual leadership whose exclusive authority is weakening, All of these allow a multiplicity of voices and opinions in general and regarding individual political views (Zicherman and Cahaner 2012; Leon 2014; Malach and Cahaner forthcoming; Caplan 2003, 2007). Thus, despite the various measures of isolation, the ultraorthodox are to a great extent exposed to what is going on in Israeli society and to societal changes within it. This has resulted in shifting public opinion within the ultraorthodox population to the right for two reasons. First, the right-wing discourse in Israel which has expressed a growing distrust and ever-growing hostility toward non-Jews has also influenced the ultraorthodox community. This trend also corresponds to the ultraorthodox reserve regarding foreigners. The second reason is anchored in the imagery adopted from the Jewish tradition that the right-wing discourse, and particularly its leadership, often use. In comparison, the left-wing discourse is seen as devoid of any territorial affinity to the Land of Israel.

The second development is the change in Israeli iconography after 1967. Until the 1967 War, iconographic Israeli sites were related to the history of the agricultural Zionist settlements, pioneering, and "conquering the desert." The ultraorthodox could disregard these symbols, which represented places and scenes imbued, from their point of view, with illegitimate meaning related to the secular-socialist character of the agricultural settlements. When the West Bank was occupied by Israel, however, biblical sites and regions whose names run like a thread throughout Jewish history and that are anchored in Jewish religious conscious-ness resurfaced in the public's consciousness. These include the Wailing Wall, the Cave of the Patriarchs, Rachel's tomb, and more. These are not symbols that the ultraorthodox public can ignore.

The third and most significant development, as far as we are concerned here, is related to the ultraorthodox migration to the large ultraorthodox neighbor-hoods and suburban communities beyond the Green Line. The greater the number of ultraorthodox settlers in the OT or next to them is, the more the ultraorthodox population as a whole begin to fear and, as a result, object to the idea of retreating from the West Bank, as such an event would hold disastrous economic repercus-sions for tens of thousands of ultraorthodox families. At the same time, there is also a growing fear of a potentially political arrangement that would bring the Palestinian Authority, with its armed policemen, to the front doors of the ultra-orthodox communities.

It should not be controversial to assume that the process of greater identifi-cation with the settlement project among the ultraorthodox will progress the lon-ger they reside in the West Bank. The low-cost housing and the large financial benefits they receive while living there help the ultraorthodox overcome their fear of "provoking the gentiles," repress the security risk, and further radicalizes them to the right (Atkes and Friedman 2005). The possibility of a future evacuation could pose a real threat to the economic existence of many ultraorthodox fami-lies, and their relevant political positions are shaped accordingly (Cahaner and Shilhav 2013).

Data gathered in a survey conducted at the end of 2014 in the new ultraor-thodox cities of Modi'in Illit, Beitar Illit, Elad, and Ramat Beit Shemesh (the latter two are ultraorthodox cities within Israel proper), showed that 77 percent of the residents located themselves on the right wing of the political spectrum. In Beitar Illit, 87 percent stated that they hold right-wing positions and in Modi'in Illit the number stating so was 67 percent (Cahaner 2014a).

As we have shown, the ultraorthodox population has undergone a significant transformation in political orientation, from a moderate political position to a more right-wing stance regarding the Israeli-Palestinian conflict and the future of the OT. The ultraorthodox population did not arrive in the West Bank identi-fying with the political Right, but as time went by, it has shifted closer to this camp out of a common interest in the future of the settlements. While the main motivation for their residents to settle beyond the Green Line remains the urgent need for housing, the ultimate result of this trend has been a more general rightward shift in political orientation throughout the ultraorthodox society.

The Settlements and the Changing Geography of Ultraorthodox Society

How did the participation of ultraorthodox communities in the settlement enterprise change the geography of the ultraorthodox society? One way to respond to this question is to consider the settlements in relation to the concepts of "gated community" and "suburb." Gated communities present a model of a gated environment that aims to segregate the inside from whatever is outside. These communities—whether they are quality-of-life communities, communities of the elite, or security communities (Blakely and Snyder 1997)—may be located either far from the city or within the urban center (Wu and Webber 2004; Handel 2014; Salcedo and Torres 2004; Rodgers 2004). Suburbs, on the other hand, offer an abundance of housing in return for a greater distance from the city that permits commuting at an ever-growing price of time and distance. Its character is defined primarily by the population's interests and values as they manifest themselves through time and in reaction to spatial constraints (Rosen and Razin 2008).

Ultraorthodox settlements can be regarded as "gated suburban communities." On the one hand, like all settlements in the West Bank, they constitute gated communities and fit the definition of ideological-security enforcement (Handel 2014). On the other hand, they are not isolated from the suburban experience and essence, since they very much function as a suburb of Jerusalem and Bnei Brak and they interact with these cities in a way that is much more characteristic of a suburb than a separated gated community (Cahaner and Shilhav 2012a, 2012b; Shilhav 1997). As in many cases, the new ultraorthodox suburban cities were a physical expression of the inability of the main city to address within its limits all the needs of the different populations (Loibl and Toetzer 2003; Frey 1992). Like most suburban communities, the new ultraorthodox cities are homogenous in population, a fact that not only addresses the wishes of most of the residents to live next to those who are culturally and economically similar to them, but also the desire to distance themselves from those who are different from them, with the associated social and political implications of this trend.

The model of "suburban gated communities" seems to fit the exigencies of the ultraorthodox community. However, it also poses a challenge to their traditional fabric as the migration of many of the younger ultraorthodox generation from the large, protective, established spaces to the new ultraorthodox suburbs has the potential for initiating far-reaching social, economic, cultural, and political changes. In particular, this trend represents a potential challenge to both the internal cohesion of the ultraorthodox society and their relative insulation from the larger Israeli society. Suburbs can become disconnected from the inner city and metamorphose from bedroom communities into self-sufficient centers in terms of services and economic activity (Frey 1992; Loibl and Toetzer 2003; Hasson and Choshen 2003). Indeed, it is possible to see in the new ultraorthodox cities the development of institutions and services that will continue to increase their independence in the future, and, potentially, disrupt or reformulate preexisting hierarchies. The ultraorthodox society has been traditionally described as marked by a condition of "complementary segregation" (Shilhav 1991): a society that exists in a condition of relative insulation and self-segregation but at the same time relies on external support in all the areas that the community lacks in the surrounding urban context. The creation of new ultraorthodox towns detached from a wider, nonultraorthodox urban fabric can potentially constitute a challenge to this traditional model of complementary segregation. Leaving traditional strongholds such as Bnei Brak and Jerusalem for the new, scattered ultraorthodox neighborhoods and suburbs potentially grants the individual and the community significant spatial mobility, which may weaken the sociocultural supervision of the community and create cracks in the "the walls of holiness" that had hitherto protected the established ultraorthodox spaces (Rosen and Razin 2008)—and especially for the younger generation, which is exposed to the media, is knowledgeable about Israeli political and social life, and encounters the complex Israeli reality more directly than its elders do (Shilhav 1991, 1997).

Recent research, however, has shown the resilience of these arrangements, albeit in a wider, multicommunity system on a metropolitan scale. First, the potential autonomy of large centers such as Beitar Illit and Modi'in Illit from the wider ultraorthodox community is mitigated by the existence of a strong network of metropolitan relations, in which established centers ("the metropole" of the ultraorthodox community) serve as a kind of "feeder pipeline" to the new suburban cities. Jerusalem and Bnei Brak serve as countrywide centers for the ultraorthodox in most areas of life, and the new suburban cities are strongly linked to these cities, which serve as a point of origin for their residents, and in which the significant ultraorthodox educational institutions, their spiritual leaders, and a wide range of commercial services and places of employment are located. Research shows that from a spatial point of view, Beitar Illit is economically, socially, and culturally linked to Jerusalem, while Modi'in Illit sits on the geographic "watershed line" and is affiliated with both Jerusalem and Bnei Brak (Cahaner 2009, 2014b).

Second, the system of complementary segregation that has developed at the urban level is largely replicated on a metropolitan scale. Ultraorthodox suburban cities depend largely on nonultraorthodox centers along the Jerusalem-Tel Aviv axis, which represent the economic, financial, and administrative center of gravity of the country. Nonetheless, the demographic size of the ultraorthodox community, the separate spaces that it has created in the new suburban ultraorthodox cities, its unique patterns of consumption, and its political clout as well have allowed it to demand—and receive—adaptations of many market components to its unique requirements and patterns of consumption. Thus, the community has developed into an almost autonomous, separate market. While not an autarchic economy, it is based for the most part on the general economy, which prepares designated products for the ultraorthodox population. Thus, although the ultraorthodox do not require doctors and nurses who are religious, the health services in the ultraorthodox neighborhoods and communities adapt to their unique character; colleges and universities adapt their curriculum and classes to the character of the male and female ultraorthodox students; hi-tech companies fashion the work place to adapt to the needs of ultraorthodox women, and large food companies dedicate manufacturing lines that provide special kosher certifications (Algazi 2006; Cahaner 2009; Cahaner and Shilhav 2012b).

Designated public transportation plays a crucial role in maintaining strong links between ultraorthodox centers on both sides of the Green Line and in reproducing the model of complementary segregation at the metropolitan level (Cahaner 2009, 2014b). According to Handel (2014), the model of gated communities connected by a designated network of transportation and transportation routes enhances the continuity and stability of the group's space. As far as ultraorthodox settlements are concerned, the provision of designated public transportation (subsidized by the state) that serves only the ultraorthodox population and is adapted to its gender and modesty requirements has paved the way to fully integrate ultraorthodox settlements in the metropolitan fabric through the creation of a contiguous, stable, economic-social space for the ultraorthodox population; at the same time, it minimizes interaction with the general public and therefore enables the self-segregation of these communities. In this respect, the ultraorthodox society has largely proved able to abandon a logic of strict territorialism and settle outside the traditional urban boundaries, as long as the conditions necessary for its existence are preserved.

Third, the migration to the suburbs has proven unable to break the relative insulation of ultraorthodox society—indeed, it has apparently reinforced it. The findings of a study on the consolidation of the ultraorthodox suburban cities in 2007 and a follow-up study in 2014 show that the establishment of homogenous ultraorthodox cities creates sealed enclosures, whose purpose is to contain the ultraorthodox population exclusively; indeed, these cities are developing capacities and infrastructure intended to preserve an isolated, separate, and closed urban environment that is self-sustaining, thus lessening daily contact with other populations (Cahaner 2009, 2014a). As we have seen, the model of complementary segregation has not been called into question by the establishment of ultraorthodox settlements as suburban localities, but rather has been reproduced at metropolitan scale. An additional factor reinforcing the tendencies toward segregation has to do with the fact that migration to the suburbs is often motivated by the desire by young parents to prevent exposure of their children to the secular population and its way of life. In other words, a process has been created that strengthens the ultraorthodox tendency to segregate, distance, and close itself from the surrounding space (Cahaner and Shilhav 2012a; Alfasi, Flint Ashery, and Benenson 2013; Flint, Benenson, and Alfasi 2012). While the process of modernization will continue to affect the ultraorthodox communities on both sides of the Green Line, it seems that at least in the ultraorthodox settlements, the trends toward increasing insulation will remain comparatively stronger in the next future.

Conclusion

This chapter examined changes within the ultraorthodox community that occurred as a result of its migration beyond the Green Line within the past two decades in light of two fundamental questions. First, has the community's political orientation changed following its participation in the colonization of the OT? Second, to what extent has the creation of large new towns in the West Bank transformed the ultraorthodox space?

Regarding the first question, the data presented here show that throughout the years a rightward shift has occurred in the political positions of the residents of the ultraorthodox settlements. It can be therefore concluded that participation in the settlement enterprise has changed the political outlook of ultraorthodox society: out of a common interest in the future of the settlements, it has certainly moved closer to the position of the political Right. In this respect, the peculiar nature of ultraorthodox settlements seems to have created a sort of intermediate category and outlook of the ultraorthodox settlers regarding the settlement project. These are defined by a different mix of motivations to settle ("necessity" as a category in between quality of life and ideology); a particularistic worldview that informs the community's adhesion to the settlements' enterprise; the transformations of contemporary ultraorthodox society; and the peculiarities of the geopolitical reality of the OT and the spatial patterns of ultraorthodox settlements.

Regarding the second question, the chapter has outlined how the development of large suburban settlements such as Modi'in Illit and Beitar Illit presents significant challenges for a society that has previously lived in the protective shade of the "walls of holiness" of established ultraorthodox centers such as Jerusalem and Bnei Brak—challenges that can potentially disrupt the internal hierarchies and dynamics of ultraorthodox society and force it to dilute its insulation from the wider Israeli-Jewish society. However, the data presented seem to suggest ultraorthodox communities have successfully met these challenges; despite being usually characterized as very territorial, the ultraorthodox society has proved able to considerably expand and transform its traditional patterns of settlements. Thanks to their internal cohesion and demographic strength—and, crucially, the provision of publicly funded government services—it has rebuilt its "walls of holiness" at metropolitan scale. This ensures the development of a coherent ultraorthodox space, with the traditional centers of Bnei Brak and Jerusalem functioning as "inner cities" of a large and expanding ultraorthodox suburban system. Participation to the settlement enterprise did not open up ultraorthodox space to a more intense exchange with the Israeli-Jewish society as a whole, as might have been predicted; indeed, the "suburban gated communities" that have been built for the ultraorthodox settlers have reinforced previous pattern of segregation. Although one can still find in the ultraorthodox settlements signs of the modernization and Israelization occurring in ultraorthodox society, these trends are apparent within the ultraorthodox settlements in a lesser and diminished extent.

Finally, the peculiarities noted with respect to ultraorthodox settlements raise the question of similarity of the former to the other settlements established in the OT. A quick examination reveals four fundamental aspects. The first is the almost infinite flexibility of the ultraorthodox public in regard to geography, since it seems open to reside in various places, as long as the basic services are provided and continuous transportation to its core cities are maintained. This is contrary to the religious-national settlements, in which the location of the settlement is of the highest importance, at the level of the region and even the basic division within it (Weiss 2011; Leon 2015b). A second difference derives from eliminating the accepted dichotomy between ideological and quality of life settlements, because the ultraorthodox settlements present a model in which this distinction is not by any means clear-cut. This joins other recent studies which demonstrate the weakness of this entrenched dichotomy. Leon (2015b), for example, argues that the national-religious "settler movement" has always combined elements of social mobility and political ideology. He points out that one cannot ignore the important role that Jewish settlement in the West Bank and Gaza played in the upward social mobility of disadvantaged groups from Israeli society. The establishment and expansion of settlements such as Ariel and Ma'ale Adumim during the past decades were no doubt a part of the ideological commitment of the right wing in Israel to the realization of the idea of "Greater Israel." However, these places also allowed the state to provide settlers a path to rapid social mobility by offering cheap housing for marginalized groups in Israeli society. For instance, Ma'ale Adumim was a place in which second-generation Oriental Mizrachi Jews could realize the dream of becoming part of the Israeli middle-class by purchasing a spacious apartment; in Ariel, new immigrants from the Former Soviet Union could locate in a cheap urban space close to the centers of employment in the heart of the country (Leon 2015b; Weiss chapter five).

A third difference is that compared to the rest of the settlements, which function as employment suburbs for the cities in the heart of the country, the ultraorthodox settlements function as independent, almost autarchic economies. Finally, we can note a great deal of similarity between the ultraorthodox settlements and the religious-national ones. Both are markedly segregated from their surroundings, whether Palestinian or Jewish; both constitute somehow "ideological" gated communities (although in the ultraorthodox case the ideology is religious-social); in both cases a designated network is deployed between the communities with which they maintain clear affiliation and which allows the minority to maintain a kind of autarchic economy through complementary spatial segregation. These characteristics correspond to the characteristics of gated communities in other parts in the world (Handel 2014).

The study of ultraorthodox settlements—currently the most stable anchor for the growth of Jewish communities beyond the Green Line—illustrates yet another crucial dimension of the heterogeneity of the settlers population; furthermore, it shows the flexibility of Israel's settlement policy in the OT and its success in co-opting sectors of the Israeli population that had little interest in the ideological and strategic agenda of colonization. At the same time, it shows how economic and demographic trends in Israel (namely, in the ultraorthodox communities) were reflected in the development of the settlement policy; in turn, the participation of ultraorthodox communities to the settlement enterprise transformed the ultraorthodox society itself, and its existence in the broader context of the Israeli society as a whole.

Note

1. With a population of more than 150,000 residents, Bnei Brak is the second largest ultraorthodox city after Jerusalem, and hosts many of the central religious, social, and cultural institutions of the ultraorthodox society in Israel.

References

Alfasi, Nurit, Shlomit Flint Ashery, and Itzhak Benenson. 2013. "Between the Individual and the Community: Residential Patterns of the Haredi Population in Jerusalem." *International Journal of Urban and Regional Research* 37 (6): 2152–2176.

Algazi, Gadi. 2006. "Matrix in Bil'in: A Story of Colonial Capitalism in Current Israel." *Theory and Criticism* 29: 173–192. [Hebrew.]

Atkes, Dror, and Lara Friedman. 2005. *The Ultra-Orthodox Population in the Settlements. Peace Now.* Accessed January 31, 2016. http://peacenow.org.il/eng/content/ultra-orthodox-jews-west -bank.

Blakely, Edward J., and Mary G. Snyder. 1997. "Divided We Fall: Gated and Walled Communities in the United States." In *Architecture of Fear*, edited by Nan Ellin, 85–99. New York: Princeton Architectural Press.

Cahaner, Lee. 2009. *The Development of the Spatial and Hierarchic Structure of the Ultra-Orthodox Jewish Population in Israel*. Haifa: Haifa University. [Hebrew.]

———. 2014a. *Dedicated Survey of the Residents of the New Ultra-Orthodox Cities*. Jerusalem: Jerusalem Institute for Israel Studies. [Hebrew.]

———. 2014b. *National Master Plan for Public Transport in the Ultra-Orthodox Sector: Report A (Internal Report)*. Jerusalem: Ministry of Transportation. [Hebrew.]

———. Forthcoming. "From a Geography of Religious Segregation to a Geography of Class Distinction: Space and Social Stratification in Ultra-Orthodox Society in Israel." In *Class, Religion and Social Stratification in Israel*, edited by Shlomo Fischer and Nissim Leon. Jerusalem: Van Leer Institute/HaKibbutz HaMeuchad.

Cahaner, Lee, and Yosef Shilhav. 2012a. "Development of the Ultra-Orthodox Space in Israel." In *The Production of Space in Israel: The Map of Settlements and Land*, edited by Shlomo Hasson, 319–338. Tel Aviv: Keter.

———. 2012b. "From Ghetto to Suburb: Changes in Ultra-Orthodox Space in Israel." In *From Survival to Consolidation: Changes in Israeli Haredi Society and Its Scholarly Study*, edited by Jimmy Kaplan and Nurit Stadler, 252–272. Tel Aviv: Van Leer Institute/HaKibbutz HaMeuchad. [Hebrew.]

———. 2013. "Ultra-Orthodox Settlements in Judea and Samaria." *Social Issues in Israel* 16: 41–62. [Hebrew.]

Caplan, Kimmy. 2003. "Studying Israeli Haredi Society: Characteristics, Achievements and Challenges." In *Israeli Haredim: Inclusion without Assimilation?*, edited by Emmanuel Sivan and Kimmy Caplan, 224–278. Jerusalem: Van Leer Institute/Hakibbutz Hameuchad. [Hebrew.]

———. 2007. *Internal Popular Discourse in Israeli Haredi Society*. Jerusalem: Zalman Shazar Center.

CBS. 2008, 2013, 2014. "Statistical Abstract of Israel." Jerusalem: Central Bureau of Statistics.

Flint, Shlomit, Itzhak Benenson, and Nurit Alfasi. 2012. "Between Friends and Strangers: Micro-Segregation in a Haredi Neighborhood in Jerusalem." *City and Community* 11 (2): 171–197.

Frey, William H. 1992. "Minority Suburbanization and Continued 'White Flight' in U.S. Metropolitan Areas: Assessing Findings from the 1990 Census." Paper presented at the *Annual Meetings of the Population Association of America*, Denver, Colorado, May 2, 1992.

Handel, Ariel. 2014. "Gated/Gating Community: The Settlement Complex in the West Bank." *Transactions of the Institute of British Geographers* 39 (4): 504–517. doi: 10.1111/tran.12045.

Hasson, Shlomo, and Maya Choshen. 2003. *The Socio-Spatial Structure of the Tel Aviv Metropolitan Area*. Jerusalem: Floersheimer Institute for Policy Studies. [Hebrew.]

Leon, Nissim. 2014. "A Society of Scholars: Is There a Future?" *Akdamut* 29: 44–129. [Hebrew.]

———. 2015a. "Rabbi'Ovadia Yosef, the Shas Party, and the Arab-Israeli Peace Process." *Middle East Journal* 69 (3): 379–395.

———. 2015b. "Self-Segregation of the Vanguard: Judea and Samaria in the Religious-Zionist Society." *Israel Affairs* 21 (3): 348–360.

Loibl, Wolfgang, and Tanja Toetzer. 2003. "Modeling Growth and Densification Processes in Suburban Regions—Simulation of Landscape Transition with Spatial Agents." *Environmental Modelling and Software* 18 (6): 553–563.

Malach, Gilad, and Lee Cahaner. "Touches of Modernity or Modern Ultra-Orthodoxy? A Numerical Assessment of Modernization Processes in Ultra-Orthodox Society." *Democratic Culture.* [Hebrew.] Forthcoming.

MoH. 2015. *Strategic Plan for Housing for the Ultra-Orthodox Population (Internal Report).* Jerusalem: Ministry of Housing/The Haredi Institute. [Hebrew.]

Rodgers, Dennis. 2004. "'Disembedding' the City: Crime, Insecurity and Spatial Organization in Managua, Nicaragua." *Environment and Urbanization* 16 (2): 113–124.

Rosen, Gillad, and Eran Razin. 2008. "Enclosed Residential Neighborhoods in Israel: From Landscapes of Heritage and Frontier Enclaves to New Gated Communities." *Environment and Planning A* 40 (12): 2895–2913.

Rosen, Gillad, and Anne B. Shlay. 2010. "Making Place: The Shifting Green Line and the Development of 'Greater' Metropolitan Jerusalem." *City and Community* 9 (4): 358–389. doi: 10.1111/J.1540-6040.2010.01344.X.

Rotem, Tamar. 2003. "Us? Settlers? Heaven Forbid!" *Haaretz,* June 29. [Hebrew.]

Sadan, Ezra, Amiram Gonen, and Yakir Plessner. 2011. *Planning an Ultra-Orthodox City Compared to a City Designed as an Ultra-Orthodox Mosaic.* Tel Aviv: Sadan Lowental. [Hebrew.]

Salcedo, Rodrigo, and Alvaro Torres. 2004. "Gated Communities in Santiago: Wall or Frontier?" *International Journal of Urban and Regional Research* 28 (1): 27–44.

Shilhav, Yosef. 1991. *A Town in a City: The Geography of Separation and Integration.* Jerusalem: The Jerusalem Institute for Israel Studies. [Hebrew.]

——. 1993. "The Emergence of Ultra-Orthodox Neighborhoods in Israeli Urban Centers." In *Local Communities and the Israeli Polity,* edited by Efraim Ben-Zadok, 157–187. New York: State University of New York Press.

——. 1997. *Governing and Managing a Haredi (Ultra-Orthodox) City.* Jerusalem: The Floersheimer Institute for Policy Studies. [Hebrew.]

——. 2001. *Territorial Iconography: Geographical Symbols of Jerusalem. A Jewish-Israeli Perspective.* Jerusalem: The Jerusalem Institute for Israel Studies. [Hebrew.]

——. 2007. "Landmarks for Zion: Territorial Commemoration in Jewish Tradition." In *Myth, Language and Memory in Forming Awareness in Israel,* 58–66. Tivon: Oranim College/Yad Ben-Zvi Institute.

Shoshana, Avi, and Limor Samimian-Darash. 2014. "Governing Heterogeneous Populations: 'Separate and Unequal' in Israel." *Sociology* 48 (6): 1139–1155.

Shragai, Nadav. 2003a. "One of Every Two New Settlers is Ultra-Orthodox." *Haaretz,* September 26. [Hebrew.]

——. 2003b. "Without the Ultra-Orthodox Jews, the Settlers' Internal Migration Balance Would Be Negative." *Haaretz,* July 13. [Hebrew.]

——. 2007. "Orthodox Jews Are Responsible for Half the Growth in the Settler Population." *Haaretz,* August 24. [Hebrew.]

Stern, Eli, and Shlomit Canaan. 2006. *The Housing Needs of the Ultra-Orthodox Sector.* Jerusalem: Ministry of Housing. [Hebrew.]

Weizman, Eyal. 2007. *Hollow Land: Israel's Architecture of Occupation.* London: Verso.

Wu, Fulong, and Klaire Webber. 2004. "The Rise of 'Foreign Gated Communities' in Beijing: Between Economic Globalization and Local Institutions." *Cities* 21 (3): 203–213.

Zicherman, Haim, and Lee Cahaner. 2012. *Modern Ultra-Orthodoxy: The Emerging Haredi Middle Class in Israel.* Jerusalem: Israel Democracy Institute. [Hebrew.]

8   Beyond Gush Emunim

On Contemporary Forms of Messianism among Religiously Motivated Settlers in the West Bank

Assaf Harel

Undoubtedly, research on the post-1967 settlement enterprise is characterized by a disproportional amount of attention that is directed toward religiously
motivated settlers. Even though the vast majority of the settler population is
Haredi or secular, much has been written about the rise of Gush Emunim (bloc
of the faithful) and its intimate ties to Rabbi Avraham Yizhak Kook, Rabbi Tzvi
Yehuda Kook, and Merkaz HaRav Yeshiva (Aran 2013; Feige 2009; Gorenberg
2006; Lustick 1988; Newman 1986; Ravitzky 1996; Rubinstein 1982; Schwartz
2009). Gush Emunim was officially founded in 1974, but continued settlement visions and practices that began in 1967 at Kfar Etzion. It propagated a messianic
theology that binds redemption with the maintenance of a physical union between Jews and the biblical Land of Israel, a union that would move history to its
redemptive end. Similarly to the sacred land, which forms the spatial counter-
part of the messianic age, the Jewish state becomes an object of sanctification, a
political manifestation of divine teleology. Within this theological worldview,
the profane shimmers with sparks of holiness and the present saturates with
messianic signs of redemption (Ravitzky 1996).

It is hard to overemphasize the impact of the religious politics of Gush Emunim upon the geopolitics of the region, Palestinian lives, the democratic qualities
of the Israeli state, and the shaping of Judaism as well. When this significance is
coupled with the intellectually and emotionally enticing power of such a socio-
culturally potent movement, it is quite understandable why Gush Emunim dominates scholarly work on post-1967 settlers. However, the narrow focus on Gush
Emunim marginalized other important aspects of settlement realities such as the
contribution of neoliberal governance to settlement growth (Weiss 2011). Moreover, Gush Emunim was often identified as a fundamentalist movement (Aran
1991, 1997; Feige 2009; Inbari 2007; Lustick 1988; Sivan 1995). This, in turn, facili-

tated the perception of settlers as radically different from other Israelis, construed their beliefs as a deviation from Judaism, and represented their settlement practices as distinct from those conducted on the other side of the Green Line (Dalsheim 2011; Fischer 2007; Rosenak 2013; Roth 2013). In short, the use of the fundamentalist framework emphasized differences over similarities.

Interestingly, the scholarly gaze at Gush Emunim generally grew at a time when Gush Emunim ceased to exist as a movement in the early 1980s and its power was diffused among varying (yet related) rabbinical figures and political bodies such as the Yesha Council and Amana (Dalsheim and Harel 2009). Still, even though it no longer exists, Gush Emunim survived discursively as a trope and theoretically as a Weberian "ideal type," which subsumes all religiously motivated settlers. One of the primary consequences of this sustained presence of Gush Emunim is a continued homogenization of an otherwise heterogeneous population whose internal composition remains sociopolitically important. Today, the religiously motivated settler population is divided among theological and ideological lines that relate among other issues to the meaning of redemption, its relation to the state of Israel, and to questions of control and sovereignty within the Israeli-Palestinian space.

This ethnographically grounded chapter aims to move beyond Gush Emunim and reviews four forms of messianism among settlers: the disavowed messianism of settlers in Alon Shvut; the neo-Hassidism of Rabbi Yitzhak Ginsburgh, Rabbi Menachem Froman, and their followers; and the mystical statism of Rabbi Tzvi Tau. In arguing for the persisting but altered centrality of messianism within the settlement enterprise, I call attention to contemporary changes within the religiously motivated settler population. Finally, this chapter raises the possibility of an emergence of post-Zionist messianism among settlers. That is, messianism that is closely related to growing alienation from Zionist politics with secular characteristics and aspires to end the role of secular Zionism within the redemptive process.

The reasons for the current messianic diversity among settlers can be traced at least to the Zionist project and its attendant religious sanctification, which laid the ground for ensuing tensions between earthly realities and transcendental ideals (Ravitzky 1996). These tensions were further heightened when territorial politics were paired with messianic convictions following the two wars (1967 and 1973) from which Gush Emunim was born. And so, starting with 1982 and culminating in 2005, a series of Israeli territorial withdrawals were bound to catalyze changes that are tied to religious attempts to reconcile the real with the ideal (Inbari 2014). Nevertheless, the sociocultural dynamics that appertain to religiously motivated settlers do not necessarily stop or begin at the Green Line. They are related to changes within the Israeli society at large, such as liberalization processes and the decline of the secular Zionist settlement ethos (Fischer 2007). Even more so, they are part of broader global processes that are imbricated with the greater world of Jewish orthodoxy that touch, for instance, upon issues such as the place of the individual within the collective, the status of women, and the nature of the relations to the secular and non-Jewish world. At the same time, because settlement realities impact local and global realities, settlers are themselves powerful agents of change and the religiously motivated ones are especially so.

The attempt to measure ideological differences among religiously motivated settlers in quantitative terms is very difficult due to at least two interrelated reasons: there is a lack of statistical data of ideological variations within the Jewish population of the West Bank, and sociocultural identity is a fluid and hybrid category. Nevertheless, based upon the religious character of individual settlements, it is commonly estimated that religiously motivated settlers comprise about a third of the approximately 360,000 West Bank settlers.[1] About half of them belong to the mystical circle and the other half belongs to the nonmystical stream of religious Zionism (e.g., the historical offshoots of Mafdal—the national-religious political party—along with the Mizrahi religious stream, which should not be confused with "mizrahi" as an ethnic identity). Alon Shvut can be understood as paradigmatic of the nonmystical stream of religious Zionist settlers while Rabbi Tau and his circle comprise a growing stream of a religiously conservative form of Kookist mystical messianism. In contrast, the followers of Rabbi Ginsburgh and Rabbi Froman constitute the contemporary fringes of religiously motivated settler life and number no more than few hundreds. However, their significance does not necessarily correspond to their size: just as Gush Emunim emerged as a small movement at first, they too may attest to the emergence of messianic forms that may gain stronger hold in the future.

Religiously motivated settlers are typically described as "messianic," a term that is commonly loaded with negative connotations: irrationality, mysticism, apocalypticism, and so forth. Although I do not contest the messianic label that is ascribed to settlers, I do view the associated stigma as a common expression of a modernist construction of the religious subject as primitive and irrational (Harding 1992). Moreover, I suggest that a heuristic differentiation between messianism and redemption as reflecting the relations between means and end can assist this review of the contemporary messianic phenomena among settlers. Therefore, I treat here messianism as a complex of revolutionary ideas, sentiments, and practices that are oriented toward redemption (Idel 2000). Messianism can thus be understood as the human force that drives the redemptive process as a journey toward personal, collective and universal fulfillment.

Messianism is more than a belief in a messianic figure (Idel 2000). It is a temporal phenomenon in which the present loses presence as it gets caught between the weight of a glorified past and the alluring power of the longed-for (and often utopian) future. At the same time, the realization of messianism translates into a practice that shifts the center of activity almost exclusively into the present, which becomes a temporal arena where reality is both negated and fulfilled as part of a revolutionary practice with redemptive ends.[2] Messianic practices are therefore often described as having "a distinctive time perception," which is "informed by an acute sense of imminence and urgency" (Kravel-Tovi and Bilu 2008, 64). Indeed, as demonstrated by Gideon Aran (2013), in its early days, a significant number of members and supporters of Gush Emunim was characterized by mystical passion and conviction of a pending redemption. Nevertheless, today, rather than exhibiting an acute sense of urgency, some religiously motivated settlers feel relatively complacent about their present conditions, while others do not seek an immediate revolution and act slowly and patiently toward redemption. Consider Alon Shvut, one of the more elite religious Zionist settlements.

Redemption Instead of Messianism: The Bourgeoisification of Settler Life

Alon Shvut was established in 1970, when Yeshivat Har Etzion, the first *yeshivat hesder* in the West Bank, moved there permanently from Kfar Etzion.[3] The relations between Gush Emunim and Alon Shvut are complex. For example, although the Yeshiva and Alon Shvut were established before Gush Emunim, one of the founders of the Yeshiva, Rabbi Hanan Porat (1943–2011), was among the founders of Gush Emunim, which sometimes established settlements through confrontation with legal authorities.[4] Yet, Alon Shvut was established following a governmental decision that designated it as the communal center of Gush Etzion: a settlement bloc south of Jerusalem that was lost during the 1948 war—a day before the Israeli declaration of independence—and resettled again after the Israeli victory in 1967.

Today, Alon Shvut functions as the unofficial capital of the area. It is the home of university professors, politicians, prominent rabbis, and judges, too. Many of Alon Shvut's residents see themselves as different from other settlers. This particular sense of identity is tied to the historical coupling of the fall of Gush Etzion and the Israeli declaration of independence, which transformed into a central element of the Zionist ethos of heroic sacrifice and national revival. In accordance, the "return" to Gush Etzion following the 1967 War fulfilled not only the religious desire to return to the biblical homeland, but also the Zionist desire to return to the ruins of the settlements that were lost in 1948. Alon Shvut is perceived by its residents as more Zionist in comparison to other settlements because its story predates Gush Emunim and blurs the historical lines between settlement acts that were carried out before and after 1967.

People in Alon Shvut often pride themselves on their rational and nuanced worldview, which confronts the complexities that may emerge from the contradictions between the secular and religious domains of life. Furthermore, in valuing Judaism as a religion of reason, people in Alon Shvut sometimes denounce

Kabbalah—Jewish mysticism—for being an irrational deviation from the rational essence of Judaism.[5] "There is a big gap in my knowledge," admitted Rabbi Cohen, one of my interlocutors "and it has to do with Kabbalah. I hardly know anything about it." He sees the engagement with mysticism as an irrational fascination with esoteric knowledge that takes away from the "beauty and depth of the Torah." Another settler was more blatant and said, "this [Kabbalah] is just superstitious nonsense. . . . Hocus Pocus," thus expressing an unabashed disregard to the mystical component that was so central to Gush Emunim's Kookist political theology and remains integral to Hassidism. Similarly, messianism is often denoted as a mystical sentiment with disastrous historical implications and when asked whether they consider themselves messianic, many of my respondents were quick to reject the messianic label.

"Are you messianic?" I asked Rabbi Cohen one day as I sat with his family around the dinner table. After a short moment of contemplation, he answered succinctly, "I am not messianic, but I believe in redemption." He explained that for him the term "messianism" connotes mystical zealotry. He believes in redemption as the ingathering of exiles and the creation of Jewish sovereignty in Eretz Israel, but opposes religious explanations that rely on mystical readings of reality. He does not live in Alon Shvut because he believes it will hasten the arrival of the Messiah. "But don't you believe in the Messiah?" I asked, somewhat confused. "Doesn't the belief in the Messiah form one of the central tenants of Jewish faith?" "Yes," he answered, "I do," but did not continue his explanation. I could see he was feeling uneasy talking about this subject.

Yifat, Rabbi Cohen's wife, noticed the tension and intervened. "I believe in the Messiah," she said authoritatively. "It is a source of hope, of endless optimism, even in the darkest moments. It is a force that strengthened Jewish communities throughout the ages." "But what does it mean for you to believe in the coming of the Messiah?" I pushed further, and she expounded: "I believe that one day we shall live in a better world, in a reality that is more spiritually connected to God. That one day we will be part of an ethical society that will allow the emergence of a just leader. But who knows when this will happen. No one can tell for certain. . . . All we can say that these are days of redemption, but we cannot take them for granted, and we should cherish the fact that we are free people." I sought further clarification: "So why are these days the days of redemption?" "The undeniable fact is that we returned to Eretz Israel from all across the world, and we have a state of our own. We are free people at last, and this is a blessed deviation in Jewish history."

In general, settlers in Alon Shvut prefer to talk about redemption rather than messianism. Messianism is discursively rejected, denied, or downplayed, while redemption is emphasized and elevated as a more meaningful and accurate religious Zionist value. This morally loaded distinction between messianism and redemption echoes the ways in which Zionist thinkers sought to simultaneously identify, but also distinguish the Zionist endeavor from Jewish messianism. Messianism was construed as a passive, irrational, and apocalyptic yearning, while Zionism was said to constitute a redemptive break from these mythical-religious elements because it formed an active and politically rational realization of the messianic myth (Raz-Krakotzkin 2002). In contrast, Zionism was considered among mystical religious Zionist circles as messianism in itself, as the political embodiment of divine will. Moreover, following the settlement project of Gush Emunim, messianism is commonly conceived these days in the vernacular as an active mystical act of "hastening the end," while redemption is associated with a more passive and rational yearning toward a just future. Thus, settlers in Alon Shvut evoke redemption as part of their effort to distinguish themselves from other settlers, align more closely with the state, and present themselves as respected and enlightened global citizens. However, as an emblem of the successful institutionalization of religiously motivated settlement life, Alon Shvut materializes the normalization of messianism.

Alon Shvut is revolution incarnated, complacent and self-confident about the future. This confidence is quite merited. All of Israel's prime ministers since the late Yitzhak Rabin declared that any peace agreement with the Palestinian Authority would include Gush Etzion within the boundaries of Israel. In accordance, although they may worry about the prospects of territorial withdrawals from the West Bank, they are not personally threatened by it.[6] As a case in point, during the 2010 festive celebrations of Alon Shvut's fortieth anniversary, a "time capsule" was buried in the ground on the lawn by the main synagogue in the Old Neighborhood. It carries colorful drawings from the preschoolers of the present to the preschoolers of Alon Shvut in 2050. This elaborate performance of confidence in the future of the settlement is tied to the generally politically passive spirit of Alon Shvut. For example, the guidelines of the settlement's email list prohibit the publication of political content. The political purpose of these antipolitical guidelines is to orient online communal discussions around the mundane and reduce internal frictions, an act that ignores the politically laden nature of the settlement. In practice, the messianism of settlers in Alon Shvut can be understood as messianism turned ordinary, contented, self-assured, and somewhat unaware of itself: bourgeois life as the face of a religious revolution. This is a far cry from the messianic excitement that is associated with the early days of Gush Emunim.

"Religious Zionism Revealed Its Whole Pathetic Being": Rabbi Ginsburgh and the "Hilltop Youth"

The messianism of Alon Shvut, whose discursive disavowal constitutes a central method of its routinization, can be contrasted with the explicit messianism of many of the settlers who are inspired by the teachings of Rabbi Yitzhak Ginsburgh. Rabbi

Ginsburgh first entered public consciousness in 1994, when he published "Baruch Ha'Gever" (Blessed Is the Man), in which he explains why the murderous acts of Baruch Goldstein, a settler who in 1994 killed twenty-nine Palestinians at the Cave of the Patriarchs in Hebron, may be considered a sacred act of martyrdom. In 2009, he made national and international headlines again following the publication of *Torat Hamelech* (The King's Torah), a halakhic book that was authored by two of Rabbi Ginsburgh's close followers. The book discusses halakhic laws of killing non-Jews (gentiles) and argues, for example, that "there is justification for killing babies if it is clear that they will grow up to harm us" (Elitzur and Shapira 2010, 207). Rabbi Ginsburgh expresses his support of the book in its opening pages.

Rabbi Ginsburgh is affiliated with Chabad Hassidism and some of his followers even believe that he is the eighth Rebbe, that he embodies the spirit of the Messiah. Although Rabbi Ginsburgh does not declare himself explicitly as the Messiah, he is the head of Derech-Chaim (Way of Life), a religious movement with an unequivocal goal: to transform Israel into a Jewish monarchy. The movement seeks to make Rabbi Ginsburgh the president of this Jewish state and fulfill the Deuteronomy (17:15) command to "set a king upon yourself" (Giladi 2014, 8–9). Due to his messianic project, Rabbi Ginsburgh has uneasy relations with Chabad.[7] Some see his activities as undermining the sacred status of the seventh Rebbe. Still, he is widely acknowledged as one of the most creative and prolific Jewish thinkers of this generation, a Jewish mystic who is occupied with conceptualizing the relevance of Kabbalah to all aspects of life. His teachings weave together the messianic politics and intellectualism of Chabad, the joyous spiritually of Breslov Hassidism, the settlement theology of Rabbi T. Y. Kook, and a religious radicalism that marks a departure from statist orientations of Gush Emunim (Fischer 2007; Garb 2009; Huss 2007).

Rabbi Ginsburgh is interested in creating a contemporary Jewish consciousness that is disconnected from the secular influences of Zionism (Tamari 2014). Unlike Rabbi A. Y. Kook and his adherers at Gush Emunim who saw redemption as predicated upon cooperation between secular and religious Jews, Rabbi Ginsburgh sees Zionism and its secular orientations as a corruptive force, an unholy *klipa* (husk/shell). *Klipa* is a kabbalistic term for impure and wicked forces that imprison and feed upon the sparks of the divine light. The separation of the holy sparks from their husks is the essence of redemption. Rabbi Ginsburgh uses the nut and its shells as a parable of the Jewish return to Zion. The *klipa* reflect an outward concealment of a sacred inner truth. Like the nutshell, a *klipa* was required at first for the protection of the fledgling Jewish sovereignty. Now, however, Zionism and its secular offshoots operate to imprison, contaminate, and suffocate the pure seed from which the true Jewish sovereignty must spring forth (Ginsburgh 2005). The shell must be broken. Through its false secular principles,

Zionism created a separation within Jewish unity, casting many Jews into spiritual exile. In contrast to religious Zionist thought, Rabbi Ginsburgh's mysticism construes Zionism as a malignant force that should be actively opposed and destroyed (Inbari 2009).

Rabbi Ginsburgh's teachings resonate among a younger generation of settlers who are associated with the hilltop youth phenomenon. "Hilltop youth" is a colloquial term that refers to settlers who live in small and isolated outposts that are often illegal even under Israeli law. Not all of these settlers are young, not all of them follow Rabbi Ginsburgh, and not all of these outposts are built on hilltops. The term, "hilltop youth," however, does capture the romantic and religious desire of these settlers to connect to nature and depart from the organized structures of power of the older and more established settlements. These outposts are often the consequence of private initiatives of individuals and small groups that act without the financial support of the Israeli government and in opposition to the general plans of regional settlement councils. The outposts are usually located amid areas heavily populated by Palestinians, and their houses are spaced out to achieve more freedom and land control. In contrast to the well-developed, concrete-filled, red-roofed, and fence-bounded settlements, their houses are simply built, often by their own inhabitants, in a manner that blends esthetically with the surrounding environment (Fischer 2005; Tzfadia, chapter 6).

The hilltop youth phenomenon grew in opposition to the urbanized and conventionalized lifestyle of the older settler generation and is related to another religious phenomenon: neo-Hassidism. Neo-Hassidism is defined by Tomer Persico (2014, 287), a leading Israeli scholar of religion, as "the deliberate and conscious attempt to draw inspiration, tools and cultural capital from early Hassidic texts and practices in order to bring about a contemporary spiritual revival." In the last two decades, in a somewhat belated response to the advent of postmodernity, more and more religious Zionists became attracted to Hassidism and began to become more critical, for example, of all-encompassing and collectivist notions of redemption in search for more personal meanings (Fischer 2011). Like the hippie movement of the 1960s and the more contemporary New Age movement, the settlers of the hills seek more intimate and authentic religious experiences and draw on Hassidic tradition as a spiritual means of connecting to self, place, and God.

The desire for personal spiritual fulfillment is not disconnected from the theological-political realm. A growing number of religiously motivated settlers is becoming ever more disillusioned with the Israeli state, seeing the state as ceding to secular and gentile values instead of Jewish ones. This process of disenchantment with the state increased in scale and theological diversity following the unilateral disengagement of Israel from the Gaza Strip (Inbari 2014). Itzik lives in one of the outposts of Yitzhar,[8] a Hassidic-oriented settlement, which is widely considered to be the most extreme right-wing settlement in the West Bank.

I asked him to talk about the similarities and differences between settlements and outposts like his, and he elaborated further:

> The outposts are trying to do what the settlements did before and the Zionist pioneers before them. And just as the settlements see themselves as the continuation of the Zionist enterprise, and there are those who oppose the settlements because they endanger the Zionist project itself, the outposts continue the religious Zionist settlements. But, [the outposts] receive opposition from within religious Zionism because they endanger the religious Zionist settlement. . . . Religious Zionism is characterized by the refusal to reach a real confrontation with the state. . . . During the disengagement, religious Zionism revealed its whole pathetic being. People spoke about the importance of democracy, about the importance of not refusing [military] orders. If you struggle . . . you have to make sacrifices. . . . If you are going to struggle, struggle, if not, then leave, this is what they didn't get.

As Itzik and his friends see it, Zionism acts against the interest of the Jewish people, erases the religious meaning of life in this age and place and partakes in the destruction of Jewish life in Judea and Samaria, the biblical cradle of Jewish civilization. In collaborating so closely with Zionist institutions, religious Zionism is seen too as colluding against Judaism itself.

Rabbi Ginsburgh's admirers on the hilltops lack his theological knowledge and sophistication. Nonetheless, inspired by his teachings, some of them engage in "Price Tag" acts. "Price Tag" is the economic euphemism given to violent actions of vandalism and revenge that include property and bodily harm and even murder, which are carried out primarily against Palestinians and non-Jewish places of worship.[9] In addition to intimidating Palestinians, these violent acts are meant to hasten the redemptive process through a radicalization of the Israeli-Palestinian conflict that will create conditions for a new political order. Although these acts receive much opposition from within the Zionist and religious Zionist establishments, Itzik, like many of his friends, believe these actions reflect the inner will of the Jewish people. Thus, according to this messianic worldview, the Israeli state is no longer a facilitator of the redemptive process, but an obstacle that must be "rectified" and overcome as soon as possible, even through violent acts that fulfill a still unconscious Jewish will.

"The Heart of the Conflict Is Also the Heart of the Solution": Rabbi Froman and Land of Peace

The neo-Hassidic counterculture of settlement life expands beyond Rabbi Ginsburgh and his young devotees. In fact, the neo-Hassidic occupation with mystical spirituality is also a defining trait of a group of settlers with political and religious outlooks that stand in opposition to Rabbi Ginsburgh's messianic project: Rabbi

Menachem Froman (1945-2013) and his circle of students. Rabbi Froman was a student of Rabbi T. Y. Kook at Merkaz HaRav Yeshiva, among the first members of Gush Emunim, and the chief rabbi of Tekoa, a mixed settlement of religious and secular people in eastern Gush Etzion. Rabbi Froman dedicated his life to peace, which may seem strange indeed: a settler and a peace activist. A man full of ostensible contradictions, he supported the establishment of a Palestinian state, but was opposed to the evacuation of settlements. He was willing to stay and live as a Jewish minority under Palestinian sovereignty, a minority that would ensure the existence of Palestinian democracy and would act as a bridge for peace between two states. Rather than seeing settlements as an obstacle for peace, he would often say, "the settlers could be the fingers of the Israeli hand held out for peace." The idea of fingers did not reflect for him a means of tearing apart Palestinian territorial contiguity and facilitating Israeli control, but instead represented contact and sensitivity.

At the center of Rabbi Froman's notion of peace was the idea that in addition to its territorial, economic, and national dimensions, the Israeli-Palestinian conflict is religious at its core, and therefore, as much as religion acts a force of violence, it can also act as a force of peace (Dalsheim 2014; Gopin 2002). This notion of peace drew upon Jewish Hassidic traditions, especially from a kabbalistic theosophy of the *sefirot* that sets the unification of oppositions as the goal of redemption.[10] For example, the gendered dynamics of the *sefirot* were translated by him into the relations between conquest and land. He saw conquest as a masculine value of expansion and control. Land, in contrast, represented for him the feminine value of restriction and reception. He understood the important redemptive task of this age as a movement away from masculine values toward feminine ones, a movement from the conquest of land to the love of the land. He argued that this movement from masculine rule over place to feminine love of place—from territorial notion of ownership to territorial notions of belonging—is the condition that would allow Israelis and Palestinians to share the same space peacefully (Froman 2014).

In 2010, Eretz Shalom (Land of Peace), a settler movement, was established to materialize Rabbi Froman's vision of peace.[11] Eretz Shalom seeks to bring about peace "from below," through meetings between settlers and Palestinians that would foster good "neighborly relations." Rather than constituting solely a cause for friction, the geographic proximity between settlers and Palestinians is understood by these settlers as containing a unique potential for local forms of cooperation—from commerce to faith-based encounters—that rely upon shared values such as love of the land and shared religious beliefs. These, in turn, are believed to increase settler recognition of the Palestinian political condition, foster a sense of local responsibility among settlers, facilitate Palestinian recognition of settlers' deep ties to the land, and help the creation of a new community of settlers and Palestinians, one that finds a way to cohabit the same space as equals under the law.

"The reality is that no one is going to go away," argued Noah, one of the founding members of Eretz Shalom and a resident of an outpost in the southern part of Gush Etzion. According to him, "the idea that Palestinians can suddenly disappear or move somewhere else belongs to the past as much as the idea of set-tlements disappearing like in the Gaza Strip. Too much energy is being futilely spent on changing the unchangeable. Instead, we must accept reality and invest energy in making it better." "There are many people who think that you live on stolen Palestinian land," I told Noah. "Before I built my house here," he explained, "I checked the maps to see that that land belongs to no one." "But you are an ex-ception," I answered. "So many settlements were built on Palestinian land. And many would argue that all of Judea and Samaria is Palestinian land." "This is one of the main problems, of the sins that we are here to change," was his response. "We are too obsessed with taking control over the land instead of realizing that there is enough land for everyone. We have to stop thinking about the land in terms of ownership and start thinking about it in terms of belonging."

Ronen is a twenty-four-year-old settler who lives in an outpost north of the settlement of Efrat in Gush Etzion. As a second-generation settler, he sees himself as indigenous to the place as much as Palestinians are. "I was born here," he stated authoritatively, "and I believe that dwelling here is part of a religious commandment, that this is sacred land, and all the regular clichés." But he also believes that "the heart of the conflict is also the heart of the solution." "This is not an ideology," he explained, "but a daily reality I try to practice. I try to know my Palestinian neighbors, to learn about their lives and become a friend." Ronen participated in several meetings between settlers and Palestinians. Yet, in these meetings he found the means not only to fulfill collective ideals but also more personal ones. "I like to think that I am representing the interests of all settlers," he explained, "but the truth is that this is part of my personal journey to under-stand the meaning of being Jewish."

During my fieldwork, I participated in a series of dialogue meetings between settlers and Palestinians. These meetings lasted for seven months and much can be said about the ensuing settler-Palestinian dynamics, but for the purpose of this chapter, it should be noted that the meetings exposed disagreements among settlers about the desired political resolution of the conflict. Some echoed Rabbi Froman's position and viewed the two-state solution with a Jewish minority in Palestine as an ideal situation, while others emphasized the intricate binational composition of the Israeli-Palestinian space and imagined a regional confederation that included the Palestinian populations of the Jordanian Kingdom as well. Then there were those who said the conflict cannot be resolved anytime soon, and therefore the best that can be currently achieved is the building of mutual trust, good neighborly relations, and the alleviation of Palestinian suffering through removal of movement restrictions and legal obstacles such as limitations on construction and access to land.

Indeed, most of the settlers agreed that regardless of geopolitical solutions, the conflict cannot be resolved any time soon. In this they reflected a common settler position as well as the opinion of Rabbi Froman, who used to caution, "slowly, slowly with peace." Rabbi Froman saw peace as a religious ideal of wholeness and unity rather than partition, one that is intrinsically tied to the redemptive aim of the messianic mission. Seeing peace as a spiritual utopia, he warned against the hastening of the end, thus offering a political-theological stance that subverts both the messianic urgency that typified Gush Emunim and the political imperative of the Israeli liberal Left. This stance was encapsulated by one of the settlers who during a very heated session posed an ultimatum to the Palestinians: "do you want peace now or peace here?" Peace was construed as a problem of time in opposition to space, as a problem of progress that was dependent upon Palestinian willingness to patiently wait until the ground conditions would allow the emergence of peace from below, from the local people themselves rather than from politicians alone.

The realm of theology does not easily correspond to the realm of practice. It is therefore difficult to clearly demarcate the lines that connect and separate the more quotidian politics of Eretz Shalom and its more mystical dimension. Nevertheless, many members of Eretz Shalom are inspired by Hasidic traditions and their connection to the land involves a mystical romanticism that in some cases translates into an arguably post-Zionist willingness to choose land over state. According to this position, within the redemptive process, the sacredness of land weighs heavier than the sacredness of state. In addition, the kabbalistic unification of opposition forms an important component of their consciousness, and their encounter with Palestinians, with the Other, was perceived not only as a political event of national significance, but also as a spiritual event with personal ramifications. In this regard, it is important to notice how regardless of obvious differences, Rabbi Froman, Rabbi Ginsburgh, and their respective followers represent two complimentary sides of the same neo-Hassidic phenomenon. They both develop from the collectivist, nationalist, and statist attitudes of Gush Emunim's Kookist ideology and contain a critique of the bourgeoisification of religiously motivated settlement life. And, they offer alternative visions of redemption that give room to individual expression and fulfillment.

Sacred State, Profane Politics: Rabbi Tau's Circle

Another manifestation of settler messianism is the Hardal phenomenon. Hardal is the Hebrew acronym of national Haredi, a religious stream that is characterized by a strict observance of Jewish laws, especially on question of modesty, separation between sexes and the intermingling of secular ideas and texts with religious study (Cohen 2005; Sheleg 2000). In this regard, Hardals are much closer to the ultraorthodox ways of Haredi Jews. However, some Hardals, especially those who are associated with Rabbi Israel Tzvi Tau, sanctify the state even as they reject its secular ways. Rabbi Tau was one of the oldest and most respected students of Rabbi T. Y. Kook at Merkaz HaRav. However, the passing away of Rabbi Tzvi Yehuda in 1982 was followed by internal divisions among his older students. Eventually, in 1997, Rabbi Tau and several other rabbis left Merkaz HaRav after a plan to open a religious teachers college inside the yeshiva. For Rabbi Tau, this plan constituted an intermingling of the sacred with the profane, of the pure and the impure, a defilement of the most important yeshiva within the Jewish world. The yeshiva was to be dedicated solely to Torah study, while the teachers college would include secular ideals and practices, such as granting bachelor of education degrees.

Rabbi Tau established yeshivat Har HaMor (literally, mountain of Myrrh), a *yeshivat hesder* known for its strict adherence to Rabbi T. Y. Kook's vision of the state as "the pedestal of God's throne in this world." It has become since then the originating yeshiva of several other yeshivas known as *yehivot hakav* (the yeshivas of the line), the yeshivas that follow Rabbi Tau and his hardline separation between the secular and religious domains of life (Rosenak 2013). For example, unlike other *hesder* yeshivas, students of *yeshivot hakav* serve only in religious military units and do not normally enroll in universities. Rabbi Tau and *yeshivot hakav* are also the most visible of the statist Hardal stream. Just as Rabbi A. Y. Kook saw sacredness with the secular Zionist endeavor (Ravitzky 1997; Schwartz 2009), their understanding of Judaism is informed by kabbalistic theologies that find the sacred within the profane. And, unlike Hardei Jews, they see themselves as the true followers of Rabbi A. Y. Kook and believe that settlement of the land advances redemption.

Rabbi Tau and his supporters are able to sanctify the state in spite of its profane ways through a mystical reading of reality that becomes a primary prism through which religious meanings are derived: political realities transform into a mere outward appearance that stands in opposition to a hidden sacred content. Like Rabbi Ginsburgh with his mysticism, Rabbi Tau is invested in creating a Jewish consciousness that is not polluted by the secular world (Fischer 2007). However, while the former sees the confrontation with Zionism as central to redemption, the latter advocates a nonconfrontational approach with the state as part of a religious worldview that sees redemption unfolding organically, in a slow and gradual manner. Thus, soldiers and officers who belong to the statist Hardal stream participated in the evacuation of settlements during the Disengagement Plan. Many cried while doing this. A few did tell their commanding officers they lacked the power to participate in the destruction of settlements, but explained their inability to obey orders as an emotional problem rather than an ideological act of refusal (Sheleg 2004).[12] This is another significant change from the days of Gush Emunim during which mystical convictions allowed activists to carry out settlement acts against the authority of the state because these were believed to fulfill the redemptive mission that state officials failed to recognize.

Nevertheless, not all of the Hardals sanctify the state, and some have ceased to see it as a primary vehicle of redemption. This, for example, is the case of those settlers who live in the outposts of Yitzhar and are also associated with neo-Hassidism. At the same time, there are neo-Hassidic settlers who oppose religious conservatism. And, to make matters more complicated, just as not all religious Zionists are settlers, not all neo-Hassidics and Hardals are settlers as well. When considering the fluid qualities of these religious identities, it is not surprising that Gush Emunim still remains the primary category of identifying religiously motivated settlers. The discursive survival Gush Emunim permits the freezing of settlers in space and in time and thus facilitates the ability to make sense of people who are threatening to the liberal-progressive researcher not only because of their messianic project and its impact upon Israeli-Palestinian realities, but also because they constitute a population whose geographic boundedness does not easily correspond to its sociocultural complexity.

Conclusion: Settler Messianism beyond Zionism?

Similarly to religious Zionism and settlers, Gush Emunim was never a homogenous entity and contained inner tensions and dilemmas from its early days. However, the religiously motivated settler population and its messianism are more diversified today than before. While these changes are tied to a myriad of global and local processes—such as the advent of postmodernity and a concomitant personal search for religious self-realization beyond the level of the collective—they are also endemic to settlers themselves. For example, with the desire of Gush Emunim to become the vanguard that unites Jewish orthodoxy and Zionism transforming over time into a movement that divided Israeli society and spurred Palestinian national aspirations, some settlers attempt to distance themselves from those who they consider to pose a messianic threat to both Zionism and the settlement enterprise. This is the case of Alon Shvut, a religious Zionist emblem of the bourgeoisification of settlement life, which engendered, in turn, a counterreaction that is manifested in the hilltop youth. Likewise, the Ginsburghian territorialization of Chabad's messianism would not have been possible without its material and ideological formations in the West Bank as much as the Fromanesque desire for peace would not have been possible without the emergence of a second and third generation of settlers who view their indigeneity and religiosity as a potential source of connection rather than confrontation with Palestinians.

If one cause for the contemporary changes among religiously motivated settlers is to be signaled out above the rest, it is the religious Zionist interweaving of the sacred with the profane realm of politics, which was destined to produce incongruities between religious expectations and political outcomes. While settlements continue to slowly grow, they do not grow as fast as most settlers desire. This relative slowness along with territorial withdrawals have put a great strain upon the messianic connection between state and land. Thus, Rabbi Froman's willingness to live as a Jewish minority within a Palestinian state (a willingness that can be conceived as post-Zionist), Rabbi Tau's mystical withdrawal from secular influences, and Rabbi Ginsburgh's messianic project of undoing Zionism and establishing a Jewish monarchy are all different reactions to a perceived conflict between Jewish ideals and political realities that are brought into sharper relief within the Occupied Territories.

These tensions and conflicts complicate relations between redemption and the state. Within statist and relatively nonmystical settlements like Alon Shvut, there is a tendency to reduce and even deny the revolutionary essence of the settlements and to emphasize redemption as an ideal that connects settlement with Zionism. Within Rabbi Ginsburgh's circle, the state is perceived as an obstacle to redemption, and the messianic act is aimed at a revolution of Zionist institutions and consciousness. While some of Rabbi Ginsburgh's followers seek to hasten redemption, within the close circle of Rabbi Froman, the messianic activity does not seek to hasten the end. Nonetheless, it seeks to challenge contemporary secular politics that discount the centrality of religion as a force of peace rather than violence alone. Rabbi Tau believes as well in a slow redemptive process, but is interested in a revolution that will unfold organically without endangering the stability of the sacred state. Regardless of obvious differences, Rabbi Tau's interest in the creation of a Jewish consciousness that is not contaminated by secular influences can be understood as a post-Zionist messianism that is not disconnected from the post-Zionism of Rabbi Ginsburgh.

Since the "biblical Land of Israel" forms the spatial component of the messianic phenomena, the relation to the land offers another revealing way of further identifying contemporary variations among religiously motivated settlers (Inbari 2014). In Alon Shvut, settlement acts are understood as religiously meaningful ways of strengthening Jewish sovereignty, as a nonmessianic fulfillment of redemption. Among the more mystical streams of settlers, the tensions between messianic aspirations and territorial politics are more acute and the reactions are more diverse. For example, Rabbi Tau and his followers oppose the establishment of a Palestinian state. And, like all mystical settlers, they believe in the immanent sacredness of land. However, when it comes to territorial withdrawals and the dismantling of settlements, Rabbi Tau advocates a nonconfrontational attitude toward the state. In contrast, for many of Rabbi Ginsburgh's admirers, violence constitutes a legitimate means of expanding settlement and protecting the eternal Jewish bond to the land. The two former positions can be compared in turn to Rabbi Froman and his circle, for whom the sacred connection to the land is a matter of belonging rather than ownership, a belonging that is even stronger than political rule and recognizes the parallel bond of Palestinians to the same land.

Together with a few other rabbinical figures, Rabbi Froman's support of the two-state solution stands as an exception to the rule among settlers. For most of them, like many other Israelis, the possibility of losing Jewish majority or the damage to the democratic character of the Israel is not as threatening as the idea of a Palestinian state. Many believe that an increased Jewish population growth (through greater birth rate and immigration) along with decreased Palestinian population growth (through lower birth rate and emigration) will eventually solve the so-called demographic problem and permit the maintenance of a Jewish majority over the entire space of Israel/Palestine, with the exclusion of Gaza, for now. As far as many of them are concerned, this demographic trend, along with increased Palestinian personal rights and limited national rights, will permit Jewish control of land and enable Palestinians to be better off than most of the Arabs in the neighboring states. They are aware of the great national and international opposition to the creeping annexation of the West Bank, but they believe they already embarked upon a journey toward redemption, a journey that contains obstacles along the way, a journey that may be elongated over time, but one from which there is no retreat.

Although religiously motivated settlers believe that redemption has already begun, they differ in their interpretation of the actions that most benefit the settlement enterprise and the redemptive process. In this chapter, I only began to scratch the surface of thick and complex layers of messianic theologies and practices that exist along with variations along socioeconomic, ethnic, generational, and geographic lines. My intention, however, was to move beyond Gush Emunim and draw rough counterlines that may shed some light about a population whose internal composition often diminishes when viewed from a far. If Alon Shvut offers one example of a successful amalgamation of messianism and Zionism, the other three groups exemplify how a growing alienation from secular Zionist politics translates differently among religiously motivated settlers.[13] A growing number of settlers embody a Jewish revolution of Zionism, which was in itself a revolution of Judaism. Perhaps the rise of messianism beyond Zionism signifies the onset of a post-Zionist era among religiously motivated settlers. The end and implications of this process remain unclear.

Notes

This chapter is based upon a dissertation that emerged from ethnographic fieldwork that was conducted in the Gaza Strip and the West Bank. The writing of the dissertation was supported by the Mellon/ACLS Dissertation Completion Fellowship from the American Council of Learned Societies (2014–2015). Fieldwork was supported by the National Science Foundation Dissertation Development Improvement Grant (award No. 1061319); the National Science Foundation Graduate Research Fellowship Program; the Bigel Endowment Award for Graduate Research in Anthropology and the Pre-Dissertation Special Study Award at Rutgers University; and, UC Berkeley's Summer Undergraduate Research Fellowship. In addition, I deeply thank the editors of this book for their help in improving this chapter.

1. There are also religiously motivated settlers among the approximately 170,000 Israelis residing at the twelve Jewish neighborhoods in East Jerusalem. However, their numbers are small in comparison to their presence in the West Bank.

2. In opposition to the claim that the post-1967 settlement enterprise constitutes a revolution of Zionism, it is possible to posit that the settlements are not necessarily revolutionary, but rather realize, complete, and solve internal contradictions within the Zionist project in relation to Judaism and the "Land of Israel." The latter claim reflects the position of many religiously motivated settlers. Nevertheless, it is important to note that unlike critical positions that point to similarities between pre-1967 and post-1967 settlement practices in order to emphasize ethical problems (especially with regard to the treatment of Palestinians and minority populations), this position commonly perceives secular Zionism as a temporary stage within the redemptive process. The revolutionary element of religiously motivated settlers' messianism is rooted within this metaphysical perspective.

3. *Hesder* yeshivas combine advanced Torah study with military service in order to provide young religious students the intellectual and spiritual tools necessary to find ideological and practical balance between piety and life in the predominantly secular army.

4. The question of relation to secular laws was a source of disagreement within Gush Emunim.

5. This position does not attest to the rationality of people in Alon Shvut or to the irrationality of other settlers. It only attests to the importance placed on rationality as a central Jewish value in Alon Shvut.

6. Nevertheless, the statist position of the settlers of Alon Shvut, that is, their close identification with Zionism and the Israeli state, is not a reflection of their confidence in the geopolitical future of Gush Etzion. Rather, it is a reflection of the general theological and sociopolitical orientations of the settlement as a community of people with similar values. For example, the settlement of Bat Ayin is located just a mile away from Alon Shvut and is therefore also set to remain within the boundaries of Israel. Yet, Bat Ayin is known as one of the more radical settlements and its residents cannot be characterized as having statist positions.

7. Rabbi Ginsburgh resides at Kfar Chabad, but is the president of Od Yoseph Chai yeshiva in Yitzhar.

8. Yitzhar was established in 1983. With a population of about a thousand people, Yitzhar is located in the northern West Bank, about five kilometers south of Nablus (biblical Shechem).

9. Many Price Tag perpetrators prefer to use the term *arvut hadadit* (mutual accountability). *Arvut hadadit* is a deeply ingrained Jewish value that construes all Jews as responsible for one another. In opposition to the economic connotations of Price Tag, the idea of *arvut hadadit* instills acts of violence with a religious sense of ethical responsibility.

10. The *sefirot* are the divine emanations of God and creation, which also operate within the soul and comprise the basis of the natural world as well. The *sefirot* are ordered as dialectical oppositions and reflect feminine and masculine qualities. According to kabbalistic traditions, creation is an erotic process that emerges from the gendered tensions within the *sefirot*.

11. The number of members in Eretz Shalom ranges from a few dozen engaged activists to a few hundred more passive supporters. After the death of Rabbi Froman, the activities of Eretz Shalom slowed down. Nevertheless, Hadassah, his widow, continues to work toward peace in his place and new local initiatives, inspired by Rabbi Froman, of cooperation between settlers and Palestinians have sprung up.

12. It should be noted that many religious Zionists rabbis called soldiers to not refuse military orders during the Disengagement Plan.

13. At the same time, this process of alienation is accompanied by the continued—and arguably quite successful—efforts of settlers to shape the state in their own image, an issue that deserves a separate investigation in its own rights.

References

Aran, Gideon. 1991. "Jewish Zionist Fundamentalism: The Bloc of the Faithful in Israel (Gush Emunim)." In *Fundamentalisms Observed*, edited by Martin. E. Marty and Scott R. Appleby, 265–344. Chicago: The University of Chicago Press.

———. 1997. "The Father, the Son, and the Holy Land: The Spiritual Authorities of Jewish-Zionism Fundamentalism in Israel." In *Spokesmen for the Despised*, edited by Scott R. Appleby, 294–327. Chicago: The University of Chicago Press.

———. 2013. *Kookism: The Roots of Gush Emunim, the Settlers' Culture, Zionist Theology and Messianism in Our Age*. Jerusalem: Carmel Press. [Hebrew.]

Cohen, Asher. 2005. "The Crochet Kipa and What Lies behind It: Multiple Identities in Religious Zionism." *Academot* 15: 6–30. [Hebrew.]

Dalsheim, Joyce. 2011. *Unsettling Gaza: Secular Liberalism, Radical Religion, and the Israeli Settlement Project*. Oxford: Oxford University Press.

———. 2014. *Producing Spoilers. Peacemaking and the Production of Enmity in a Secular Age*. Oxford: Oxford University Press.

Dalsheim, Joyce, and Harel Assaf. 2009. "Representing Settlers." *Review of Middle East Studies* 43 (2): 219–238.

Elitzur, Yosef, and Shapira Yitzhak. 2010. *The King's Torah: Rules of Souls among Israel and the Nations*. Yitzhar: The Torah institute, Od Yosef Chai. [Hebrew.]

Feige, Michael. 2009. *Settling in the Hearts: Jewish Fundamentalism in the Occupied Territories*. Detroit: Wayne State University Press.

Fischer, Shlomo. 2005. "The Moral Crisis of Spiritualism." In *Eretz Acheret*, February 28. Accessed March 26, 2015. http://acheret.co.il/?cmd=articles.144&act=read&id=591. [Hebrew.]

———. 2007. "Self-Expression and Democracy in Radical Religious Zionist Ideology." PhD diss., Hebrew University, Jerusalem.

———. 2011. "Radical Religious Zionism from the Collective to the Individual." In *Kabbalah and Contemporary Spiritual Revival*, edited by Boaz Huss, 285–306. Be'er Sheva: Ben-Gurion University Press.

Froman, Menachem. 2014. *Peace, People, Land*. Tel Aviv: Miskal–Yedioth Ahronoth Books and Chemed Books. [Hebrew.]

Garb, Jonathan. 2009. The Chosen Will Become Herds: Studies in Twentieth-Century Kabbalah. Translated by Yaffah Berkovits-Murciano. New Haven: Yale University Press.

Giladi, Atiel. 2014. "An Offer to Manage Derech Chaim Movement according to the Principles of the Jewish Governance Method." *Derech Chaim*. Accessed March 26, 2015. http://www .derech-chaim.org/wp-content/uploads/2014/02/דרך-הלמה.pdf. [Hebrew.]

Ginsburgh, Yitzchak. 2005. *Umimena Yivasha* (He Shall Be Delivered from It). Kfar Chabad: Gal Einai Institute Publications. [Hebrew.]

Gopin, Marc. 2002. *Holy War, Holy Peace: How Religion Can Bring Peace to the Middle East*. New York, NY: Oxford University Press.

Gorenberg, Gershom. 2006. *The Accidental Empire: Israel and the Birth of the Settlements, 1967–1977*. New York: Henry Holt.

Harding, Susan. 1992. "Representing Fundamentalism: The Problem of the Repugnant Cultural Other." *Social Research* 58 (2): 373–393.

Huss, Boaz, 2007. "The New Age of Kabbalah: Contemporary Kabbalah, the New Age and Postmodern Spirituality." *Journal of Modern Jewish Studies*, 6 (2): 107–125.

Idel, Moshe. 2000. *Messianic Mystics*. New Haven, CT: Yale University Press.

Inbari, Motti. 2007. "Fundamentalism in Crisis—The Response of the Gush Emunim Rabbinical Authorities to the Theological Dilemmas Raised by Israel's Disengagement Plan." *Journal of Church and State* 49 (4): 697–716.

———. 2009. *Jewish Fundamentalism and the Temple Mount: Who Will Build the Third Temple*. Albany: State University of New York Press.

———. 2014. *Messianic Religious Zionism Confronts Israeli Territorial Compromises*. Cambridge: Cambridge University Press.

Kravel-Tovi, Michal, and Yoram Bilu. 2008. "The Work of the Present: Constructing Messianic Temporality in the Wake of Failed Prophecy among Chabad Hasidim." *American Ethnologist* 35 (1): 64–80.

Lustick, Ian. 1988. *For the Land and the Lord: Jewish Fundamentalism in Israel*. New York: Council on Foreign Relations.

Newman, David. 1986. "Gush Emunim: Between Fundamentalism and Pragmatism." *Jerusalem Quarterly* 39: 33–43.

Persico, Tomer. 2014. "Neo-Hasidic Revival: Expressivist Uses of Traditional Lore." *Modern Judaism* 34 (3): 287–308.

Ravitzky, Aviezer. 1996. *The Revealed End and the State of the Jews*. Tel Aviv: Am Oved. [Hebrew.]

Raz-Krakotzkin, Amnon. 2002. "Between Brit Shalom and the Temple: The Dialectics of Redemption and Messianism in the Footsteps of Gershom Scholem." *Theory and Criticism* 20 (2): 97–112. [Hebrew.]

Rosenak, Avinoam. 2013. *Cracks: Unity of Opposites, the Political and Rabbi Kook's Disciples*. Tel Aviv: Resling Publishing. [Hebrew.]

Roth, Anat. 2013. *Not at any Cost: From Gush Katif to Amona: The Story behind the Struggle over the Land of Israel*. Tel Aviv: Miskal–Yedioth Ahronoth and Chemed Books. [Hebrew.]

Rubinstein, Danny. 1982. *On the Lord's Side: Gush Emunim*. Tel Aviv: Kibutz Meuhad. [Hebrew.]

Schwartz, Dov. 2009. *Religious Zionism: History and Ideology*. Brighton, MA: Academic Studies.

Sheleg, Yair. 2000. *The New Religious: A Contemporary Look on Religious Society in Israel*. Jerusalem: Keter. [Hebrew.]

———. 2004. "Rabbi Tau's Grey Refusal." *Haaretz*, September 14. Accessed August 23, 2015. http://www.haaretz.co.il/misc/1.1558453. [Hebrew.]

Sivan, Emanuel. 1995. "The Enclave Culture." In *Fundamentalisms Comprehended*, edited by Martin. E. Marty and Scott R. Appleby, 11–68. Chicago: The University of Chicago Press.

Tamari, Assaf. 2014. "The Place of Politics: The Notion of Consciousness in Rabbi Yitzchak Ginsburgh's Political Thought." *Israel Studies Review* 29 (2): 78–98.

Weiss, Hadas. 2011. "On Value and Values in a West Bank Settlement." *American Ethnologist* 38 (1): 36–46.

PART III

FORCED COEXISTENCE: PALESTINIANS AND JEWISH SETTLERS

9   From *Kubaniya* to Outpost

A Genealogy of the Palestinian Conceptualization of Jewish Settlement in a Shifting National Context

Honaida Ghanim

THE PALESTINIAN ENCOUNTER with the Zionist colonial project, with its varying historical forms and expressions, is a focal point in the Arab discourse in general and the national Palestinian discourse in particular. One would be hard pressed to find a Palestinian intellectual who has not written on the topic. Some have written about the development of the colonial project, its earlier stages, the plans developed to empty Palestine of its indigenous population and their effects and dynamic. Others have written about the power relations and the strategy behind the success of the colonial project, the global and regional conditions, and the cooperation between the Zionist movement and the British Mandate. However, alongside such serious scholarship, more superficial volumes have also been written, characterized by demagogical and essentialist discourse.

The result has been an overwhelming deluge of writing about Jews, Zionists, settlements, settlers, colonialism, imperialism, the historical Khaibar tribe and Ibn al-Nadhir, the Jewish plot, and Yajuj and Majuj. Instead of focusing the discussion, a discursive chaos was created. Often, the readers find themselves floundering between two polar opposites, the essentialist pole and the dynamic pole, with numerous variations and levels of complexity between them. At the one pole is a discourse in which the Zionist settler is mediated through a variety of essentialist, cultural, historical stereotypes of the Jew as avaricious, fraudulent, and traitorous. At the other pole, one finds rigorous, sociohistorical research that attempts to understand the Zionist enterprise, and its settler-colonial project in particular, as a product of social dynamics, shaped by the historical conditions and processes created at various crossroads. This body of research usually applies a structural and systemic approach, concentrating mainly on macro processes. Between the spectrum sketched by the contours of two trends, the last two decades have witnessed a growing anthropological and sociological interest in the Palestinian experience vis-à-vis the Zionist colonial project. Despite this growing interest, there is still a lack of studies that examine the process in which the image of the colonial/colony and the conceptualization and the terminology in which it is understood have been produced and developed throughout various historical crossroads.

It is possible to point out four general trends in the Palestinian research in general, and the polemical and theoretical writing in particular, concerning the encounter with the colonial project in Palestine:

1. A macro level analysis emphasizing the historically unbalanced power relations between the Zionists and Palestinians. This type of research examines the encounter at the macro level and focuses on outlining the intent and execution of the expulsion of the Palestinians from their homeland, the superiority of the Israeli military, and the cooperation between the Zionist movement and British imperialism during the mandatory period (see, for example, Qasimiyah 1996; Kanaʻnah 1992; Khalidi 1988, 2005; Masalha 1992, 1997, 2012; Shufani 2002; Tarabee 1970; Mustafa 1985; Nofal 1997; Al-Husseini 1969). This view is responsible for establishing the canonical national discourse of Palestinian historiography.

2. In contrast to the aforementioned, there is a strand of historiography that focuses on the fringes (i.e., the marginal and esoteric) of social encounters and interactions between Jewish groups or individuals and the Palestinians residing in Palestine at the end of the nineteenth and the first two to three decades of the twentieth century. This trend of studies presents an alternative history to that of the first trend, as it argues for ambivalent, tense, and complex encounters and for the construction of a Jewish-Arab identity that was abruptly interrupted by the influence of Zionism and the colonial dynamic (see, for example, Nassar and Tamari 2005; Tamari and Nassar 2003; Tamari 2004, 2011).

3. An emphasis of the resistance and resilience of the Palestinian population exists particularly in the anthropological and sociological literatures. This trend focuses on patterns of Palestinian resistance, of sociocultural confrontation and internal resilience vis-à-vis the colonial project, on national Palestinian culture that developed vis-à-vis the Zionist project, on national identity and the development of the national Palestinian movement, on the effects of resistance and conflict on social roles (including gender), on the period of the Military Administration of the Palestinian citizens in the state of Israel (1948–1966), on the oppressive encounter of the state with the Palestinian in Israel or the Occupied Territories, and the development of the colonial project at the major historical crossroads of the conflict (1948, 1967) (see, for example, Kassem 2011; Tabar 2007; El-Sakka 2013; Hammami 1990; Kanaaneh and Nusair 2010; Taraki et al. 1997; Abdo 1991; Peteet 2013; Nashif 2008; Ghanim 2009a, 2009b; Saʼdi 2013).

4. An analysis of the symbolic representations of the Palestinian image in the various Zionist colonial discourses, on the orientalization of Palestine in the colonial imagination, and on the representations of the Palestinians in the canonical culture and literature—notably Said (1983), Shulḥut (1997), Al-Shaikh (2013), Mazʻal (1985), ʻAmr and Mazal (1989).

However, despite the existence of the aforementioned stands of, it is possible to point out three deficiencies in the Palestinian research that attempts to examine and make sense of the encounter with the colonial Zionist project:

1. The hegemony of the nationalist perspective. Research focused on the Palestinians has adopted basic assumptions regarding morality and social behaviors that are anchored in the national perspective. In this context, for instance, collective behaviors of resistance were analyzed as rational, planned, and calculated as opposed to being, at times, minor, adaptive, and riddled with tensions. Critical Palestinian social and historical research lacks qualitative phenomenological research that will free itself from the national hegemony and study the establishment and construction of the image of the Other in Palestinian society.

2. An overemphasis of 1948, on what preceded the Nakba and enabled it, while overlooking the events of 1967. This focus is not coincidental and derives from the attitude toward 1948 as the watershed moment in Palestinian history, one that symbolizes the loss of the homeland and the onset of the state of existence as refugees (Zreik 1999; Kayyali 1970; Ghanim 2009a; Saʼdi 2002; Sanbar 2001). At the same time, 1967 was perceived primarily as a shameful defeat of the Arab states in a war, which in despite of it happening also on Palestinian land, was experienced mainly as an external military defeat, indicating deep corruption and constituting the point of no return in the establishment of Israel on Palestinian land (Bishara 2000).

3. A dichotomy that veers between totalization and flattening of the Jewish Other on the one hand, and on the other hand, an overemphasis of internal ruptures, particularly ethnic ones. By emphasizing social fragmentation and negation of national Israeli-Jewish identity, it assumes that the extended conflict with the Palestinian is the only cohesive element permitting the continued existence of Jewish collective identity. Among the different tensions, the one between Western and Oriental Jews is particularly stressed, followed by the ongoing conflicts between the ultraorthodox and secular Jews.

Although many publications have surveyed the image of the Palestinian in Zionist/Israeli discourse—for example, Shulḥut (1997), Mazʼal (1985), Dawabsheh (2010), Juaʼbah (2011)—few have carried out the opposite study: that is, investigate the process by which the image of the Jewish colonizer/settler and colonies/settlements in Palestinian written and oral discourse developed and changed over time. Such analysis opens possibilities for exposing the ambivalence and tensions that are embodied in this image not necessarily as an antithesis of the self, but as a complex product of relations between self and other. Here I will attempt to fill this gap by means of a qualitative study, based on interviews with three generations of Palestinians: the generation that lived before 1948 and experienced the establishment of the first Jewish settlements during the British Mandate (before the Nakba); the second generation that experienced 1967 and the beginning of the settlements in the West Bank; and the third generation that was born during the Oslo period and experienced the third generation of settlements and settlers: the generation of the "hilltop youths" and outposts.[1]

The First Pattern: *Kubaniya-khawaja* (from the Onset of Zionist Settlement to 1948)

The Palestinians have several terms and names for Jewish settlers and settlements. These terms reflect the development of the concept of the colonizer at various historical crossroads. From the beginning of the twentieth century to the 1948 War, the Jewish settlements established at the time were called, in the spoken Palestinian language, *kubaniya*. In the written language they were usually called *musta'amara* and in isolated cases *mustawtana*.[2] At the same time, the settlers themselves were referred to, especially by the rural Palestinians, by the foreign term *khawaja*. According to the contemporary Arabic lexicon Al-Ma'any, *khawaja* is a Persian surname meaning, originally, "the master" or "the honorable one." The Arabs used this word to denote a professional teacher or educator of boys. Later, the term was used for eunuchs, a use that is related to the fact that the *khawajas* became private tutors of the royal family and their appointment was conditioned upon their castration, to prevent forbidden relations with the daughters of the royal family.[3] In Greater Syria, the cloth merchants, most of whom were Jews, were called *khawaja* (Al-Qasmi and Khalil 1988). In the court records of the Ottoman Period, the term was used for Jews, Christians, and foreigners. In many Arab societies, the term was used for foreigners. In this context, all the British as well as the Europeans who arrived to the region on missionary work were thus referred to with this term and, later on, so were the Jews who came from Europe.

In the vernacular, the term that served the Palestinians to describe the Jewish settlement until 1948 was *kubaniya*. This is a mixed foreign term, whose exact etymology is difficult to ascertain, although most people believe that it originates from the English word "company." Comparisons of this term with other uses in colloquial Arabic strengthen this claim. In colloquial Egyptian, *kubaniya* means a government company, and in daily use the water and electricity utilities are called *kubaniya*. Others believe that the term is derived from the word "camp," referring to military camps. This conceptualization was applied to the Jewish Zionist settlement but not to the old Jewish settlements, such as in Tiberias or Hebron. In this context, many of the Palestinian testimonials present a distinction between various types of Jews based on their affiliation with the Zionist colonial project. This is how Anwar El-Khatib describes life in the Old City of Jerusalem before the Nakba: "At the time, within the walls of the Old City, there lived Yemenite and Bukhari Jews with whom we had good relations, despite the massacre of the Jews in Hebron in 1929. We did not see American or Polish Jews . . . all were local Jews, we even called them Jewish Arabs" (quoted in Davis [2010, 82]).

In the interviews I conducted with Palestinian refugees from Haifa that reside in the West Bank city of Ramallah, they related that their parents used to call the Jews that came from countries such as Syria, Egypt, and Yemen *"Yahud awlad Arab,"* meaning Jews who are sons of Arabs, while the European Jews were perceived as foreign. According to one of the interviewees, the Arab Jews also were suspicious of the European Jews and thought that they had come to the country to enslave them.

The accumulating evidence regarding the social relations that prevailed between the Jewish immigrants from Europe and the Palestinians are also not unequivocal. It is possible to point out a distinction in the discourse used by villagers next to whom Jewish communities were established, residents of these communities, and their Jewish residents. Raya, an eighty-six-year-old refugee from the destroyed village of Abu-Shosha, next to which Kibbutz Gezer was established, lives with her extended family in Jalazone refugee camp (near Ramallah) and lost three of her brothers in 1948—two were murdered in cold blood by Hagana forces that invaded the village, and one fell in the battles of Bab El-Wad. She says: "The residents of Gezer and ourselves were friendly, they used to come and spend the nights, they had a kubaniya nearby. I remember that their commander was named Meir and he used to say, 'my friend, we and you do not fear each other'" (Raya, interview; June 14, 2015).[4] Raya added that the Haganah forces did not want the residents of Gezer to maintain social relations with the Arabs.

The distinction between different types of Jews subsided as a result of the increase in Zionist settlement activity and local resistance. According to Hillel Cohen (2015), the deterioration of inter-communal relations began with the events of 1929, a sort of small-scale civil war, in which local Jews were attacked alongside the new Jewish immigrants, considered foreign to the land. These events, which terminated the Jewish settlement in Hebron and harmed the native Jewish groups in Jerusalem and Acre, were a strategic turning point that contributed to creating a stronger separation between Arabs and Jews on a religious-ethnic basis. In this period local Jews left (and were removed) from the Palestinian social fabric and conclusively embraced the Zionist project. The effect of this collapse had important consequences. To a great extent it matched the fundamental tenets of Zionist ideology, which strove to organize the Jews under one national, ethnic umbrella, and it made it impossible to argue for an inclusive local identity that united Jews and Arabs. Furthermore, it blurred the line between the colonial and the national: Jews stopped being divided into local and foreign, Arabs and *khawajat*; they all became Zionists, as the colonial and local fused. Notably, the symbolic retreat of the local Jews from their Arab identity paralleled their physical relocation from mixed communities, as Jews began to depart the Palestinian (physical) space and converge into Jewish spaces that were termed, colloquially, *kubaniya*. On the eve of the war, in 1948, Jews and Arabs already lived, for the most part, in separate places and regions.

If we were to adopt Hillel Cohen's argument, according to which 1929 marked the beginning of the Zionization of the local Jews and thus also marked the collapse of the Palestinian distinction between local and *khawaja* Jews, then 1948 marked the total victory of the *kubaniya* as a colonial paradigm. Following the destruction of Palestinian society and its national liberation project on one hand, and the establishment of the State of Israel on its ruins on the other, the *kubaniya* model was applied to 78 percent of Historic Palestine. The *kubaniya* spread across space, regarding it as its exclusive property. The political sovereignty of the *kubaniya* organized as Jewish sovereignty, and the laws were engineered so as to permit the institutionalization of the exclusive sovereignty. Thus, while the refugees were not permitted to return, Jews received the automatic right to immigrate. Applying the logic of *kubaniya* to the space was bidirectional: not only on the part of the settlers but also by the natives-turned-refugees, who perceived the state that was established through the preceding medium of the *kubaniya* and the Israeli Jew through the medium of the *khawaja*.

The Second Pattern: *Al-Musta'amara* (from 1948 to 1967)

The Palestinian Nakba created a new national and social reality. Instead of one society living in one territory, Palestinian society divided into four separate groups living within different contexts: the Palestinian refugees that settled in Arab countries, the Palestinians in the Gaza Strip living under Egyptian rule, the Palestinians in the West Bank living under Jordanian rule, and the Palestinians living in the State of Israel. The new daily conditions of existence for each group, along with the development of the Palestinian national movement and culture, made their mark on the conceptualization of the Jewish settlement that had by then developed into a state. This was reinforced by the specific international context in those years, namely the global struggle against colonialism.

In this context, the daily living conditions of the Palestinians that following the Nakba had become Israeli citizens dictated a gradual shift to a different conceptualization. As part of the new status and power relations, the epithets *khawaja* and *kubaniya* tended to fade out of the colloquial discourse, as the Palestinians living in Israel began to adopt the official names of the communities that were established and with which they had functional relations. At the same time, among the rest of the Palestinians that were left out of the new state's borders, the term "Jew" came to be used in the spoken language to refer to both Israel and its inhabitants. Concurrently, the terms *musta'amir* and *musta'amara* turned into the central terms in the national and cultural Palestinian discourse, primarily outside of Israel.

The structural changes experienced by the Palestinians after the Nakba in Israel turned them from farmers to wage earners in the Israeli cities. If prior to 1948 there were Palestinian cities that were a part of the organic space, after the Nakba, they had to locate themselves within Israeli space. They began becoming familiar with the places in which they worked; the name of their employer; the names of the streets where governmental agencies, Israeli hospitals, and police stations were built; the names of the Jewish doctors; and the Hebrew term for the village's military commander.

The employment relations that developed between the Palestinians and the Israeli-Jews following the absorption of the remaining Palestinians as manual laborers in 1948 located them in the bottom of an hierarchical, ethnic relationship. The employer was Jewish and the employee was Arab. In the colloquial language, the Palestinians used the term *mua'lem* (work manager) to denote the Jewish employer. In a way, the conceptualization of the Jew as *mua'lem* served as an interesting return to the original etymological meaning of *khawaja* as teacher (also *mua'lem*); however, now, the power relations had been turned on its head. While the *khawaja* had been marked as external and foreign, and thereby was castrated, the *mua'lem* now signified the ruling class. The term *kubaniya* also all but disappeared from daily language, gradually devolving into the sole use of adults who lived before 1948. At the same time, the epithet *khawaja* continued to be used in spoken language to denote foreigners. My father, rest his soul, would justify the conservative social attitude towards us by saying that he was not a *khawaja* and would never become one! In the Palestinian discourse that developed among other Palestinian groups, in parallel to the colloquial Palestinian discourse in Israel, the terms *musta'amara* (colony) and *musta'amarin* (colonizers), which had been used before the Nakba only in the written language, became the central concepts in the national Palestinian discourse that referred to Jewish existence in Palestine. This conceptualization was shaped in the context of global struggles for liberation from Western colonialism in the 1950s and 1960s, most centrally the Algerian struggle, which became a model for Palestinian resistance (Sayegh 1965). The conceptualization of Jewish existence in Palestine as a colonial one reflected the Palestinian national project at the time, which envisioned the liberation of Palestinians from Zionist colonialism, as it was formulated in the national charters in 1964, 1965, and 1968, and which became the founding document of the Palestine Liberation Organization. According to Article 6 of the charter from 1968: "The Jews who had been permanent residents of Palestine until the beginning of the Zionist invasion will be considered Palestinians."[5] The Palestinian Council held in 1968 passed a resolution clarifying that: "The aggression against the Palestinian nation and its land began in 1917. Therefore, the removal of the aggression necessarily means the removal of all signs of aggression since the Zionist invasion and not since the June 1967 War." As we shall soon see, throughout the 1970s, parallel to the acceptance of a territorial compromise, a gradual change occurred in this stance.

The Third Pattern: *Al-Mustawtana* (from 1967 to 1993)

Following the 1967 War and the occupation of the rest of Palestine, new terms entered the national Palestinian lexicon: *al-mustawtin* and *al-mustawtana*, which refer specifically to Jewish settlers and settlements established in the territories occupied in 1967. Just as in Hebrew a distinction exists between the settlements established within the Green Line (*yishuv*) and those constructed outside of it (*hitnachalut*), so in Arabic a special term was allocated for the Jewish settlement in the territories occupied in 1967: *mustawtana*, which is a translation of the Hebrew term for "settlement." Classical Arabic dictionaries describe the word *mustawtin* as referring to "one who turned the land into his homeland." This description is neutral toward the act itself, as it does not testify to coercion or occupation.

The question to be asked is why did the Palestinians use new and differential terms to describe the colonial settlement project in 1967? What distinguished, from their point of view, the colonial project in 1948 from the project of 1967? Was the conceptualization a result of adopting the hegemonic Israeli discourse within the context of a newly created environment? What distinguished the 1948 settler from the 1967 colonizer? In the following, I will argue that the conceptualization reflected the new power relations created following the defeat of 1967. This process was responsible for the gradual acceptance of a political solution based on the idea of partition into two states.

The occupation of 1967 occurred nineteen years after the Palestinian Nakba and the establishment of the State of Israel in 1948. During these years a new generation of Palestinians was born and raised in the shadow of the loss of a homeland, in a state of refugeeness and foreignness. Palestinian expectations following the Nakba did not include the establishment of a state and were not formulated politically but rather as a discourse of rights, which included the return for refugees and the liberation of the homeland from the hands of Zionist colonial rule (Ghanim 2009b). From the Nakba and the establishment of the State of Israel, to the defeat of 1967 and the occupation of the rest of the Palestinian homeland, the Palestinians believed that the Zionist colonization was temporary and that the liberation of Palestine was merely a matter of time (Bishara 2000). The optimistic pan-Arab climate, the charismatic leadership of Gamal Abdel Nasser, the establishment of the Palestine Liberation Organization in 1964 and the declaration of the onset of the revolutionary struggle by the leadership of the Fatah in the beginning of 1965 greatly invigorated the Arab world in general and the Palestinians in particular. At the time, "Palestine was the compass and conscience of the Arab world," as the attitude toward the Palestinians was commonly formulated in the Arab world. The extent of the disappointment following the bitter defeat in 1967, which was termed "Naksa," was just as large as the hope that preceded it (Al-Azm 2011).

The difference in the conceptualization of the results of the 1967 War as "Naksa" and the events of 1948 as "Nakba" sheds some light on the uniqueness and different effects that these two events had on the manner in which the Jewish settlement was perceived in the Palestinian discourse.

In Palestinian literature, the Nakba refers to the disaster that befell the Palestinians in 1948, following acts of ethnic cleansing committed by the Zionist forces, which included the mass expulsion of 780,000 Palestinians, who became refugees (Abu Lughod 1971), the destruction of over five hundred villages, and the emptying of Arab cities of their inhabitants (Tamari 2002; Abd al-Jawad 2006; Ghanim 2009b; Kana'neh 1992). The Naksa, on the other hand, refers to the military defeat of the Arab armies that participated in the 1967 War and to the occupation of the West Bank, Gaza Strip, Sinai, and the Golan Heights (Ghanim 2009b; Al-Azm 2011). The bitter defeat of 1967 had a strategic effect on the Palestinian national paradigm. The desire to experience rebirth through the disaster of 1948 was revealed to be a most difficult proposition to carry out. Liberation of the homeland became distant and the pan-Arab Spring led by Nasser was routed.

After realizing the catastrophic consequences of the Arab defeat in 1967, the Palestinians gradually began to adopt the two-state solution based on territorial partition. The occupation of the rest of Palestine, following the establishment of the Jewish state on the lands of 1948, created space for a most important political maneuver of reframing Jewish colonialism among Palestinians in the national discourse, through turning Israel from a colonial force into an occupying one. Accordingly, if up to 1967 the Palestinians were fighting to liberate the homeland from the foreign colonialist, after 1967 they gradually began to reorganize their national project as one of liberation from occupation and the establishment of a Palestinian state alongside an Israeli one in the territories occupied in 1967.

The national shift toward national pragmatism and a Western and internationally-endorsed political solution also explains the gradual decline in the use of the term *musta'amara*, which is embedded in the discourse and the global struggle against colonialism, and the gradual adoption of the term *mustawtana*, which parallels the international term of "settlement." This is a relatively neutral term, which in the historical context of the 1960s does not embody any hint of legitimacy or lack thereof concerning the State of Israel itself; rather, it focuses criticism on the military occupation of 1967, which despite the uneasiness involved, is still considered in international law a permissible act that countries can commit under certain circumstances.

The differential Palestinian conceptualization of the Jewish settlement is mostly similar to the canonical Israeli conceptualization, which was arranged on the axis of time and place, separating "settlements" (in the Occupied Territories) from "communities" (in "Israel proper"). Yet, it differs in that it does not differentiate between the various Jewish communities established in the territories occupied in 1967. While in the hegemonic Israeli discourse, the Jewish settlements in the Golan Heights or the Jordan Valley are called "communities," the settlements in East Jerusalem are called "neighborhoods," and the rest of the Jewish communities in the West Bank are called "settlements"—the Palestinian discourse applies the term *mustawtana* to all of them.

The differential use prevalent in the broad Palestinian public discourse, which to a great extent corresponds to the Israeli conceptual map, has raised criticism among some of the Palestinian political and intellectual factions. Two trends in the discourse on the Jewish settlement after 1967 can be highlighted: the religious and the nationalist-intellectual. Both of these trends generally opposed the use of the term *mustawtana*, particularly the differential conceptualization of the Jewish settlement beyond and within the Green Line. These two trends have suggested alternative conceptualizations that reflect their ideology.

The Religious Discourse: *Mughtasabat* not Settlements

The various types of religious criticism adopt the terms *mughtasib* and *mughtasabat* as referring to all types of Jewish settlement. Literally, *mughtasabat* means "rape victims," while the settlers themselves are called "rapists." It is possible to find an explanation for this conceptualization in the Islamic website The Way of Islam.[6] The website presents guidelines for the correction of common mistakes in the national discourse, while at the same time offering alternative terms, which are supposed to reflect reality in an accurate and precise manner in order to prevent its distortion. In this context, the term *al-mustawtanun al-Yahud* (the Jewish settlers) is presented as a misleading term, and in its place the site suggests the term "the Jewish rapists" as a precise description. According to the website, "[the literal meaning of] mustawtin is one who turns the land into his homeland, while in Palestine, the Jews seized the land using rape and coercion, and therefore they are rapists." The site assumes an essential contradiction between turning the land into a homeland and seizing the land by force, although in practice, one can presume that such a contradiction need not necessarily exist. To the contrary, one can seize a place by force and turn it into the homeland of new settlers.

The Islamic discourse uses sexually loaded language to indicate the symbolic significance of seizing a place. Interspersing sexual motifs in the national language is not unique to the religious discourse or to Palestinian national discourse; rather, it is a foundational motif in national identity throughout the world (Hammami 2010; Yuval-Davis 1997). Nationalism, state, and citizenship were constructed as masculine motifs, while earth, land, and homeland have been constructed through feminine motifs, which include the metaphor of the homeland as mother or beloved (Ghanim 2009a) Thus, for instance, the occupation of Palestine has been described as a beloved being captured, as rape of the homeland, or violation of the collective family honor, which will be corrected only through the brave intervention of the warrior-male. Imbuing the national discourse with sexual motifs embedded in the patriarchal structure has turned the national liberation project into a male chauvinist liberation project and has completely established the homeland in the image of a raped, passive woman.

Yet, the Islamic conceptualization of the settlement project in Palestine as an act of rape and its integration into the existing masculine culture contains an inherent structural contradiction which does not accord with the customary way of dealing with rape in this culture. In an essay titled "The War of Concepts," the Palestinian author Khairi Mansour criticized the use of the term "rape" and its derivatives, arguing that: "If we accept what happened in Palestine as rape, the solution for the rape victim in our popular culture is for the rapist to marry his victim in order to cover up the shameful act. According to this logic, the peace agreements signed between the Arabs and Israel are wedding ceremonies that are publicly advertised, so that the child-to-be will not be a bastard."[7]

The Nationalist-Intellectual Discourse

The nationalist-intellectual trend also suggested discontinuing the use of the term *mustawtana* and replacing it with the conceptualization used in the past by the Palestinians to describe the Jewish settlement in Palestine: *musta'amarat* (colonies). In this context, the Palestinian sociologist Abaher El-Sakka (2013) has emphasized that the distinction that must be made is in regards to the axis of time and place: between *al-musta'amara al-ula* (the first colony) established within the Green Line, and *al-musta'amara al-thani-a* (the second colony) established in the territories occupied in 1967. As he sees it, the use of the term *mustawtana* is political, serving the political perspective that manifests in the Oslo Accords and that accepts the distinction between the various areas as a way to justify the establishment of a state in the 1967 lands, instead of calling for the decolonization of the homeland and conceptualization of the national struggle as a struggle against a colonial project. According to the researcher Abdul-Rahim Al-Shaikh (2013), decolonization does not distinguish between Tel Aviv and Ariel, both of which are belligerent colonial settlements that can be normalized only through establishing one state for Jews and Palestinians on a completely equal basis.

This is the hegemonic trend in Palestinian academia, particularly in the social sciences. Sociologists and cultural anthropologists adamantly refuse to accept the differential conceptualization that distinguishes between the 1948 and 1967 settlements. The organizing rationale of such conceptualization, at least at the level of principle, is the decolonizing rationale of the South African project and recognition of Palestinian national self-determination, which are based on a reorganization of state-citizen relations on an equal basis. The organizing rationale of the Islamic discourse, on the other hand, is *de facto* the Algerian decolonization model, which is based on the "purification of the place" from the presence of the settlers, while aiming to turn back time, to the period before colonization.

Good Settler, Bad Settler: The Birth of the *Boa'ra* ("Outpost")

With the two-state solution based on the 1967 border gaining increasing recognition, particularly after the Oslo Accords, the concept of *mustawtana* turned into the canonic, hegemonic term in the popular and public discourse, while the alternative concepts gradually turned into a mark of an unpragmatic, fantastical, and dogmatic discourse.

However, the two-state solution that the Palestinians thought they would realize following the Oslo process did not materialize, while the settlements continued to expand. Today, Jewish settlers constitute one fifth of the overall Palestinian population in the West Bank and East Jerusalem,[8] surrounding the Palestinians with their settlements and infrastructure. The Palestinians who accepted the idea of dividing Palestine and establishing a state on 22 percent of the original homeland found themselves trapped in a problematic reality. They recognized Israel's right to exist on 78 percent of their land, but while Israel disengaged from the Palestinians and built roadblocks and a separation barrier that guaranteed their separation from the state they had accepted based on the 1967 borders, the settlers surged into the area designated for the Palestinian state and took over land that was supposed to serve the basis for the minimal development of a state. Through this process, the settlers in the West Bank gradually began to represent the new face of Israel for the Palestinians and, in turn, reshaped the way in which the Palestinians in the West Bank conceptualize the settlers. Throughout the years a distinction began to develop between the different groups of settlers that expressed the power relations which manifested on the ground, in which the Palestinians found themselves at the nadir of their national project as the dream of two states gradually faded away. Concentrated in discontinuous enclaves that they manage during the day and whose integrity is violated by the free hand the Israeli army maintains in all the areas that are under security control of the Palestinian Authority. Furthermore, they have all but lost faith in their political and national leadership, which they view as subcontractors for the preservation of the occupation at worst or as an impotent leadership at best, while the political division between Gaza and the West Bank persists.

Among many Palestinians in the West Bank, the prevalent image of the settlers is that of Jews who are more religious and racist, compared to other Israeli Jews. Abdullah, a twenty-three-year-old resident of the Jalazone refugee camp, located next to the religious settlement of Beit El that was created in 1977, noted in an interview that "there is a difference between the residents of the settlements and the rest of the Israelis. The settlers are usually more religious and more racist" (interview, June 14, 2015). Samer, a forty-nine-year-old resident of Ramallah who was active in the first Intifada and spent three years in prison for being a member of the Popular Front, explains the difference between the settlers and the rest of the Israelis in the 1980s: "Before the first Intifada there were Jews who were clerks and worked in the official offices in the city and the banks, there were soldiers, and policemen, and settlers, and plain civilians. More than all of them, the settlers with the kippah were the most scary and violent, even compared to the soldiers. A kippah for us was equivalent to a violent settler" (interview, June 14, 2015).

As Samer explains, at the time, the settlers were perceived mainly through the equation that a *kippah* (the Hebrew word for *yamaka*, the Jewish head cover) equals violence. Until the First Intifada there was no clear distinction between the different types of settlers, but mainly between the settlers and other Israeli groups. While the settlers were perceived as a homogenous and religious group, the Israelis increasingly came to be perceived as a heterogeneous group. This was mainly a result of the absorption of Palestinian workers in the Israeli labor market and the human interaction between Jewish and Palestinian individuals.

Following the outbreak of the First Intifada, which abruptly interrupted the habitual social interactions between Israeli Jews and the Palestinians, and following the policy of separation and proliferation of checkpoints and strict enclosures that accompanied the failed implementation of the Oslo Accords, which increased the encounters between civilians and the military, the Palestinian lexicon expanded to include concepts of control and oppression (e.g., barrier, fence, dirt road, bypass road, invasion, identification, permission, security ban). At the same time, the complex conception of the Israeli Jews began to revert back to the image of a homogenous category of the "Yahud." In the daily language of Palestinians residing within the territories, it became customary to say, "I got a job at the Jews," or "I have permission to go to the Jews." The differential conceptualization that varies according to experience and context becomes clear when comparing the Palestinians who are Israeli citizens, the Palestinians of East Jerusalem, and the Palestinians in the rest of the Occupied Territories.

The former, who reside within the most overt manifestation of Israeli power relations and heterogeneity, almost never use the term "Yahud"; rather, they use concrete and differential concepts and names for places, peoples, and positions. Furthermore, they have assimilated numerous terms, concepts, and words from Hebrew into their daily Arabic. The Jerusalem Palestinians, who hold Israeli residence identification cards and sustain daily, functional relations with the state's institutions (e.g., Israel's Tax authority, the Ministry of Interior, Social Security) and are employed in, mostly, the Western part of the city, use a variety of concepts and nuances to conceptualize the Israeli Jews, although to a lesser extent than the Palestinians in Israel. Their language has also absorbed Hebrew terms that reflect the functional and business interactions they conduct. Some of the terms have been transformed, Arabicized, and assimilated into daily language as concepts that are not identical to their Hebrew origin, alongside terms that have been fully assimilated as is from Hebrew (Mar'i 2013a, 2013b).

At the same time, an interesting process unfolded among the West Bank Palestinians: the deconstruction of the category of "settlers" into subcategories, along with the collapse of all the Israeli-Jewish categories into one category. This process reflects, first, Israel's separation policy and construction of the barrier, which curtailed the relationships between West Bank Palestinians and the Israeli Jews, as well as the expansion of the settlements and the rise in daily violence on the part of settler groups such as "Price Tag" and the hilltop youth. These are exacerbated as a result of the rising power of the settlers in the political arena who consolidated their control over focal centers of power and decision making in Israel. The settlers, perceived primarily as a group of radical religious people, are gradually being viewed as a much more heterogeneous group that includes distinct categories of radicals and moderates, good guys and bad guys. At the same time, the subcategories of Israeli society are being merged into one category of "Yahud." Of course, this process is not uniform nor entirely one directional, but nonetheless it is a trend that reflects the prevailing disposition of the Palestinians in the West Bank.

We can learn about these differential categories of settlers and the settlements from what Abd Wadi, Head of the Village Council of Qusra, said to Israeli television in a news program that aired on March 2, 2013.[9] In this interview he compared the settlers of Esh Kodesh, recognized as an "illegal outpost" in the eyes of Israel, to those living in Migdalim, a settlement established "legally" in 1981. Both settlements were established on the lands of Qusra and both are illegal according to international law. Nonetheless, according to Abd Wadi, "Migdalim exists on our land since 1981. It is at the main entrance to our village. The residents of Migdalim enter our village, they shop in the supermarket and use the gas station. There are no problems between us and Migdalim. Esh Kodesh is an illegal outpost and they conduct repeated attacks on Qusra."

Undoubtedly, the differential conceptualization expressed by the Head of the Qusra Council is related to the direct experience of the villagers, who suffer from physical attacks and direct and consistent harassment by the residents of Esh Kodesh and the atmosphere of terror that the "Price Tag" groups have imposed upon the Palestinians. The context of the interview is an additional factor, as it was conducted by an Israeli journalist in a program broadcast to a Jewish Israeli audience, so that one can assume the head of the village was interested in arousing empathy for his people. But beyond the direct experience and the desire to arouse empathy, this distinction between two types of settlers demonstrates an interesting process in which the established settlements undergo a process of incorporation in the local discourse, as a by-product of their common economic and social interactions.

Salem, a fifty-one-year-old man from the village of Sarta, adjacent to where the settlement of Barkan was established in 1981 by a mixed group of immigrants from the former Soviet Union and the descendants of Yemenite Jews, speaks of the matter-of-fact, nonhostile relationships that exist between the village's people and the residents of the settlement. He claims that these relationships are a result of their daily interactions, created through the employment of groups of workers from his village in the settlement and the Barkan Industrial Park:[10]

> The houses of Barkan were built by the people of Sarta and at times there were people from our village who built houses on land that was confiscated from them. In Barkan there were no large [construction] companies who built the settlement; there were contractors and workers from the [Sarta] village. This activity created a direct interaction and an unmediated visual connection. This interaction softened the hostility. Almost all the people of the village knew people from the settlement. Whoever did not work in the settlement worked in the Barkan Industrial Park nearby [the settlement] and was closely familiar with the settlers.

Salem adds:

> The good relations are a product of a shared interest; there is no love here, no acknowledgment or acceptance; rather there is a direct economic interest in which the people of the village profit by working in the village and the residents of the settlement profit of course by the relatively cheap labor . . . lacking a shared interest, hostility increases . . . see for instance the relationship between the people of El-Bireh and Psagot: The relations are hostile because there is no work-related interaction, no common interest.

Furthermore, he says:

> Even though the settlers of Barkan are right-wing and religious, they pro-
> tected their workers from the radical settler thugs who were harassing
> them. They did this because they [the residents of Barkan] are smarter,
> they want the Palestinians to do their work for them, and they do. (Inter-
> view, June 15, 2015)

The violent and thuggish behavior of the hilltop youth in contrast to the
state-like attitude of the rest of the settlers who respect the official Israeli laws and
the banal employment relations positions the former as a group of law-breakers
who challenge the jurisdiction of the State of Israel, as opposed to the latter group
of "law-abiders." In the context of the differentiation between law-breaking and
law-abiding settlers, Israeli public figures, politicians, and journalists criticize the
government's incompetence toward the former and issue calls to deal with them
decisively. These voices grow louder with each "Price Tag" attack, especially if the
damage inflicted is particularly bad, as in the case of the attack on the Dawabsheh family from the Duma village in which the parents were burned alive along
with their year-and-half-old baby while their older son was fatally burned. This
case shifted the attention of the Israeli public debate to the violence of the settlers—a discourse that faded away in time.[11]

Beyond the effect of this violence on the perception of the settlers in the
Palestinian discourse, their conceptualization is largely related to the failure of the Oslo peace process and the change in the status of the settlers in
the Israeli political map—moving from a marginal force in society to a major,
highly important one. This testifies to the crucial moment in which the defeated
Palestinians begin to unconsciously whitewash the settlements by adopting the
Israeli distinction between a "normal" settlement and a "problematic" settlement,
and more concretely, between "settlement blocs" and "illegal outposts." Thus, the
demand to preserve the settlement blocs—which became hegemonic among the
Israeli public, along with the demand to dismantle the outposts—began to also
spread among the Palestinians, who have gradually accepted the idea of negotiated land swaps that would result in compensating the Palestinians with land in
return for transferring the settlement blocs to Israel.[12]

Conclusion

The Palestinian conceptualization of the Jewish community is not uniform. This
historical survey of the conceptualization's development and transformation over
time reveals a strong link among the perception and apprehension of Jews, the
attitude toward the Jewish settlers and settlements, and the development and the
complex dynamic between the Palestinian and Zionist national projects.

Until the Nakba, which marks the collapse of Palestinian society and the Palestinian national project at that time, the Palestinians referred to the Jewish settlement through the pairing of *kubaniya-khawajah*, in which the Jewish settlement is viewed, basically, as a foreign entity in Palestinian space. This attitude was directed exclusively to the Jewish Zionist settlement and not to the local Jews, who were conceptualized as Arab Jews and recognized as part of the local fabric. But this attitude, too, gradually changed, as tensions between Zionists and Palestinians began to grow until the distinction among Jews slowly faded away, and until it disappeared in 1948.

In this context, the Nakba was the strategic junction in which *kubaniya* as a colonial paradigm emerged victorious, and replaced the previous differentiation between Arab-Jews and *khawaja*-foreigners. The different categorization of Jews collapsed into one unifying category and became, in the popular discourse beyond the Green Line, *Yahud*. Among the Palestinians who remained in Israel and began to maintain daily and employment relations with the Jewish society and the state that it established, new concepts began to emerge that reflected primarily hierarchical relations. Notably among these was the term *mua'lem* that slowly replaced the term *khawajah* (interestingly, both terms denote "educator"), while the term *kubaniya* was deconstructed into the names of the kibbutzim and cities that the Palestinians began to become familiar with due to their proximity to and interaction with place. Parallel to the popular Palestinian discourse (in Israel, Palestine and elsewhere), the nationalist conceptualization that began to develop in the intellectual discourse and grew to become the ideological focal point centered on the concept *musta'amara*. This concept is embedded in the global context of the 1960s, in which many nations were liberated from colonialism and foreign occupation. The ideology that reigned then was that Palestine, similar to Algeria and other colonized countries, was subject to Zionist colonization, which must be dismantled.

This conceptualization began to peter out after the 1967 defeat. The Palestinians, who started to embrace the idea of a division based on the 1967 borders, began to conceptualize the colonial project on the two sides of the Green Line in different ways. The term used to describe the Jewish communities established in the territories captured in the 1967 war was *mustawtanat*, which is a translation of the English term "settlements." Meanwhile the concept of Zionist *musta'amarat* and *musta'amir*, which until 1967 referred to the entire Jewish community in Palestine, faded away. This decline reflected recognition of the difference between Israel and its occupation, as the national struggle began to organize against the occupation of 1967 and no longer against the colonization of Historic Palestine. Therefore, the Palestinian political lexicon and conceptualization has grown closer to the Israeli and international ones and thus facilitated the rearticulating of the national imagination and project to fit the form and currency of territorial partition and the two-state solution. The differential conceptualization of the settlements was intended to focus Palestinian resistance and to recruit international support against their establishment and against changing the demographic-ethnic reality on the ground.

Another important dimension also affected this conceptualization; namely, the absorption of the Palestinian labor force from the Occupied Territories into the Israeli labor market. This created a close encounter, a familiarity with the Israeli landscape, which turned the names of cities and the term *mua'lem* (the Jewish work manager) into part of Palestinian daily life, in a way reminiscent of the conceptualization of the Israeli Arabs in the 1960s. This post-1967 conceptualization constantly developed and changed, under the influence of the dynamics of the conflict and the Palestinian national project. Following the deterioration of the Palestinian national project and its failure to realize an independent sovereign state (a project that replaced the decolonization of Historic Palestine) and with the parallel eruption of the settlement project into the Occupied Territories and the acceptance of the principle of land swaps and settlement blocs, the Palestinians began to distinguish among the various types of settlements in a way that mirrored the grammar of the Israeli discourse. In other words, a distinction was formed between a "legitimate settlement" and an "illegal outpost." The attitude toward the settlements developed in response to the direct violence that they display and not as part of the overall national project. This is even more striking considering that the settlement blocs established by the State of Israel have seized the majority of Palestinian land and therefore endanger the Palestinian state project far more than the illegal outposts/settlements.

The outpost has become the new colonial paradigm. Currently, the Palestinians direct their criticism toward the outposts and their residents, who make their lives miserable and terrify them. At the same time the settlements are gradually becoming a relatively "normal" place. Their normalization began with the Palestinian readiness to swap land that includes the settlement blocs that occurred in parallel to the explosion of new outposts on the ground, which have sprouted like mushrooms after the rain. A situation has been created in which the outposts, in their right-wing radicalism, have overshadowed the international illegitimacy of the settlements. Thus, every stage reinvented the language that would normalize the configuration that preceded it. The outpost normalizes the settlement, which was the focal point of the Palestinian national struggle for an independent state on the land occupied in 1967, after the settlements had normalized the Jewish colonial community, which is nothing more than the foreign *kubaniya* that invaded Palestine before 1948.

Notes

1. For more on the "illegal outposts" see Tzfadia, chapter 6.
2. The Arab language has two distinct forms: written and spoken. The written language is usually literary Arabic and is the shared language of the Arab world. Spoken, popular Arabic has many, very different dialects.
3. Al-Ma'any Lexicon. http://goo.gl/ojJPwV (last accessed July 27, 2016).
4. Haganah was the pre-1948 main Jewish military organization.
5. For the full text of the 1968 Palestinian National Charter, see: http://avalon.law.yale.edu /20th_century/plocov.asp (last accessed July 27, 2016).
6. See http://goo.gl/k6BOve (last accessed January 26, 2016).
7. Khairi Mansour, 2014, "Concepts at War," *Al-Quds Al-Arabi*, August 9, http://www .alquds.co.uk/?p=204179 (last accessed July 27, 2016).
8. For recent demographic figures of the Occupied West Bank and East Jerusalem see: https://www.cia.gov/library/publications/the-world-factbook/geos/we.html (last accessed July 25, 2016).
9. The report can be viewed at the MAKO website http://goo.gl/BzTHmv (last accessed September 15, 2015).
10. For more on the hiring of Palestinian labor in the Jewish settlements see Paz-Fuchs and Ronen, chapter 10.
11. Rania Zabanah, 2015, "The Death of Ali Dawabsheh," *Al-Jazeera*, August 4, http://goo .gl/pjqxJH (last accessed January 26, 2016).
12. Ilana Ben Zion, 2013, "Palestinians Make Stiff Land Demands for Peace Deal," *Times of Israel*, October 27, http://www.timesofisrael.com/palestinians-make-stiff-land-demands-for -peace/ (last accessed July 27, 2016).

References

Abd al-Jawad, Saleh. 2006. "The Arab and Palestinian Narratives of the 1948 War." In *The Intertwined Narratives of Israel-Palestine: History's Double Helix*, edited by Robert I. Rotberg, 72–113. Bloomington and Indianapolis: Indiana University Press.

Abdo, Nahla. 1991. "Women of the Intifada: Gender, Class and National Liberation." *Race and Class* 32 (4): 19–34.

Abu-Lughod, Janet. 1971. "The Demographic Transformation of Palestine." In *The Transformation of Palestine,* edited by Ibrahim Abu-Lughod, 153–161. Evanston, IL: Northwestern University Press.

Al-Azm, Sadik. 2011. *Self-Criticism after the Defeat*. London: Saqi. [Original edition, 1968.]

Al-Husseini, Ishaq Musa. 1969. *History of the Palestinian Cause*. Cairo: The Research Institute for Arab Studies.

Al-Qasmi, Saed, and Al-A'zem Khalil. 1988. *Dictionary of Shamia Craft*. Damascus: Dar Tlass. [Arabic.]

Al-Shaikh, Abdul-Rahim. 2013. "The Palestinian Cultural Identity: Paradigms, Representations, and Resemblances." Paper presented to the Palestinian Communities, Its Representations, and the Future of the Palestinian Cause Conference, Ramallah: The Palestinian Center for Policy Research, January 17, 2013. [Arabic.]

'Amr, Yunus, and Ghanim Mazal. 1989. *The Arab in Hebrew Children's Literature.* Hebron: Hebron University Research Center. [Arabic.]

Bishara, Azmi. 2000. *The Arab in Israel: A View from the Inside.* 2nd edition. Beirut: Center for Arab Unity Studies. [Arabic.]

Cohen, Hillel. 2015. *Year Zero of the Arab-Israeli Conflict 1929.* Lebanon, NH: Brandeis University Press and University Press of New England.

Davis, Rachel. 2010. "Growing-up in Palestine before the Year 1948." In *In Jerusalem: History of the Future: Studies in Jerusalem's Past and Present Studies,* edited by Issam Nassar, 75–124. Ramallah: Institute for Palestine Studies.

Dawabsheh, Muhammad. 2010. "The Image of the Arab in Israeli Literature." *Diwan al-Arab.* Accessed September 14, 2015. http://www.diwanalarab.com/spip.php?page=article&id _article=21416. [Arabic.]

El-Sakka, Abaher. 2013. "The Palestinian Social Identity: Its Fragmented Representations and Multiple Intersections." Paper presented to the Palestinian Communities, Its Representations, and the Future of the Palestinian Cause Conference, Ramallah: The Palestinian Center for Policy Research, January 17, 2013. [Arabic.]

Ghanim, Honaida. 2009a. "Poetics of Disaster: Nationalism, Gender, and Social Change among Palestinian Poets in Israel after Nakba." *International Journal of Politics, Culture, and Society* 22 (1): 23–39.

———. 2009b. *Reinventing the Nation: Palestinian Intellectuals in Israel.* Jerusalem: Magnes Press. [Hebrew.]

Hammami, Rema. 1990. "Women, the Hijab and the Intifada." *Middle East Report* 20 (3&4): 24–28.

———. 2010. "Gender, Nakba and Nation: Palestinian Women's Presence and Absence in the Narration of 1948 Memories." In *Across the Wall: Narratives of Israeli-Palestinian History,* edited by Ilan Pappé and Jamil Hilal, 235–268. London: I. B. Tauris.

Jua'bah, 'Abd Al-Mu'ti. 2011. *The Image Precedes the Myth: An Exploratory Study of Early Zionist Films.* Ramallah: Palestinian Forum for Israeli Studies. [Arabic.]

Kanaaneh, Rhoda Ann, and Isis Nusair. 2010. *Displaced at Home: Ethnicity and Gender among Palestinians in Israel.* New York: SUNY Press.

Kana'nah, Shariif. 1992. *The Palestinian Diaspora: Immigration or Displacement?* Jerusalem: Universal Jerusalem Institute for Palestine Studies. [Arabic.]

Kassem, Fatma. 2011. *Palestinian Women: Narrative Histories and Gendered Memory.* London: Zed Books.

Kayyali, 'Abd Al-Wahhab. 1970. *Modern History of Palestine.* Beirut: Arab Institute for Research and Publishing. [Arabic.]

Khalidi, Walid. 1988. "Plan Dalet: Master Plan for the Conquest of Palestine." *Journal of Palestine Studies* 18 (1): 4–33.

———. 2005. "Why Did the Palestinians Leave, Revisited." *Journal of Palestine Studies* 34 (2): 42–54.

Mar'i, Abd al-Rahman, 2013a. "Arabs Speaking Hebrew." *Alachson.* December 30. Accessed July 26, 2016. http://goo.gl/RhaICF. [Hebrew.]

Mar'i, Abd al-Rahman, 2013b. *Wallah Beseder: Linguistic Portrait of the Arabs in Israel.* Tel Aviv: Keter. [Hebrew.]

Masalha, Nur. 1992. *Expulsion of the Palestinians: The Concept of "Transfer" in Zionist Political Thought 1882–1948.* Washington, DC: Institute for Palestinian Studies.

———. 1997. *A Land without a People: Israel, Transfer and the Palestinians 1949–96.* London: Faband Faber.

——. 2012. *The Palestine Nakba: Decolonising History, Narrating the Subaltern, Reclaiming Memory*. London: Zed Books.

Maz'al, Ghanim. 1985. *The Arab Character in Modern Hebrew Literature*. Acre: Dar al-Asswar. [Arabic.]

Mustafa, Muhammad. 1985. *Britain and Palestine*. Cairo: Dar al-Shoruq. [Arabic.]

Nashif, Esmail. 2008. *Palestinian Political Prisoners: Identity and Community*. London: Routledge.

Nassar, Issam, and Selim Tamari. 2005. *Pilgrims, Lepers and Stuffed Cabbage: Essays on Jerusalem's Cultural History*. Jerusalem: Institute of Jerusalem Studies.

Nofal, Ahmad. 1997. *The Zionist Conspiracy of the Colonisation of Palestine: An Introduction to the Palestinian Cause*. Amman, Jordan: Middle East Studies Center. [Arabic.]

Peteet, Julie. 2013. *Gender in Crisis: Women and the Palestinian Resistance Movement*. New York: Columbia University Press.

Qasimiyah, Khayryah. 1996. *The Palestinian Cause and the Hashemite Leaders: Al-Ḥusayn, 'Abd Allaah, Fayṣal, Ghazī, 'Abd Al-Ilah, 1915–1951*. Amman, Jordan: The Higher Committee for Writing about the History of Jordan, The Royal Aal al-Bayt Institute for Islamic Thought. [Arabic.]

Sa'di, Ahmad H. 2002. "Catastrophe, Memory and Identity: Al-Nakbah as a Component of Palestinian Identity." *Israel Studies* 7 (2): 175–198.

——. 2013. *Thorough Surveillance: The Genesis of Israeli Policies of Population Management, Surveillance and Political Control towards the Palestinian Minority*. Manchester and New York: Manchester University Press.

Said, Edward W. 1979. *The Question of Palestine*. New York: Vintage Books.

Sanbar, Elias. 2001. "Out of Place, out of Time." *Mediterranean Historical Review* 16 (1): 87–94.

Sayegh, Fayez A. 1965. *Zionist Colonialism in Palestine*. Beirut: Palestine Liberation Organization–Research Center.

Shufani, Elias. 2002. *Israel in 50 Years: The Zionist Project: From the Abstract to the Tangible*. Damascus: Dar Jafra. [Arabic.]

Shulḥut, Anṭuwan. 1997. *Rifts in the Eschatological Culture*. Acre: Dar al-Aswar. [Arabic.]

Tabar, Linda. 2007. "Memory, Agency, Counter-narrative: Testimonies from Jenin Refugee Camp." *Critical Arts: A Journal of South-North Cultural Studies* 21 (1): 6–31.

Tamari, Salim. 2002. *Jerusalem 1948: The Arab Neighbourhoods and their Fate in the War*. Jerusalem: Institue of Palestine Studies and Badil.

——. 2004. "Ishaq al-Shami and the Predicament of the Arab Jew in Palestine." *Jerusalem Quarterly File* 21 (2): 10–26.

——. 2011. *Year of the Locust: A Soldier's Diary and the Erasure of Palestine's Ottoman Past*. Berkeley: University of California Press.

Tamari, Salim, and Issam Nassar. 2003. *The Ottoman Jerusalem in El-Jawhariyyeh Memoirs, the Second Book of the Musician Wasif Jawhariyyeh, 1904–1917*. Beirut: Institute for Palestine Studies. [Arabic.]

Tarabee, Hamad. 1970. *Palestine in Zionist and Colonialist Plans (1922–1870)*. Cairo: Research Institute of Arab Studies. [Arabic.]

Taraki, Lisa, Rita Giacaman, Rema Hammami, Penny Johnson, and Iṣlāḥ Jād. 1997. *Al-Mar'ah Al-Filasṭīnīyah: Al-waḍ' Al-rāhin*. Bīr Zayt: Barnāmaj Dirāsāt Al-Mar'ah, Jāmi'at Bīr Zayt. [Arabic.]

Yuval-Davis, Nira. 1997. *Gender and Nation*. Vol. 24. Cambridge: Cambridge University Press.

Zreik, Raef. 1999. "From an Arab Viewpoint." *Haaretz*, April 20. [Hebrew.]

10 Integrated or Segregated?

Israeli-Palestinian Employment Relations in the Settlements

Amir Paz-Fuchs and Yaël Ronen

I<small>N</small> JULY 2015 the Israeli National Labor Tribunal (NLT) denied a claim for statutory labor rights under Israeli law, submitted by three Palestinians employed in a factory in the Nitzanei Shalom industrial area in the West Bank. The tribunal held that the industrial zone was part of a joint enterprise agreed upon under the Israeli-Palestinian Interim Agreement of 1995, the purpose of which was to supply jobs to Palestinians. For that reason, Jordanian, rather than Israeli law, should apply.[1] This ruling is yet another block in the jurisprudential wall gradually evolving in the West Bank between Israelis and Palestinians. This chapter explores the juxtaposition of different areas of law that inform this phenomenon, namely labor law, international law, and conflict of laws, in the context of Israel's settlements policy.

There is no shortage of scholarly literature and policy papers documenting, analyzing, and informing employment relations, and the relevant legal regimes regulating these relations in domestic and regional contexts. The situation is quite different where international conflicts are concerned. In such contexts, economic relations among the civilian population are perceived at best as secondary in importance to humanitarian and security concerns. This hierarchy is largely justified, since the political and military instability caused by conflict puts life itself at jeopardy. However, the matter is different in a situation of occupation, when hostilities give way to stability. Moreover, in a situation of prolonged occupation, economic relations may become increasingly woven into the fabric of the legal structure of the conflict. In the territories occupied by Israel, an important political and economic reality is the employment of Palestinians by Israelis (individually or through Israeli-owned corporations), within the Israeli settlements and outside them.

The inherent challenge of regulating employment relations in a situation of occupation is exacerbated in the West Bank by two unique characteristics of the Israeli occupation. The first is the fact that there are many Israeli employees within the occupied territory, working in the same industries and work places as the Palestinians, sometimes shoulder to shoulder, oftentimes as superiors within the workplace. Second is the incongruity between the geographical location in which the employment of Palestinians takes place and the manner in which that location is perceived. Despite their legal status as foreign territory, the settlements and their adjacent industrial areas are socially and politically perceived by many Israelis as incorporated within Israel. Consequently, employment relations maintained in the settlements are regarded largely as an intra-Israeli matter insofar as concerns Israelis, with the presence of Palestinian parties constituting a foreign element, even though legally the situation is the exact converse.

In 2007 the Israeli High Court of Justice (HCJ) addressed some of the challenges that this unique work environment creates, in its *Worker's Hotline* ruling.[2] The court was faced with the question of whether Israeli or Jordanian law applied to the employment of Palestinians working in Israeli-run establishments within the settlements, alongside Israeli employees. The court attempted to give legal expression to the social reality according to which the settlements are part of Israel, by refusing to attach weight to the difference in nationality between employees, and applying to all of them the same legal order, the Israeli one. However, in doing so it disregarded the economic incentives that underlie the employment of Palestinians by Israelis. The sustainability of the court's ruling was therefore subsequently challenged through diverse legal constructs. This chapter traces the evolution of the 2007 ruling in the practice of employers and other economic actors and in related jurisprudence and examines its ramifications.

We begin with brief accounts of the Palestinian labor market in the West Bank, and of the legal order that regulates labor relations in that territory. We then trace the developments in case law that have informed the law applicable to the employment of Palestinians by Israelis, focusing on the effect of the 2007 ruling in *Worker's Hotline*. We suggest that the interpretation and application of this ruling by relevant actors, as it has been confirmed in subsequent decisions of the lower labor tribunals, has followed the letter of *Worker's Hotline* but at times diverged so greatly from its spirit, that it may pave the way to results that are the opposite of the approach that the HCJ was advocating.

Palestinian Labor in the Occupied Territories

Israel's conquest of the West Bank and the Gaza Strip in 1967 had an immediate impact on the labor economies in these areas. The most striking feature of the consolidation of occupation was Israel's attempt to improve the population's standard of living and individual prosperity, even as it undermined the Palestinian population's attempts to create a self-sufficient and independent economy, and stifled industrial and agricultural development (Gordon 2008).

Life in the Occupied Territories became intimately linked to Israel, as their residents developed, with Israeli encouragement and coercion, a dependence on Israel for basic commodities, employment, and access to services and commerce (Swirski 2008; Gordon 2008). This dependence has not gone unnoticed. Already at the outset of the occupation, an Israeli government publication stated that "naturally and unavoidably the [occupied] territories are becoming dependent upon Israel for all their economic and service needs."[3] Israel acted proactively to limit the viability of Palestinian agriculture and industry. As early as one week after the 1967 War ended, on June 18, 1967, Israel issued a military order that made it illegal to conduct business transactions involving land or property, to conduct electric maintenance work or connect a generator, or to plant new citrus trees or replace old nonproductive trees, without a permit (Gordon 2008).[4] In subsequent years, Israel continued to regulate Palestinian agriculture in minute detail and restricted Palestinian access to markets for agricultural products (Van Esveld 2015, 23). In addition, it has blocked investments in civil infrastructure needed for the economic development of the Occupied Territories (Gordon 2008). This policy of "antiplanning" (Weizman 2007, 97) and "de-development" (Gordon 2009, 239, 247; Roy 1995, 4, 128), together with the open borders policy between Israel and the Occupied Territories, has led to an incremental reliance of the Palestinian workforce on work in Israel (Mundlak 1998). And so, by 1971, 11.8 percent of the Palestinian workforce was employed in Israel, rising to 39.2 percent by 1987. This large proportion of workers employed outside their territory is unparalleled. Some estimate that after taking into account unregistered workers, the figure was closer to 70 percent (Lein 1999). Combined, these policies led to the integration of the Palestinian economy into the Israeli economy (Paz-Fuchs and Ronen 2012).

Since the First Intifada in 1987, and even more significantly since the eruption of the Second Intifada in 2000, entry of Palestinians into Israel has been greatly curtailed, and the employment of Palestinians in Israel has fallen dramatically. As a coping mechanism, many Palestinians resorted to self-employment and to agriculture. The prospect of self-sustenance based on those, however, was significantly hindered by the construction of the Separation Barrier in the West Bank, beginning in 2003, and by the related regime of restrictions on movement within the West Bank. These restrictions, unprecedented in the history of the occupation in their scope, duration, and severity (Barsella 2007, 12–20), have changed not only the physical, but also the social and economic landscape of the West Bank. They separate Palestinian residents of the West Bank from their land, and cut them off from the West Bank hinterland, thereby inhibiting the possibility of land cultivation and making a living off agriculture (ILO 2015). Similarly, many Palestinians cannot maintain their own businesses, since movement of goods has become prohibitively expensive; tourism has become nonexistent; and employees cannot commute and are forced to seek work close to home. In a survey that focused on the consequences of the Separation Barrier, 55 percent of participating West Bank residents reported that its most immediate effect was on their place of employment and livelihood (Kimhi 2006, 40). Palestinians have therefore increasingly been forced to take up work in settlements and Israeli-run industrial zones (ILO 2015, para. 75), despite their moral and political reservations (Abdallah 2014), and for less than the Israeli minimum wage (Kanafani and Ghait 2012, 21). Indeed, as Israeli settlement in the West Bank deepened, especially in the 1990s, Israeli businesses became increasingly aware of the opportunity of lower employment standards a few miles from home. According to the Palestinian Central Bureau of Statistics, 20,300 Palestinians were employed in the settlements with permits in the second quarter of 2015 (PCBS 2015, 5) and an estimated ten thousand others were employed in the settlements without permit, most of them in the Jordan Valley (ILO 2015). The Israeli Civil Administration, which grants permits to Palestinians, cites similar figures: 25,756 in November 2014 (Knesset 2014), with the numbers continuously rising since then. In other words, 4 to 6 percent of working Palestinians are employed by Israeli settlers and corporations in the West Bank (ILO 2015, paras. 30, 37). Specifically in Area C, which includes the agriculturally developed Jordan Valley, 24 percent of working Palestinians are employed in the settlements or their industries (OCHA 2013). Insofar as particular sectors are concerned, the data are somewhat limited. The Palestinian Central Bureau of Statistics, which as far as we know is the only institution that traces the employment realities in the West Bank, does not distinguish between Palestinian employment in Israel and Palestinian employment in settlements (or in Israeli-owned industries in the West Bank). According to its Labor Force Survey of 2015, 63.2 percent of Palestinian workers in Israel and the settlements were employed in the construction sector (PCBS 2015, 17). Trailing far behind were the mining, quarrying, and manufacturing industries (13.7 percent); agriculture, fishing, and forestry (9.8 percent); commerce, restaurants, and hotels (8.5 percent); and services and other branches (4.8 percent) (ibid.).

It has been argued that Israel intentionally obstructed the development of an independent Palestinian industry so as to inhibit economic competition and to guarantee the regular supply of cheap labor for Israel and Israeli businesses (Gordon 2008). As one employer candidly argued before the HCJ in *Worker's Hotline* (in an effort to convince that his reasonable expectation was to rely on, and benefit from, cheap labor), private businesses relocated to the West Bank in order to benefit from the lower standard of living, the captive labor market, and water and land resources (Hever 2010; Bichler and Nitzan 2001). Worryingly, in 2013, the Regional Labor Tribunal accepted a defendant employer's argument that Israeli law should not be applied to the employment of the Palestinian claimants, among other reasons because that would lead the employer into financial crisis and possibly even to bankruptcy.[5]

The vast majority of scholarship, reports, and journalistic portrayals have focused on the dire situation of Palestinian workers, including the impact of their being employed by Israeli settlers (Van Esveld 2015). While much of this literature focuses on the military and governmental regulation of Palestinian labor, a comprehensive analysis of the Israeli-Palestinian economic relationship requires that a more detailed account be taken of the contractual aspect of Palestinian employment, namely vis-à-vis Israeli employers. There is no comprehensive data on the number of Israeli employers in the West Bank. Alongside the Civil Administration (the military entity that governs the daily matters in the West Bank), which is a significant employer in its own right, hundreds of Israeli private sector employers operate in settlements, industrial zones, and agricultural areas such as the Jordan Valley. Who Profits, a nongovernmental organization dedicated to documenting the commercial involvement of Israeli companies in the Occupied Palestinian Territories, details 465 such companies operating in settlements, industrial zones, and agricultural areas. In addition, there are numerous nonincorporated, individual employers. An important factor, which has received almost no attention whatsoever, is the fact that in many cases, Israelis also work in the same places of business, whether alongside the Palestinians, performing similar tasks, or, more frequently, in different positions, often hierarchically higher ones. Consequently, there are two different—but not fully segregated—sets of labor relations: one between Israeli employers and Israeli employees, and another between Israeli employers and Palestinian employees.

The Law Applicable to Employment in the West Bank

Under the law of occupation, the occupant "shall take all the measures in his power to restore, and ensure, as far as possible, public order and safety, while respecting, unless absolutely prevented, the laws in force in the country."[6] The "laws in force in the country" are Jordanian (in the West Bank) or Egyptian (in the Gaza Strip, relevant to the present discussion with respect to the period prior to the 2005 disengagement).[7] This provision of the law of occupation was endorsed by the Israeli military government in a proclamation issued immediately upon the entry of the Israel Defense Forces into the West Bank and the Gaza Strip, which stipulated that "[t]he law which existed in the Region on June 7, 1967, shall remain in force."[8]

However, four additional layers of law apply. The first layer consists of over two thousand military orders adopted through the years, which regulate various areas of life. Among those, some amend the territorially applicable Jordanian labor law, such as with respect to work accidents,[9] sick pay,[10] compensation claims, and certain procedural rights.[11] These orders largely duplicate Israeli legislation. While military orders apply, as such, to the entire occupied territory, their subject matter may be more specific. Thus, two major orders specifically regulate the relations among Israelis within the Israeli settlements across a host of issues. These orders intentionally duplicate Israeli legislation, thereby creating "the law of the exclaves."[12] It is they which form the basis for the perception that Israeli law governs life in the settlements, despite their different constitutional status (military orders rather than parliamentary legislation). Similarly noteworthy are the 1982 Order on Employment of Workers in Certain Places (Judea and Samaria) and its 2007 amendment. The 1982 order imposed an obligation on Israeli employers within the settlements duplicating Israel's Minimum Wage Law.[13] In 2007, following the *Worker's Hotline* ruling, the order was amended to extend the obligation to Israeli employers anywhere within the West Bank (importantly, including in the industrial zones).[14] The general implications of this order are noteworthy. First and foremost, the order comprehensively protects Palestinian employees by focusing on the identity of the employer and preempting efforts to place Israeli corporations outside the settlements and thus outside the reach of the earlier order. On the other hand, this may arguably be the most direct form of creeping annexation, as Israeli law effectively applies throughout the West Bank, albeit on a personal basis rather than on a territorial basis.

A second layer of norms is Israeli legislation that has been expressly extended to apply only to Israeli residents of the West Bank, on a personal basis. This layer consists of fewer than twenty laws on issues such as taxation, criminal liability, military conscription, social security, and national elections. There is no such legislation in the realm of employment law. However, since 2013, there have been several efforts to legislate an automatic extension of all Israeli laws, past and future, to Israeli settlers. These efforts have been motivated primarily by the desire to expand the protection of Israeli labor law to Israeli workers, and in particular Israeli female workers, in the settlements. These efforts have, to date, been blocked by the attorney general and by centrist ministers who warned that the application of Israeli law in the West Bank may have international legal ramifications, including charges of creeping annexation (Lis and Hovel 2013).[15] More recently, the principal political instigators of the initiative have abandoned it, following pressure from Israeli employers of Palestinian employees who object to the additional costs that such legislation would impose on them (Levinson 2015). The government has so far limited itself to duplicating the Israeli Women's Employment Law into a military order. The order applies the protection under Israeli law to "persons employed by an [Israeli or an Israeli corporation] employer outside the municipalities' territories."[16] This ostensibly covers Palestinian women employed by Israelis in Area C.[17]

The remaining two layers of legal norms are less known, perhaps because they are relevant specifically to employment law, and both are contractual. The first is collective agreements that in domestic industrial relations apply to all individuals employed by an employer who is party to a collective agreement. Insofar as employment in the West Bank is concerned, they are of limited relevance, since the employers there are small private corporations and are rarely bound by collective agreements;[18] interesting legal challenges may nonetheless arise where the state (e.g., the Civil Administration) is concerned.

The final layer of legal regulation is the individual employment contract. The remainder of this chapter focuses on the law applicable to such a contract when the parties are an Israeli employer and a Palestinian employee.

The Law Applicable to Contracts of Employment of Palestinians by Israeli Employers in the Settlements: *Worker's Hotline*

Parties to an agreement are generally free to decide on the particular law that would apply to their relations, irrespective of the territorially applicable law. This freedom is generally constrained only by public policy considerations, according to which an agreement would be held suspect if it appears to deny basic, fundamental rights that would apply had it not been for the stipulated choice of law. Where an agreement does not stipulate the law applicable to it, the choice-of-law rules common to most states, including Israel, provide that the law governing a contract is the one to which the contract is most closely related when a weighted contact count is performed.

Until 2007, few if any of the employment contracts in use by Israeli employers in the West Bank contained provisions determining the law applicable to them. Indeed, many contracts were concluded orally. It was neither disputed as a matter of fact, nor controversial as a matter of policy, that the employment of Israelis (by Israelis) was governed by Israeli law. This is the law to which the contract is most closely linked, first and foremost through the expectation of the parties. By the same token, it was probable that Palestinians employed by Palestinians were (and still are) employed under Jordanian law. Any controversy on this (which would not likely reach adjudication in an Israeli court) would be beyond the scope of this chapter. More significantly, however, prior to 2007, the unarticulated practice was that Palestinians were employed under Jordanian law (as modified by military orders, for example on the payment of Israeli minimum wage) also when their employers were Israelis, including when the workplace was a settlement or an Israeli-owned industry situated elsewhere in the West Bank.

Matters supposedly changed dramatically in 2007, following the HCJ's ruling in *Worker's Hotline*.[19] The case originated in five judgments of regional labor tribunals, which applied Israeli law to the labor relations between Palestinian residents of the West Bank and their Israeli employers in the settlements. In the *Giv'at Ze'ev* case,[20] the Jerusalem regional labor tribunal ruled in favor of fourteen Palestinian cleaners employed by the Giv'at Ze'ev Municipal Council, who claimed minimum wage, pension, travel expenses, convalescence pay, holiday pay, severance pay, advance notice, and wage incentives, all under Israeli law. In another case, the Tel Aviv regional labor tribunal ruled in favor of a Palestinian employee of Abir Textile Industries Ltd., an Israeli firm located in the Barkan industrial zone in the West Bank. The employee claimed advance notice, severance pay, compensation for delay in wages, pay in lieu of annual leave, and minimum wage, all under Israeli law.[21] In *Aqua*, the Tel Aviv regional labor tribunal ruled in favor of a Palestinian working for an Israeli company located in the Ma'ale Efraim industrial zone, who demanded benefits under Israeli law after being dismissed.[22] In *Tzarfati Car Services Ltd.*, a Palestinian employed by an Israeli garage located in the Ma'ale Adumim industrial zone demanded severance pay and social benefits under Israeli law. The Jerusalem regional labor tribunal rejected the employer's claim that Israeli labor law did not apply. Lastly, in *Nituv Management and Development Ltd.*, the Tel Aviv regional labor tribunal denied a request for summary dismissal filed by the respondent company, which was based on the claim that the 1963 Israeli Severance Compensation Law did not apply to a Palestinian employee.[23]

The employers in the five cases appealed to the NLT. The NLT chose to deal jointly with the question whether it was Israeli labor law that applied to the employment by an Israeli corporation or public employer of Palestinians within a settlement in the West Bank. Noting that in none of the cases had there been either written contacts or an express stipulation of the applicable law, the NLT applied the traditional, contact-based approach to identifying the law to which the contracts were most closely connected. It proceeded from the presumption that the contract is governed first and foremost by the law of the place of performance;[24] it then examined whether under a weighted contact count there was a country other than Jordan to which the contract was more closely connected.[25] The NLT held that the specific contacts to Israeli law, namely the identity of the employer, the currency of payment, the language of documents, the adherence to Israeli days of rest, and even payment of tax in Israel, were not indicative of the applicable law. In contrast, the contacts to Jordanian law included the facts that the contracts were performed in the West Bank, which was also the place of contracting; that the place of business of the employer was the West Bank;[26] and the fact that the employees were Palestinian residents of the West Bank. On this basis, the NLT concluded that the contracts were more closely connected to Jordanian law.[27]

The NLT's judgment was appealed before the HCJ by *Worker's Hotline*, an Israel nongovernmental organization. The HCJ reversed the decision, holding that the labor relations between the Israeli employers and the petitioning Palestinian employees were more closely connected to Israeli law than to Jordan and its law.[28]

The HCJ instructed that the following principles should be observed in deciding the applicable law in labor relations. First, if the parties agreed that a certain law would apply, such as Jordanian law, then as a rule, the parties' choice
should be respected. However, in light of the inherent power disparities between
the employer, who drafts the contract, and the employee, who has little choice but
to sign it, courts should exercise a degree of caution before taking the agreement
as conclusive.

If, however, the parties did not stipulate which law would apply, the court
should apply the legal system that is closest to the contract as identified through a
weighted contacts count. Relevant contacts would include the place of signing,
the place of negotiation, the place of the contract's execution, the identity of
the parties including their nationality and place of residence, the language of the
contract, the currency for payment, and where taxes were to be paid. The court
emphasized that the territorial contact, namely that the work was to be carried
out in the settlements where Jordanian law was the territorial law, is of limited
weight in this context, since within the settlements there are already different legal
orders applicable to different populations. Instead, other contacts, such as the
currency of payment, the fact that documents relating to the work were in Hebrew,
the fact that days of rest were determined according to Israel's calendar, and that
in one case an employee even paid tax in Israel, were decisive. The court also stated
that policy considerations may impact on the contact count. Specifically in the
context of labor law it mentioned the importance of equality, namely the need to
give equal pay and working conditions for equal work. In the specific context, it
held that the same *law* should apply to workers doing the same work side by side.
Since it was clear that the employment of Israelis by Israeli employers (whether
within the settlements or elsewhere) was governed by Israeli law, equality would
require that it apply also to the Palestinian employees.

In an earlier publication (Paz-Fuchs and Ronen 2012), we surmised that an
Israeli employer might abide by the *Worker's Hotline* and still manage to evade
the reach of Israeli law with respect to its Palestinian employees even while
applying Israeli law to its Israeli employees, in one of two fashions. The first is
through an explicit agreement with the Palestinian employees that Jordanian law
would apply to their employment. The other is through the employment of Palestinian manpower companies as intermediaries, so as to increase the weight of
contacts that pull toward Jordanian law. We now assess recent jurisprudence in
light of our estimates, and add two additional factors discernible in the tribunals'
analyses: the limited role attached to the principle of equality, and the importance
attached to the place of work.

Before proceeding, it is important to clarify the significance, in our view, of
the determination as to whether Israeli law or Jordanian law applies to the employment of Palestinians by Israelis. We do not hold that either law should neces-

sarily apply to the employment of Palestinians by Israelis, either within the settlements or outside them. Each case should be decided independently, in light of the choice-of-law rules, which regulate the law applicable to transnational interactions. Those acknowledge that when a situation has links to a number of legal orders, any number of factors may affect the decision which legal order would apply, including the identity and characteristics of the parties involved. The analysis may result in different legal orders governing apparently similar situations. While this in itself is not objectionable, the application of different legal orders is objectionable where the factors chosen are extraneous to the context at hand. We hold that in the case of employment, the nationality of the employees is an extraneous factor, which must not be given effect, directly or indirectly; moreover, we argue that equality among employees within the same business is (as the HCJ held) a consideration in itself. Neither of these arguments advocates that Israeli law should necessarily apply to the employment of Palestinians (nor, in fact, to that of Israelis).[29] They do advocate, however, that if Israeli law is unfailingly and sweepingly applied to Israeli employees, then the application of another law to Palestinians is suspect. Moreover, we argue that the decision whether Israeli law or Palestinian law applies should take into account the wider economic context, rather than merely focus on the Palestinian labor market, and that disingenuous distinctions among coemployees should be scrutinized with care.

Notwithstanding our indifference as to which of the two legal orders should apply so long as it applies uniformly to employees within the same establishment, it is worth noting that the choice between the legal orders affects not only the primary, substantive norms, but also the secondary ones, which concern enforcement. Israeli labor law enforcement agencies are empowered to enforce only Israeli law. A holding that Jordanian law applies inherently denies Palestinians the protection of these enforcement agencies. Whether Israel has an obligation to enforce labor law in the West Bank irrespective of its normative source is a complex issue beyond the scope of this chapter. For our present purposes, it is sufficient to emphasize that no such enforcement takes place. Indeed, even where Israeli labor law does govern, five years after the *Worker's Hotline* ruling it was reported that "Israeli employers in settlements and industrial zones in the West Bank continue to routinely deny the rights of their Palestinian workers. . . . The vast majority of workers earn less than the minimum wage, their wages are withheld from time to time, their social rights are denied and they are exposed to dangers in their workplaces."[30] Enforcement of statutory employment rights is entrusted to the Civil Administration. The work of the Civil Administration in this regard was the subject of severe criticism by the Israeli State Comptroller (2011, 1663–1699). The latter noted, inter alia, that Israeli labor law is enforced only where Israeli workers are concerned, but not to protect Palestinian workers (1674). With regard to minimum wage (which has been extended through a military order to all persons employed by Israelis throughout the West Bank), the State Comptroller noted that no inspections had been carried out for years.

In the agricultural sector, much of the focus has been on the date farms in the Jordan Valley. A 2015 report by Human Rights Watch documents, not for the first time (see Worker's Hotline 2009), the extent of hazardous conditions that workers in those farms are exposed to (Van Esveld 2015). Date farm workers are not provided with access to medical care, are not compensated for their injuries, and are even refused sick pay for work-related absence due to injuries. While the date farm industry abuses have been repeatedly exposed, they are not isolated. Similar practices take place in other areas of the Jordan Valley, and with other crops (Van Esveld 2015, 45–46). There is an additional aspect that distinguishes the date industry. Many workers in this sector are children, some as young as eleven years old. The general minimum age for employment under Israel law is fifteen, although children are allowed to work in undemanding roles, and during vacation, from the age of fourteen. Health and safety hazards are more harmful to them because of their age. They are at higher risk of contracting a long-term illness, cancer, neurological problems, and infertility. They also earn less than the Israeli minimum wage. In fact, most earn about one-half of the Israeli teenage minimum wage and some earn one-fourth of that wage.

Interestingly, while the Human Rights Watch report is very critical of the exploitation endured by Palestinian workers and, by implication, the lack of enforcement of Israeli laws, its authors clarify that they "do not call on Israel to extend its domestic legal order, including workers' rights protections, into occupied territory. The international law of belligerent occupation, applicable to the West Bank today, prohibits Israel, as the occupying power, from extending the jurisdiction of its domestic laws into Palestine as though it were the sovereign" (Van Esveld 2015, 5). The avoidance of creeping annexation is thus a prominent political and legal concern.

The Aftermath of *Worker's Hotline*

Express Agreements

One way in which an employer can stay true to the letter of *Worker's Hotline* yet circumvent its spirit is by entering into an express agreement with the Palestinian employee on the applicable law, even while Israeli employees continue to be governed by Israeli law. In *Worker's Hotline*, the court clarified that barring exceptional circumstances, courts would give effect to an express agreement.[31] In fact, since the *Worker's Hotline* ruling has been published, a new practice has been adopted by Israeli employers, of signing written contracts with their Palestinian employees, which expressly stipulate that their relations would be governed by

Jordanian law.[32] The *Mahisan* ruling is particularly interesting, and worrying, in this respect. The case involved 110 workers employed by the Israeli Civil Administration itself. Guided by the ruling in *Worker's Hotline*, the Civil Administration drafted contracts in Arabic for its Palestinian workers, which included a provision that prescribed Jordanian law as the law of the contract. The regional labor tribunal confirmed the validity of the stipulation, without addressing the obvious power disparities that, in this case, are threefold: employer-employee; Israeli-Palestinian (in the context of the occupation); and the powerful position of the employer, the Civil Administration, in regulating the lives of the employee in all aspects of life, including those which are unrelated to work itself (e.g., authorization of permits, supply of water and electricity). In a different jurisprudential approach, the regional labor tribunal in *Haled* took an intermediary approach, refusing to regard the stipulation on the applicable law as trumping the issue. Instead, it factored the stipulation into the contact count, thus awarding it some weight but not an absolute one.[33]

Recourse to Palestinian Intermediaries

A second tactic for avoiding the application of Israeli law to an employment relationship with Palestinian employees is through recourse to manpower agencies and service providers, a highly prevalent technique in the domestic Israeli labor market (Mundlak 2008). These firms are often used for "payrolling" purposes only, creating the appearance of the agency or service provider as the legal employer, thereby allowing the true employer to circumvent obligations based in collective agreements that would otherwise apply (Deakin 2001; Fudge 2006).[34] In the context of choice-of-law rules, hiring an intermediary Palestinian company as a service provider or manpower agency, which in turn would hire Palestinian employees, may enable an Israeli employer to manipulate the contact count away from Israeli law. Nongovernmental organizations have begun to collect evidence of this practice (Worker's Hotline 2009) and have estimated that Israeli companies employ 30 percent of Palestinian workers through Palestinian contractors (Worker's Hotline 2012, 41).

The obvious conclusion is that unless tribunals look at apparently innocuous agreements in context, Israeli employers can abide by the dictates of *Worker's Hotline* and still offer their employees terms that are acceptable only under Jordanian law, simply by incorporating a Palestinian company as an intermediary. A possible avenue for escaping such a harsh conclusion may be in an interim ruling given by the regional labor tribunal in 2009 according to which the strong involvement of the Israeli employer in the day-to-day employment regime demanded viewing the former as a "joint employer," alongside the Palestinian contractor, who was only formally involved.[35] This idea, of viewing the end-user and the contractor as joint employers, has been floating in academic scholarship (Davidov 2006; Prassl 2015). It is amply complicated in domestic situations, and the introduction of conflicting legal orders would introduce an additional layer of complexity. For example, one may ask whether the inclusion of the Israeli company as a joint employer brings with it the whole gamut of Israeli labor law.

Parsing Equality

A central principle that governed the HCJ's *Worker's Hotline* ruling was the principle of equality, according to which Israelis and Palestinians employed in the same work by the same employer should be governed by the same legal order. Two issues that concern the application of equality in this context merit elaboration here. First is that in the employment context, equality normally refers to *terms and working conditions*. This demand was not raised, and therefore not addressed, in any of the cases that have reached the tribunals to date. Instead, Palestinian employees demand, and tribunals at times approve, the application of the same *law*. In *Masa'ad*,[36] for example, the regional labor tribunal cited the fact that Israelis and Palestinians worked for the same employer as justifying its decision to apply Israeli law to the Palestinian employees. But the tribunal did not inquire whether the Israeli employees were paid *more* than the minimum wage, or whether they were provided other benefits above and beyond statutory requirements, while those benefits were denied to the Palestinians employees.

A second issue that arises is the comparators used when evaluating a claim of discrimination. In *Worker's Hotline*, the court noted that the Palestinian petitioners did the same kind of work and for the same employers as did the Israeli employees, and were thus entitled to have the same law applied to them. In subsequent case law, various efforts have been made to qualify this statement. For example, in *Dynamica*, the court reiterated the *Worker's Hotline* conclusion that Israeli and Palestinian workers may not work under different laws, but it found that "unlike the situation in *Worker's Hotline*, where Palestinian and Israeli workers were employed together, here *only Palestinian workers* are involved." Consequently, applying Jordanian law to the contracts of the Palestinian employees was not discriminatory.[37]

Moreover, employers have at times relied on the fact that Palestinians and Israelis did different work—for the same employer—to justify divergence from the principle of equality. In some cases, this claim was accepted by the tribunals, in a manner that, with due respect, constitutes a fundamental misunderstanding of the role of equality when considering the law that should apply. In *Haled*, for example, the regional labor tribunal held that although there were Israeli workers in the factory, the fact that they were at a managerial level, and thus not executing "equal work," was reason enough not to apply Israeli law to Palestinians while it did apply to Israeli employees.[38] The same reasoning was applied in *Madnabe*, first by the regional labor tribunal[39] (2013) and later (2015) by the NLT,[40] which held that different legal orders could apply to the Palestinians and to the Israelis since the Israelis were employed "in roles different to those of the appellants" (not even managerial), "and thus not comparable to the work they do."[41] Yet the difference in the type of work that is performed, which is amply relevant in the context of terms and conditions (such as pay), is entirely irrelevant when the demand is for application of the same legal order. In the latter case, public policy considerations favor applying the same law to all workers in the same workplace, *regardless of their particular role*. In *Masa'ad*, the tribunal correctly held that applying different law to Israelis and Palestinians would be discriminatory since no relevant difference between them has been proven.[42] In *Balal*, the tribunal was even more explicit, stating a distinction based on national origin is unacceptable in light of the principle of equality, irrespective of the different positions that employees held.[43]

Perhaps the most worrying statement in this respect was made by the NLT, which held in one case that the relevant comparison is not between Palestinians and Israelis working for the same employer, but between Palestinians working for Israeli employers and Palestinians working *for Palestinian employers* in the same industrial area.[44] This is a rare occasion where comparisons are made across employers, solely on the basis of the employees' nationality, and, in defiance of the principles of labor law, to the detriment of the employees.

Why are courts carving out a crucial exception in a way that would significantly limit the application of the principle of equality? We can only surmise that at least one of the background considerations is the worry, always present, of creeping annexation. If the principle of equality indeed requires the application of Israeli law to every place of employment where Israelis work alongside Palestinians (regardless of their respective roles), the implication would be that Israeli labor law apply to the vast majority of undertakings in Area C. Despite the fact that such application would primarily benefit Palestinian workers, the general political and international legal implications are also relevant. The issue has been, as expected, very contentious politically. For while Palestinians object to the annexation of Palestinian land by applying Israeli law through Parliament, the effects of the judicial rulings is tantamount to these very measures. The response from the Palestinian Authority was to try to get to the root of the problem, inter alia by considering a ban on Palestinian employment in the settlements (*Al-Monitor*, February 18, 2014). However, in light of the high rates of unemployment throughout the West Bank, and the comparatively higher wages in Israeli industries than in the Palestinian ones, this measure has proven politically unrealistic (Issacharoff 2010). Additionally, and more cynically, in carving out such an exception, tribunals have taken into account the argument put forward by Israeli employers, time and again,[45] that a blanket application of Israeli law to Palestinian workers would have devastating implications on business profitability.

Location

In *Worker's Hotline*, the HCJ emphasized that in the Israeli settlements, where military orders duplicated Israeli law insofar as concerns Israelis, the relevance of territorial law was of little weight. Looking to the other contacts invoked in that case, the court found weighty links with Israeli law. However, the court's *rejection* of the territorial link has been implausibly used in subsequent jurisprudence to substantiate the *significance* of territorial links, in a variety of ways.

One such use is in the automatic linkage between performance of work on the territory of a settlement and the applicability of Israeli law.[46] In light of the fact that the settlements constitute "legal exclaves" where the expectation of Israelis is on many levels that Israeli or Israeli-like law apply, this decision is not substantively questionable,[47] although the overriding weight attached to that link is problematic as it may be viewed as creeping annexation. Indeed, by applying Israeli law on a quasi-territorial basis, the tribunals render any proposed distinctions between Israeli and Palestinian employees immaterial insofar as concerns employment within the settlements themselves, thereby reinforcing the principle of equality.

More disturbing, however, is the converse determination: that where the issue is employment outside the settlements, Israeli law does not apply to the contract, at least prima facie. One of the first of such cases to reach the NLT was *Az-Rom*, which concerned employees in the Erez industrial area which was located in the Gaza Strip prior to Israel's disengagement from the area. The NLT distinguished the case from *Worker's Hotline* by stressing that the industrial zone in question was *intentionally* not included within the jurisdiction of the Israeli exclaves, and that the territorial link was determinative in deciding that Egyptian law should apply.[48] More recently, in *Madnabe* (2015), the NLT held that employment of Palestinians by Israelis in an industrial zone in the West Bank was governed by Jordanian law since the industrial zone was not within a settlement.[49] This deduction was neither stated nor implied in *Worker's Hotline*. On the contrary, the HCJ stated the limited significance of the territorial link as a contact to Jordanian law within the settlements; it certainly did not uphold its exclusivity to employment relations outside the settlements. The rulings of the labor tribunals are not even consonant with the military order of 2007, which extended Israeli minimum wage to employment by Israelis anywhere in the West Bank, an order that implicitly acknowledged that the specific location of work within the West Bank was of minor significance compared with the identity of the employer.

The element of location was decisive in *Haled* and in *Mahisan*. In *Haled*, the regional labor tribunal made a significant effort to determine whether the relevant factory was situated in an "Israeli exclave." Upon reaching the conclusion that it was not, and that it was sufficiently remote from any such exclave, the tribunal decided that Jordanian law should apply. This conclusion was reached, it should be stressed, despite the fact that the employer was Israeli, that the contract was written in Hebrew, as were the pay slips and attendance sheets; and most importantly, that the area was secured in a manner that Palestinians (but not Israelis) required permits to enter into it. As noted, in *Mahisan*, the employer was the Civil Administration itself, which is headquartered in a military base outside the Beit-El settlement. The regional labor tribunal stressed that the military base is not located in the "Israeli exclave" and therefore Israeli law would not apply.[50] These cases, especially the latter one, contrast interestingly with a ruling of the NLT confirmed by the HCJ over four decades earlier: in *Kiryat Arba*, the HCJ dealt, for the first time, with a labor dispute between the Civil Administration and Israeli employees in a settlement. The court held that Israeli employees of the military commander, who applies his authority in area under its control, are subject to Israeli labor law.[51] Thus, not only was the identity of the employer and the employees significant, but also the fact that the work was conducted in an area under the authority of the Israeli military commander. This rationale, however, would justify the applicability of Israeli law everywhere in the West Bank, at the very least in the industrial areas and in the rest of Area C, where the Palestinian Authority exercises no territorial authority but only a small number of powers limited only to Palestinians. *Mahisan* diverged from the jurisprudence of the HCJ and of the NLT even more astoundingly, in holding that employment by the Civil Administration—an organ of the Israeli military government—is a contact to *Jordanian* law, since the Civil Administration "replaces the Jordanian sovereign that preceded the Israeli military forces."[52]

Concluding Observations

The jurisprudence of the regional labor tribunals is by no means uniform, and, moreover, only the jurisprudence of the NLT and the HCJ is binding law. And yet, when taken as a whole, the decisions of the tribunals paint a picture that may not be fully consonant with *Worker's Hotline*'s spirit, even if they are in line with its word. Two phenomena are tentatively emerging. One concerns the territorial aspects in the application of Israeli law, the other concerns the role of equality in the decisions of the courts.

Territorial application of Israeli law: In *Worker's Hotline* the HCJ held that within the West Bank settlements, the link to the territorial law of the place of work is of little significance because there is no uniform law, and different laws apply to Israelis and Palestinians. Therefore, Jordanian law (which is the territorial law of the entire West Bank) cannot be presumed (as was done by the NLT) to apply. Since *Worker's Hotline*, however, labor tribunals do attach significance to the law of the place of work,[53] supposedly in reliance on *Worker's Hotline*, except that insofar as concerns the settlements, they consider Israeli law to be that law rather than Jordanian. Labor tribunals have begun regarding Israeli law as the territorial law in the settlements, and holding that outside the settlements, Israeli law necessarily, or at least presumptively, does not apply.[54] The incremental application of Israeli law through a territorial or quasi-territorial basis can arguably be characterized as creeping annexation of the settlements. Importantly, this quasi-territorial expansion is limited to Israeli exclaves even when equality concerns call, in our view, for a wider application of Israel law, namely also outside the exclaves.

Equality: In *Worker's Hotline* the HCJ emphasized that the principle of equality dictates that differences of nationality may not result in the application of different legal orders to persons performing similar work; yet "similar work" has been interpreted with such parsing that in practice, differences of nationality do effectively have normative consequences in all but a very narrow category of cases. We critiqued as irrelevant the distinction that the tribunals make among employees within the same business according to the specific work that they perform and the comparison to Palestinians employed in Palestinian-owned industries in the same area.

But the parsing of circumstances goes further, for example in the reference to the purpose of the work. The fact that Palestinians are the beneficiaries of the work performed has been cited as a relevant contact in the weighted count.[55] Taking this position to its logical conclusion, it would suggest that Palestinian and Israeli workers in the famed SodaStream factory could be subjected to different laws if Palestinians were designated to production lines that would be marketed to Palestinians, and Israeli workers to productions lines that would "benefit" the Israeli population. Similarly, in *Madnabe*, the NLT confirmed that Israeli law should not apply to Palestinian employees in the industrial zone inter alia because the zone was established to provide work for Palestinians. This statement is peculiar both descriptively, as the zone obviously benefits the Israeli economy no less than it benefits the Palestinians,[56] and normatively, since, as we noted, such a consideration is foreign to labor law principles and ought not appear in a labor contract contact count.

After half a century of occupation and a growing interdependence of the populations and their economies, the tribunals view themselves as forced to make principled legal determinations so as not to hinder a functioning economy, in very irregular circumstances. We identified two emerging principles: the quasi-territorial application of Israeli law in the settlements, and the limiting of the principle of equality. Both differentiate between Israelis and Palestinians, each raising particular concerns. The application of Israeli law to the settlements on a territorial basis smacks of annexation, which has serious political consequences. The differentiation between employees on the basis of national affiliation raises a different set of concerns, namely the undermining of universal human rights principles through legal segregation by the application of different legal orders to different people within the same territory.

Notes

1. Labor Appeal 10736-12-13 Madnabe (July 10, 2015).
2. HCJ 5666/03 Worker's Hotline v. The National Labor Tribunal et al. (2007), para 10.
3. *Three Years of Military Government 1967–1970: Data on Civilian Activities in Judea and Samaria, The Gaza Strip and Northern Sinai* (Tel Aviv: Coordinator of Government Operations in the Administered Territories, Ministry of Defence, 1970), 4.
4. Military Order 25, 1967; Military Order 427, 1971.
5. Regional Labor Case 2106/10 Madnabe v. Yamit Water Filtering (T.A., Nov. 3, 2013), para 14. The ruling was confirmed by the NLT. The latter's decision neither reiterated nor expressed objection to this reasoning, Madnabe (2015) (*supra* note 1).
6. Convention (IV) respecting the Laws and Customs of War on Land and its annex: Regulations concerning the Laws and Customs of War on Land 1907, Oct. 18, 1907, 36 Stat. 2227, T.S. No. 53. See also Geneva Convention (IV) Relative to the Protection of Civilian Persons in Time of War, art. 64, Aug. 12, 1949, 75 U.N.T.S. 287 (hereinafter Fourth Geneva Convention).
7. The present analysis will focus on the West Bank, given that since 2005, there is no Israeli civilian presence within the Gaza Strip. It will also disregard Palestinian law, which does not apply to Israelis or in the Israeli settlements.
8. Proclamation regarding Government and Law Arrangements (West Bank Region) (No. 2) 5727-1967 of June 7, 1967.
9. Order regarding Work Accident Insurance (Judea and Samaria) (No. 662), 5736-1976, June 22, 1976, Order regarding the Labor Law (work accidents) (Judea and Samaria) (No. 663), 5736-1976, June 22, 1976 and No. 663, June 22, 1976, as well as subsequent amendments to the Jordanian 1960 Labor Law (*supra* note 20).
10. Order amending the Jordanian Labor Law, Law No. 21 of 1960 (Amendment No. 6) (Judea and Samaria) (No. 1133), 5745-1985, Mar. 1, 1985.
11. Order amending the Jordanian Labor Law, Law No. 21 of 1960 (Judea and Samaria) (No. 439) 5731-1971, Aug. 5, 1971 and Order amending the Jordanian Labor Law, Law No. 21 of 1960 (Amendment) (Judea and Samaria) (No. 825) 5740-1980, Feb. 20, 1980.
12. Order on Administration of Municipal Councils (Judea and Samaria) 1981, No. 892 (Isr.), Order on Administration of Regional Councils (Judea and Samaria) 1979, No. 783 (Isr.).
13. Order regarding Employment of Workers in Certain Locations (Judea and Samaria) (No. 967) 5742-1982, Mar. 3, 1982, Article 3 (hereinafter Order No. 967).
14. Order regarding Employment of Workers in Certain Locations (Amendment No. 3) (Judea and Samaria) (No. 1605) 5788-2007. Nov. 7, 2007, Article 6, adding Article 3B to Order No. 967.
15. Letter from the Israeli Attorney General to the Secretary of the Government, Re: Comments on the Government's Agenda for Sept. 1, 2013 (Aug. 29, 2013).

16. Order 1730 (28.12.2013), Article 1.

17. Israelis presumably do not maintain business in Areas A or B.

18. But see Balal and Others v. Even Bar Ltd. And another, Jerusalem Regional Labor Tribunal Case 2548/08 and others (June 13, 2013) para. 88, where the tribunal held that extension orders (which are signed by the Minister of Employment, and extend collective agreements to employers who have not signed collective agreements) apply on the ground that the applicability of Israeli law extended to all Israeli law regulating the employment relationship, regardless of the place of contracting.

19. *Worker's Hotline* (*supra* note 2).

20. Labor Court Case 55/3-100 to 55/3-113 Giv'at Ze'ev (Dec. 28, 1997) (Isr.).

21. Labor Court Case 57/3-2981 Abir Ltd. (Dec. 14, 1997) (Isr.).

22. Labor Court Case 300309/99 Aqua Print Ltd. (June 10, 2001) (Isr.).

23. Labor Court Case 35/3400 Nituv Management and Development (Feb. 1, 1998) (Isr.).

24. *Worker's Hotline* (*supra* note 2), para. 14; Civ App 419/71 Menora v. Nomikos 26(2) PD 527, 531 [1972] (Isr.); Rome Convention on the Law Applicable to Contractual Obligations, 1980 O.J. (L 266) 1; 1998 O.J. (C 027) 34 (consolidated version), arts. 4(1), 6(2); Restatement (Second) of Conflict of Laws, § 188(2)(c) (1971).

25. Labor Appeal 300050/98 Giv'at Ze'ev v. Mahmoud, 38 Labor Judgments 577 (Isr.), para. 24.

26. A contact that largely duplicates the former.

27. *Giv'at Ze'ev, supra* note 25, para. 31.

28. *Worker's Hotline* (*supra* note 2), paras. 25 and 26.

29. Labor Appeal 244/99 Zorba v. The Civil Administration (June 24, 2003), para 7.

30. *Worker's Hotline* (*supra* note 2), paras. 37 and 38.

31. *Worker's Hotline* (*supra* note 2), para. 23.

32. Regional Labor Case Morad Haled v. Tal-El Collection and Recycling (Tel Aviv, 2013); Regional Labor Case 3452/09 Jahalin v. Municipality of Ma'ale Adumim (Jerusalem, Feb. 3, 2011); Madnabe (2015) (*supra* note 1); Regional Labor Case 2727/09 Tareq Mahisan v. the Civil Administration (Jerusalem, 2014).

33. Haled, id, para 19.

34. And in the present context see Regional Labor Case 3105/07 Muna Mahmoud al-Samarat et al. v. Eitan and Yinon Agriculture Ltd. (May 24, 2009), para 50.

35. Id, para 56. Since the case was settled out of court, no final ruling was given on the matter. See also Regional Labor Case 4773—09-11 Rabah v. Gottfeld (Tel Aviv, April 23, 2013), para 8.

36. Regional Labor Case Ibrahim Masa'ad v. Kibbutz Galgal (2011).

37. HCJ 1234/10 Dynamica 2002 Ltd. v. the Civil Administration (2010), para. 12.

38. Haled (supra note 32), para 21.

39. *Supra* note 5.

40. Madnabe (2015) (*supra* note 1).

41. See also Mahisan (*supra* note 32), para 13.

42. Masa'ad, *supra* note 36, para 26. And similarly when comparing Palestinian employees with Thai employees see Rabah (*supra* note 35), para 16.

43. Balal (*supra* note 18), para 67.

44. Labor Appeal 207/08 Az-Rom v. Ashkanta (Jerusalem, Jan. 13, 2012), para 64.

45. Madnabe (2013), (*supra* note 5); see also Labor Appeal 1342-01-11 Basharat v. Bali (Nov. 26 2013), para 10.

46. Regional Labor Case 2320-09 Bani Udda v. Naor (Jerusalem, April 24, 2012), paras 27 and 28. The tribunal went so far as to hold that Israeli law applied from the time that *Worker's*

Hotline was handed down, despite noting that the parties were in agreement that Jordanian law applied to their relations, para 7.

    47. For example, Labor Appeal 256/08 Koka v. Schwartz (Feb. 23, 2011), para 32.

    48. Az-Rom (*supra* note 44), para 58.

    49. Madnabe (2015) (*supra* note 1).

    50. Mahisan (*supra* note 32), paras 12 and 13.

    51. HCJ 663/78 Kiryat Arba Administration v. the NLC and Rachel Klein 33(2) PD 398 [1979] (Isr.), para 5.

    52. Mahisan (*supra* note 32), para 14. This construct was rejected in Zorba (*supra* note 29), para 7.

    53. Regional Labor Case 10736-05-11 Udda v. Shmuel (Aug. 30, 2013), para 5.

    54. Mahisan (*supra* note 32), para 11, Madnabe (2015) (*supra* note 1).

    55. Mahisan (*supra* note 32), para 12. For a milder articulation of this notion see Az-Rom (*supra* note 44), para. 53; Regional Labor Case 10736-05-11 Udda (*supra* note 53), paras. 4 and 5.

    56. In Balal, the tribunal held that the fact an Israeli employer in an industrial area set up within the municipal area of a settlement made the company part of the Israeli market, thereby constituting a link to Israel. Balal (*supra* note 18), para 61.

References

Abdallah, Jihan. 2014. "A Palestinian Contradiction: Working in the Settlements." *Al-Monitor*, February 18. Accessed January 31, 2016. http://www.al-monitor.com/pulse/originals/2014/02 /settlements-palestinians-occupation-israel-sodastream.html.

Barsella, Anat. 2007. Ground to a Halt: Denial of Palestinians' Freedom of Movement in the West Bank. *B'Tselem.* http://www.btselem.org/download/200708_ground_to_a_halt_eng.pdf.

Bichler, Shimshon, and Jonathan Nitzan. 2001. *From War Profits to Peace Dividends.* Jerusalem: Carmel. [Hebrew.]

Davidov, Guy. 2006. "Enforcement Problems in Informal Labor Markets: A View from Israel." *Comparative Labor Law and Policy Journal* 27 (1): 3–26.

Deakin, Simon. 2001. "Commentary: The Changing Concept of the 'Employer' in Labour Law." *Industrial Law Journal* 30 (1): 72–84.

Fudge, Judy. 2006. "The Legal Boundaries of the Employer, Precarious Workers, and Labour Protection." In *Boundaries and Frontiers of Labour Law: Goals and Means in the Regulation of Work*, edited by Guy Davidov and Brian Langille, 295–316. Oxford: Hart Publishing.

Gordon, Neve. 2008. *Israel's Occupation.* Berkeley: University of California Press.

———. 2009. "From Colonization to Separation: Exploring the Structure of Israel's Occupation." In *The Power of Inclusive Exclusion: Anatomy of Israeli Rule in the Occupied Palestinian Territories*, edited by Adi Ophir, Michal Givoni, and Sari Hanafi, 239–268. New York: Zone Books.

Hever, Shir. 2010. *The Political Economy of Israel's Occupation.* London: Pluto Press.

ILO. 2015. *The Situation of Workers of the Occupied Arab Territories.* Geneva: International Labor Office. doi: ILC.104/DG/APP

Issacharoff, Avi. 2010. "PA Lightens Ban on Working in the Settlements to Ease Palestinian Unemployment." *Haaretz*, December 28. Accessed January 31, 2016. http://www.haaretz .com/israel-news/pa-lightens-ban-on-working-in-settlements-to-ease-palestinian -unemployment-1.333439.

Kanafani, Nu'man, and Ziad Ghait. 2012. *The Economic Base of Israel's Colonial Settlements in the West Bank*. Ramallah: Palestine Economic Policy Research Institute.

Kimhi, Israel, ed. 2006. *The Security Fence around Jerusalem: Implications for the City and Its Residents*. Jerusalem: Jerusalem Institute Israel.

Knesset. 2014. *Parliamentary Committee for the Problem of Migrant Workers*. Jerusalem: Knesset. [Hebrew.]

Lein, Yehezkel. 1999. "Builders of Zion: Human Rights Violations of Palestinians from the Occupied Territories Working in Israel and the Settlements." *B'Tselem*. Accessed January 31, 2016. http://www.btselem.org/publication/43.

Levinson, Chaim. 2015. "Right-Wing Israeli Party Drops Bid to Have Labor Law Apply in West Bank." *Haaretz*, July 21. Accessed January 31, 2016. http://www.haaretz.com/israel-news/.premium-1.666995.

Lis, Jonathan, and Revital Hovel. 2013. "Passing Bill on Women's Rights in the West Bank Could Be Seen as Annexation, AG Warns." *Haaretz*, September 1. Accessed January 31, 2016. http://www.haaretz.com/israel-news/.premium-1.544597.

Mundlak, Guy. 1998. "Power-Breaking or Power-Entrenching Law—The Regulation of Palestinian Workers in Israel." *Comparative Labor Law Journal and Policy Journal* 20 (4): 569.

———. 2008. "Israeli System of Labor Law: Sources and Form, The." *Comparative Labor Law Journal and Policy Journal* 30 (2): 159.

OCHA. 2013. "Area C Vulnerability Profile." *OCHA*. Accessed January 31, 2016. https://http://www.ochaopt.org/documents/ocha_opt_fact_sheet_5_3_2014_en_.pdf.

Paz-Fuchs, Amir, and Yaël Ronen. 2012. "Occupational Hazards: Labor Rights in the Occupied Territories." *Berkeley Journal of International Law* 30 (2): 580.

PCBS. 2015. *Labour Force Survey*. Ramallah: Palestinian Central Bureau of Statistics.

Prassl, Jeremias. 2015. *The Concept of the Employer*. Oxford University Press: Oxford.

Roy, Sara. 1995. *The Gaza Strip: The Political Economy of De-development*. Washington, DC: Institute for Palestine Studies.

State Comptroller. 2011. *Annual Report No. 62 for 2011*. Jerusalem: State Comptroller.

Swirski, Shlomo. 2008. *The Cost of Occupation—The Burden of the Israeli-Palestinian Conflict: 2008*. Tel Aviv: Adva Center. Accessed January 31, 2016. http://adva.org/wp-content/uploads/2014/09/costofoccupation2008fullenglish-1-.pdf.

Van Esveld, Bill. 2015. "Ripe for Abuse: Palestinian Child Labor in Israeli Agricultural Settlements in the West Bank." *Human Rights Watch*. Accessed January 31, 2016. https://http://www.hrw.org/report/2015/04/13/ripe-abuse/palestinian-child-labor-israeli-agricultural-settlements-west-bank.

Weizman, Eyal. 2007. *Hollow Land: Israel's Architecture of Occupation*. London: Verso.

Worker's Hotline. 2009. *Palestinian Workers in West Bank Settlements—2008*. Tel Aviv: Worker's Hotline.

———. 2012. *Employment of Palestinians in Israel and the Settlements: Restrictive Policies and Abuse of Rights*. Tel Aviv: Worker's Hotline.

11 Jerusalem's Colonial Space as Paradox

Palestinians Living in the Settlements

Wendy Pullan and Haim Yacobi

THE "SATELLITE NEIGHBORHOODS"—the settlements built from 1967 in East Jerusalem—are, arguably, the place where one finds the deepest fissures between Jewish and Palestinian attitudes to the occupation. Approximately one-third of all settlers live in those large bedroom suburbs in annexed East Jerusalem. For most Jewish Israelis, these are satellites or simply neighborhoods of the capital, a reality of "facts on the ground" and now well absorbed into the everyday urban fabric. Israelis distinguish them from the rest of the settlements in the West Bank. Their Jewish-only populations tend not to be radical and many consider themselves apolitical; these residents live in the settlements because they can enjoy good housing stock at favorable prices, resulting in larger houses, often with gardens, than would be available inside the city's Green Line. For Palestinians, the settlements are built on stolen land, their land. For them, these neighborhoods are colonies and the result of a long occupation that cements its processes of domination through planning and building.

Yet, despite these characterizations, this bilateral opposition is not as well defined as might seem. Some Palestinians, either Israeli citizens or those holding Jerusalem Residency Certificates, have moved into the Jewish settlements in Jerusalem. According to the available data at the end of 2008 (CBS 2008), approximately 4,500 Palestinians live in the city's settlements. They too wish to avail themselves of the superior facilities available in the settlements. Abowd (2007, 1025) suggests that these areas offer urban services and goods that make them attractive for many Palestinians "whose options in Arab neighborhoods are not uncommonly more expensive and difficult to access." Good quality housing in Palestinian East Jerusalem is in short supply. Poor services and a housing shortage are a result of both Israeli policy and practice that has left the Palestinian parts of the city underdeveloped since 1967. This has resulted in anomalies in the segregated housing profile of the city. Although quantitatively the data might be considered a marginal phenomenon, qualitatively, we suggest it is significant for a highly divided city such as Jerusalem, and more generally, for the study of the dynamics of Israel's occupation.[1] Moreover, the "normalization" of the occupation

and colonization of East Jerusalem is described in the literature as a static phenomenon, overlooking microscale analysis of everyday life in the city, and its
effect on urban praxis.

In this chapter, we highlight the paradox of Jerusalem's colonial space; on the
one hand, the Israeli settlements in East Jerusalem were planned, designed, and
marketed as part of the attempt to Judaize the city, while on the other hand, Palestinians who move to these enclaves cross an invisible boundary to become one
with the "settlers." In other words, although the settlements are usually considered as the place of ethnic separation, the long-term effects of Israeli policy has
caused some infiltration of Palestinians into these segregated areas. Whether this
phenomenon has created the possibility for greater integration is doubtful and
will be something that this chapter interrogates. A parallel situation applies to
the academic literature on the settlements, where the analysis is often separated.
We offer a different, complementary view, pointing to a more nuanced understanding of the urban dynamics of occupation and conflict while looking at a set
of inversions (Palestinian settlers in a Jewish settlement). As we will illustrate, it
is the very particular urban condition of a neighborhood/settlement, and the
various legal statuses of its inhabitants, that open possibilities for the Palestinian
population. Paradoxically, the attempt to politically and territorially annex East
Jerusalem makes it harder to fully Judaize it.

Our focus on a neighborhood scale as a means of understanding the very extensive colonial settlements around Jerusalem is far from arbitrary. Rather, the
concept of neighborhood, as a social and spatial entity, is discursively linked to
modernity, modern planning, and certainly nationalism (Gillette 2010). Since the
end of the nineteenth century, the design of modern neighborhoods was at the core
of urban planning; its vision was not only the physical improvement of housing
conditions, it also extended to *civitas*, the shared community of citizens (Gillette
2010, 2). Yet, Western planning ideologies in colonial contexts inherently embody
cultural imperialism and thus present a utopian idiom of neighborhood that is
based on a homogenous social entity; against such a background, a community
where its dwellers are strangers to each other is thus rendered problematic. In other
words, there is a hegemonic assumption behind colonial planning, and a sense of
community is taken to refer to the same ethnic, national, racial, or class group.

Based on extensive fieldwork carried out from January 2006 to July 2013,
which included documentation, quantitative data collection, archival research as
well as in-depth interviews, this chapter focuses on French Hill, the neighborhood
that was the first settlement of the Israeli Judaization of East Jerusalem. Israelis
consider it to be politically and culturally part of unified Jerusalem. Established according to modern planning episteme, this neighborhood is inhabited by Jewish
residents, but as noted, it is undergoing a process of demographic transformation as

Palestinians, both with Israeli citizenship and Jerusalem Resident Certificates, have been moving there in recent years.

Indeed, as we will detail, despite the escalating violence following the First Intifada and especially the Second Intifada and the ongoing discourses of enmity, Israeli residents in French Hill found themselves facing a dilemma: "to sell or not to sell," using Rabinowitz's words (1994), property to Palestinians.[2] While such a dilemma has been explored by several studies in relation to Jewish-Arab mixed cities (Yacobi 2009), we suggest that the case of French Hill may exhibit some differences to areas inside Israel. For if we consider the matter in terms of Palestinian sensibilities, the question of whether "to buy or not to buy" property becomes one of existential concern, as French Hill is one of the first settlements built on occupied Palestinian land in East Jerusalem, as well as a neighborhood ostensibly built for, and offering public services to, Jewish residents only. For Palestinians who consider buying into French Hill, the fear of being branded a collaborator will always lie just below the surface of everyday life.

New Colonialism: The Establishment of a Modern Neighborhood

Despite the fact that the colonization of East Jerusalem was declared in a 1968 government decision taken at national level, it is the professional knowledge of experts that contributed to the implementation of such policy. The first step was the use of the legal system; in January 1968, the Land Ordinance for expropriating land through the Planning and Construction Law 1965 was invoked. This allowed the expropriation of land for public use without any specified use, whether for housing, parks, or infrastructure. As a result of this act, 3.345 km^2 were expropriated in the first instance, including the area to become French Hill, in the northern part of "unified Jerusalem."

French Hill stands at a critical topographical point for the newly expanded Israeli Jerusalem. From it, there is a visual axis to the Old City, while at the same time, the neighborhood pivots between the main road to the northern West Bank and to the south, East Jerusalem. It is also on the road that connects Mount Scopus, and its Hebrew University campus, with Israeli West Jerusalem. The connections help to reinforce an Israeli weak spot from the divided topography of 1948–1967 and point toward future settlement. Certainly, the location of Jerusalem's new neighborhoods, including French Hill, did not depend upon the availability of land or planning logic, but rather it was part of Israel's explicit policy.

The initial demographic objective for French Hill was designed to house 2,400 Jewish families. This number increased later due to a decision to allocate 3.7 km^2 to the expansion of the Hebrew University Campus (Yacobi 2008). Public buildings such as schools and kindergartens were located on the east slope of the hill, protected from the western wind, and the housing zones were designed around the hilltop.

In December 1969, the Rogers' Plan (after U.S. Secretary of State William Rogers) was published, calling for a shared administration of the city by representatives of the three main religions. Such a recommendation was rejected by the Israeli authorities and as a result the aspirations for low-rise housing in French Hill were pushed aside and three to four additional floors were added to each building to intensify the Jewish presence in East Jerusalem. In the case of French Hill, housing was a key player, and the geopolitical effect of modern architecture and planning has had to do with the ability to produce not only a tangible manifestation in territory, but also "new forms of collective association, personal habit and daily life" (Holston 1989, 31). This is noticeable in the planning outline of French Hill where the southwest side of the neighborhood was left vacant to enable a view toward the Old City and the Temple Mount. Moreover, the attempt to create a visual axis between the frontier new settlement and the historical center of Jerusalem's Old City contributed to the symbolic construction of the settlement being part of "united Jerusalem."

The attempt to colonize East Jerusalem was not just territorial, but also to create a new sense of belonging and superiority among the Jerusalem (Jewish) inhabitants in their new neighborhoods. Thus, for example, special attention was given to the new street names that were named after military events understood by Israelis to be heroic, such as: Mavo Hamaavak (the Struggle Alley), the Partizan Alley, Mavo Hahitnadvut (the Volunteering Alley, commemorating Jewish volunteers during World War II), and HaEtzel and HaLehi Streets, recognizing Jewish militant groups who fought the British for independence in the late 1940s (Report from the Committee of Names and Streets, No. 47, 14.5.1973, Jerusalem Municipality Archive).

To sum up this section, locating French Hill as the first settlement after the 1967 war to link West Jerusalem and the Hebrew University Campus on Mount Scopus had a fundamental role in the process of the Israeli territorialization of the city. It marked the edges of the "unification" of the city post-1967, and through the planning apparatus produced a seemingly natural and historically based frontier, which enabled the extensive development of Jewish neighborhoods on Palestinian expropriated land. By so doing, an ongoing process of normalizing the occupation of East Jerusalem was taking place, producing a new cognitive map of a unified Jerusalem as the Jewish capital.

The Urban Frontier

The location of French Hill with its proximity to a number of Palestinian areas, such as Issawiya and Shuafat, meant that total control or removal of Palestinians in the Jewish neighborhood would be difficult or impossible. Both geographically and symbolically, the frontier location of French Hill is significant; it is geographically surrounded by contested landscapes, today including a portion of the separation wall.[3] It watches (and is indeed watched by) Shuafat, the nearby Palestinian refugee camp, and it marks the edge of the city as it is situated by the main road that leads to the Judaean Desert. Indeed, as argued by Pullan (2011), studies of contested frontier zones tend to focus on states or regions rather than cities, where, according to Ron (2003) the colonial frontier is conceived as a remote and radicalized region, a resource of Terra Nullius. On the other hand, despite strict attempts to command urban frontiers through controlling practices such as planning, housing regulations, etc., cities do not normally have the apparatus available to states to control frontiers (Pullan 2011). The situation of French Hill is an example of such an urban frontier. There, the increasing movement of Palestinians into the neighborhood is a result of the geopolitical conditions where Israeli surveillance and control over East Jerusalem's Palestinian neighborhoods cause unequal distribution of resources and infrastructure, poverty, social, and physical deterioration.

A closer view of daily activities reveals that Palestinian presence in the neighborhood is due to public services that are located there. For example, the local commercial center in HaEtzel Street serves not just Jewish inhabitants, but also Palestinians from nearby neighborhoods such as Issawiya, Shuafat, Beit Hanina, and Beit La'hiya as customers. The local branch of HaPoalim Bank, in HaHaganah Street serves both the Jewish and Arab population, as does the post office in HaHail Street, and a car insurance agency that is owned by a Palestinian. The unequal distribution of infrastructure and services between West and East Jerusalem is indeed one of the main reasons why Palestinians cross the border (Conflict in Cities interviews archive, Northern Site, file 14, 2005).

The proximity of the French Hill neighborhood to the Hebrew University Campus attracts Palestinian students (the majority of which are Israeli citizens) who rent accommodation in the neighborhood. Sharing apartments is very common, and there are some cases of mixed Palestinians and Israelis. HaEtzel and Bar-Kochva Streets are the most common areas for students, due to their proximity to the university and because they are relatively cheap. No formal Palestinian residency statistics exist, but from a survey of names on mailboxes in these streets, we learned that the number of Palestinians living in this area is stable. For example: in 17 HaEtzel Street, five out of twenty-four apartments had Arabic names written in Hebrew characters on their mailboxes in 2005, with six Arabic names in 2010. In 16 HaEtzel Street, four out of twenty-one apartments had Arabic names written in Hebrew characters in 2005 and two in 2010. In 16 Bar-Kochva Street, one out of twelve apartments had an Arabic name written in Hebrew letters on their mailbox and the same in 2010. The Palestinian students use all the facilities in the area, including the bank, post office, supermarket, and some coffee shops (Saja Kilani, interview, August 8, 2006). This is perceived as a threat by some Jewish residents: "I went to the café in the commercial center; it was full of Arabs. I didn't feel comfortable and thus I asked for a takeaway coffee. . . . We don't [want to] drink coffee in Ramallah. There is an economic interest for the shops in the commercial center and thus Arabs are there" (Bracha, interview, January 29, 2006). Like other colonial cities, despite the spatiopolitical divisions along ethnonational and racial lines (Robinson 1997), there is an ongoing flow of labor (in the Jerusalem case, Palestinian workers) to the "white neighborhoods" (in Jerusalem, to French Hill and many other Jewish neighborhoods). This was observed as early as the beginning of the 1970s (*Giv'aton*, the French Hill local newspaper, March 1975, Jerusalem Municipality Archive).

From the early 2000s, during the escalating violence and tension between Israel and the Palestinians, the frontier characteristics of the French Hill area attracted some major Palestinian bombings and other attacks.[4] Hence, the Palestinian presence in French Hill was heavily contested and feared by many Israelis. One of these conflicts was around the presence of Palestinian children and youth in a playground situated at the edge of the neighborhood that faced east toward their own village of Issawiya and was far superior to any play area in their own vicinity. As a result of continued protests by the Jewish residents of French Hill, the Jerusalem Municipality removed most of the playground furniture to stop the Issawiya children from coming to this playground. The displeasure of some of the Jewish population in the neighborhood at the use and/or appropriation of space by Palestinians is expressed in the words of Uri Michaeli, the head of the local municipality of the French Hill neighborhood at that time:

> Gan Hashlosha was built as a memorial for three soldiers who were killed in Lebanon. No one has ever forbid Issawiya's children from entering the playground and they were welcomed at first, but in the last two years the place has become a real bother. Issawiya's children took over the playground, drove out the Jewish children with threats and knives, teased the adults and harassed the girls. Whole families started coming to the playground, although it has no sanitary facilities for so many visitors. The children of French Hill stopped coming. The activity in the garden lasted till late at night, with shouting and screaming, until many of the neighbors seriously considered moving from their houses. (Interview, September 29, 2000).

Indeed, below the surface of these arguments, there is an additional layer, elusive but also significant, that is linked to the fear and anxiety associated with the presence of the Other. As the works of Sandercock (2000) and Bauman (2006) reveal, the fear of the Other is a central component in the discourse of urban politics. Furthermore, the presence of fear in urban space is not a simple reflection of social reality but rather itself a mechanism that produces "reality," one that is mediated through discourses of fear and order. This is illustrated in the words of the then head of the communal administration of French Hill: "Tomorrow I will be asked to open an Arab school, and the day after to build a mosque. Each person should live in his neighborhood—as I do not want to have Haredim [ultraorthodox Jews] here neither do I want Arabs . . . I am afraid that French Hill will be occupied by Issawiya" (Gideon Yeger, cited in Hasson 2009).

Fear in its political dimension is intensified when the city undergoes significant transformations that produce political discourse that is, in turn, shaped by those that fear. To some extent, the presence of Palestinians coming from the neighboring Palestinian districts, as well as Palestinian students renting apartments and using public space in French Hill is a good example of the way in which the discourse of fear focuses on the "what and whom" we should be afraid of. For Israelis fear is mostly intermittent, sometimes suppressed through their culture of occupation, but occasionally made immediate and visible through challenges like the situation in French Hill. Because they are under occupation, the fear of Palestinians could be seen as more consistent and unbroken, but for them as well, French Hill makes it clear and visible as they venture into "enemy" territory with only limited means of escape or relief. Important to both groups, and to our discussion here is the spatial dimension of fear, which "does not just involve a relationship between the individual and a variety of societal structures; it is embedded in a network of moral and political geographies" (Smith and Pain 2008).

Strategies for Survival

It is important to reiterate the primary reason why most Palestinians have moved to French Hill: they desire a better place to live. Homes and neighborhoods, with a good level of housing stock and neighborhood services, are generally denied to them in their own communities. But although French Hill offers better physical accommodation, is it a better place to live? This may be considered from two points of view, Israelis and Palestinians in French Hill, and the Israeli reaction to their inroads. With respect to the latter, opposition has become more entrenched and more vocal. While the presence of Palestinians in public spaces such as the French Hill commercial center and playground might be perceived by Jewish residents as a relatively minor phenomenon that can be controlled, the permanent presence of Palestinians who buy and rent property in the neighborhood is a much more contested subject. There has been not only an institutionalized attempt to severely limit Palestinians from living in property in areas designated for Israeli habitation, but also an extensive public discourse intended to reinforce the ban; for example, in September 2010, a public "Rabbis' Letter" called for Jews not to let Arabs rent apartments in their communities.[5] This declaration states that anyone renting his apartment to an Arab is doing harm—both in the eyes of God and for his fellow man.

As far as Palestinians are concerned, the advantages and disadvantages of living in French Hill are far more complex. The wider geopolitical conditions with respect to the city of Jerusalem should also be noted here as a central component in the explanation of this phenomenon. For many years, the Israeli authorities have pursued a policy of limiting new housing in Palestinian areas of Jerusalem, and more recently, the demolition of homes built without permits. For Palestinians who have the blue Jerusalem residency identification card, living outside Jerusalem's new borders endangers their status as Jerusalemites, while for Palestinians with Israeli citizenship this new reality complicates their mobility.[6] Hence, after the construction of the wall began, thousands of Palestinians returned to the city in order to protect their residency status as well as some of their rights. As a result, there has been an intensification of the housing shortage in East Jerusalem, with an accompanying rapid increase in housing prices of about 50 percent (IPCC 2005) that created pressure on the housing market. All of these factors have resulted in some Palestinians with Jerusalem identification cards or Israeli citizenship, who have the economic ability, moving into Jewish neighborhoods.

This phenomenon reveals further complexities: Israeli Palestinians, who have a longer history of living near or next to Israelis and usually speak fluent Hebrew, tend to be more comfortable with such a move. Jerusalem Palestinians, who may or may not speak good Hebrew and live under more recent and harsh occupation, with pressure from their fellow Palestinians to avoid fraternizing with Israelis, are not. At the same time, it should be noted that this is an upper middle class practice; mortgages are generally not available for such purchases by Palestinians, and cash payments are the norm. Yet, although economic means makes the endeavor possible, the potential for political pitfalls is evident in an interview (April 13, 2010) with Mustafa, a Palestinian who is an Israeli citizen, who moved to the French Hill in 2005: "In the year 2000 we almost bought a 'villa' in [Israeli] Pisgat Zeev. Then the Second Intifada started, there was a tension and I knew that we could not move to Pisgat Zeev. . . . So, we searched for a place we liked. We did not want to live in [Palestinian] Shuafat; the municipal services, schools and infrastructure are not good there. Because of the Intifada, there is often a flying checkpoint at the entrance to Shuafat, and if they stop you, you cannot get to work on time in the city." Mustafa notes that French Hill is close to some of the Palestinian commercial and social centers such as Sheikh Jarrah, Wadi Joz, Beit Hanina, and the main road to Ramallah, thus enabling contact with the Palestinian side, while on the other hand his family can enjoy "modern infrastructure, municipal services. Here there is security and sovereignty, it is not abandoned" (ibid.). These, as well as nearby Shuafat, are mostly middle-class Palestinian neighborhoods supplying shops and services appropriate to their residents. The geopolitics of the situation is tempered by specific needs and familiar practices.

Palestinians who wish to buy a property in the French Hill must negotiate with Jewish estate agents or deal directly with individual Jewish vendors who will often maximize their material gain in selling property to Palestinians. In some cases, they are very reluctant to sell to Palestinians. This issue was raised by Antuan, a Christian-Palestinian lawyer, and an Israeli citizen who is married to a Jerusalem Palestinian. Antuan bought his apartment in 2002; it was during the Second Intifada, and a spate of attacks and the killing of Israelis in the French Hill area brought house prices down. Despite the relatively low housing prices at that time, Antuan mentioned that some of the Israeli sellers refused to sell their apartments to Palestinians (interview, April 9, 2010).

Indeed, the discussion of the politics of "free market" dynamic vis-à-vis ethnic and racial exclusion is well known in the literature, such as the case of American racial neighborhood covenants excluding African Americans from buying or renting housing in "white" neighborhoods (Massey and Denton 1993). It compares closely with Jerusalem where the "fear of Arabness," a term coined by Dahan-Kalev (2010), is a central mechanism of racializing the Other, in other words, representing and defining Palestinians on the basis of racial categories that are used to justify social biases and discrimination.

Beyond the social obstacles, as a lawyer who represents other Palestinian families that purchase property in the French Hill, Antuan stated: "Arabs who buy here are economically stable, so they can buy every apartment they are interested in. I personally know around twenty families who bought property. . . . If you look at these families—they are each in a better economic situation than the average Israeli family. They can afford '*tosefet Aravi*'" (interview).

The Hebrew term *tosefet Aravi*, used by Antuan, has also been repeated by other interviewees. Literally meaning "an additional price for Arabs," charged by Israeli vendors, it has become a common expression, codifying the sole access of Palestinians to the housing market in Jewish neighborhoods, while financially ensuring that Palestinian buyers offer 20 to 25 percent more for property in the neighborhood. An estate agent who lives and works in French Hill states: "The Arab buyers are offering better prices than the Israelis . . . it creates a dilemma for the vendor. Some Jews will never sell their flats to Arabs, they say I'll never do it to my neighbors' but some others will. As a property agent I will never do it" (Abraham, interview, January 29, 2006). Indeed, contrary to the image of a backward or less worldly social group, as is often presented in Israeli public discourse, Palestinian residents who are economically able to buy property in French Hill are upper middle class and often better educated than the average Israeli residents; many of them are professionals or academics searching for a better housing environment, as stated by Mustafa: "We were looking for an apartment. . . . We wanted a neighborhood that we liked, with good infrastructure. French Hill is a nice place to live; the neighbors knew we are Arabs, they were nice.... All we want is to live peacefully" (interview).

But despite the fact that class and the modern Western lifestyle of the Palestinian inhabitants of French Hill is an implicit condition for their presence there, from the Jewish side it is just the beginning of a rapid slide to losing demographic dominance in the neighborhood. This dilemma, as suggested by Rabinowitz (1994) accentuates the tension between the collective ethos of Zionist territoriality and, what has become central to the Israel's economy, a capitalist mode of free housing market dynamics where personal economic gain dominates. In the words of a Jewish resident, "In French Hill, especially in Ha-Etzel Street, the process [of Arabization] is rapid. The Arabs in our area are upper middle class. They come from the North [of Israel]—one of them is a lawyer and following his arrival another member of his family joined.... It starts with the arrival of good people but I am afraid that during the years some negative elements will also live here" (Ariella, interview, January 29, 2006).

In the end, housing does not necessarily make up all of the key features of a neighborhood, and this is where hope for some further integration meets a stumbling block. According to our findings, Palestinians in French Hill do not partake of many local activities. They do not send their children to the local, Hebrew-language school: "Initially we did not want to live in a neighborhood which is entirely Jewish since there is a problem with the education of our children ... when we decided to move to the French Hill we decided to send our children to the Anglican School, though it is expensive and far away" (Antuan, interview). Beyond that, Antuan echoes a common experience among Palestinians residing in French Hill who do not socialize with Jewish Israelis, and their use of neighborhood shops and services is minimal and curtailed. Mustafa notes: "We do our shopping in Shuafat, but once a week we go to the shopping mall [in Pisgat Zeev]. We have no contact with the cultural events here, the kids do not go to after-school activities here; the piano teacher is coming to teach them here, at home; we take them to visit their [non-Israeli] friends in other neighborhoods. They have no reason to play outside" (interview). Palestinians may have moved to French Hill for better housing. But at any meaningful level, they are not recognized as welcome residents of their neighborhood and cannot participate through both their own reluctance and Israeli distrust. This leaves them isolated, even caged, as a small minority in an often unfriendly, sometimes hostile, environment.

The Possibilities for Participation

In French Hill, both rights and participation are key issues, and the Palestinians fall short in both. Much has been said of the right to the city (Lefebvre 1996) in relation to the situation of Palestinian citizens in Israel (Yacobi 2009) and here we would like to focus instead on the question of participation. This can take a variety of forms; an extensive discussion of the pros and cons of participation is beyond the scope of this chapter. However, it is worth saying that we consider it here primarily in terms of an urban culture with the necessary overtones of political life that the situation in Jerusalem dictates.

Seyla Benhabib (2002) makes the important points that participation in a culture exists from within that culture, and although by nature it is shared, it may also be contested. While clearly there is more than one culture living in French Hill, we might question to what extent the place itself offers some cultural parameters that, for Palestinians and Israelis, are in some ways shared and certainly contested. To this, we might add that participation requires some level of corporate activity or public life; it is not an individual act.

To understand how place may play a role in public participation, it is worthwhile to see French Hill as a modern Westernized neighborhood in the context of an older urban tradition of Middle Eastern cities. These cities had quarters where different ethnic groups were not necessarily rigidly divided but nonetheless recognizable as such; the cities also had areas where people mixed, mostly in market areas, including coffeehouses, baths, and water sources. They saw a variety of faces, heard different languages and accents, and to some extent they discussed or argued about the matters of the day; markets were political places. In the late Ottoman Period, Jerusalem was a more mixed city, and more nuanced in its ethnic strata (Tamari 2011).

To a large extent, a local and customary order persisted in the city although this was rarely comprehended by foreign (mostly Western) travelers who, from the nineteenth century, describe the city as having four quarters based upon religious divisions. Tamari (2011, 66) argues that the confessional city was primarily reinforced by the British after 1917. While it would be difficult to say that people had any more trust in regard for the ethnically Other than they do today, the possibilities of participating in city life were probably more institutionalized and embedded in the urban structures. We can talk about a spectrum of space from segregation, as in mosques, churches, and synagogues, to integration, as in markets. In between, people (men) frequented favorite cafes, where they met friends and acquaintances and where they knew they were welcome and avoided ones where they felt uncomfortable. On the whole, they maintained neighborly relations that formed the basis of trade, patronage, and, more generally, everyday life. In modern terminology, we could say that the city center provided places for mediating difference.

As we noted, Israel has for the most part embraced modern planning and architecture that, as disciplines, have mostly neglected such a mediated environment; at best, they have organized cities and neighborhoods in terms of functional typologies with little reflection of the nuanced social structures that are common in the Middle East. At worst, they have extended and reinforced the planning policies that separated peoples on the basis of ethnic affiliation. Following in the footsteps of British planning (Kendall 1948), the Israeli settlements in East Jerusalem have been designed as autonomous enclaves, divided from Palestinian areas by valleys and bypass roads rather than by urban places in which social and economic activity might develop. If we look today at where there is some interaction between Palestinians and Israelis, it often happens in the most mundane areas of life—markets, petrol stations, some restaurants, or in French Hill, in the supermarket, post office, and bank (Conflict in Cities fieldwork archive, Northern Site, files 4, 13, 23, 24). However, these places are relatively few, and encounters tend to be fleeting.

With respect to the geopolitics of neighborhoods, there is a clash of scales, between everyday life and the big political picture. French Hill can be said to some extent to be a microcosm of the Palestine-Israel conflict, and rather than the slow and undramatic "murmur of urban political discourse" that Appadurai (1996) claims to commonly characterize the confluence of local and global, Jerusalem's high profile means that even the most innocuous of actions are quickly thrust onto the world stage. At the same time, the lack of balance between the everyday acts of Israelis and Palestinians reflects the asymmetry of the larger political situation, and people who are caught up in these circumstances are forced to live in a big but skewed picture. In short, daily acts regularly become issues of sovereignty and, as Hannah Arendt (1989, 234–235) has made clear, plurality and sovereignty do not mix.

One might ask to what extent living in French Hill is for its Palestinian minority an act of resistance, in itself, a form of participation as a member of one's nation. For example, while many of the middle-class Palestinian residents of French Hill see their residency as a "strategy of survival," some underline the political dimension of their decision to move to a colonial neighborhood: "we broke the stereotypes against Arabs. They [the Jewish neighbors] feel that we are part of this place. . . . If you will measure the socio-economic ability of the Arabs in the neighborhood, it is much higher than the average Jewish people. . . . Our presence here has a symbolic meaning; it is even a symbolic de-colonization" (Antuan, interview).

While this may offer some satisfaction as an act of ongoing subversion, at least at a symbolic level, the problem of everyday participation in one's neighborhood and community is not solved. Rather, there is the question to what extent Palestinians need to relinquish parts of their own culture in order to achieve even a minimal level of integration. How compromised are they? To buy or not to buy becomes an existential question. This seems to be most important in the question of Palestinian polity; not only how much can they participate in Israeli culture and institutions in French Hill, but to what extent are they participant in their own culture and politics if they live in such a neighborhood? While they may enjoy some small level of acceptance within Israeli circles in French Hill, this is fundamentally opposed to the wishes of the larger Palestinian entity that desires the end of the occupation and their own liberation. Arendt's basic description of the polity of the polis as "speaking and acting together" (1989, 183) is mostly removed from the French Hill Palestinians who live apart from the wider Palestinian collective. It is at this fundamental level—not in the withholding of integration with Israelis, but in their separation from Palestinian society—that participation is primarily denied to them.

Conclusion

Ideally, the urban sphere, in its density and diversity, could serve as a space that is "open to flows of people" (Katznelson 1997, 57). Such a liberal perspective relies heavily on the belief that the city has the potential for the production of an "enabling space" that might disrupt the existing hierarchies and boundaries of ethnic and class structures. Yet, as we have detailed, such a view is only partial in the context of Jerusalem's settlements, which is divided not only along the Jewish/Arab partition but also according to other ethnic divisions that stem from the nature of the Israeli settler society.

The most significant contribution of this chapter is that it looks not solely at macro processes, namely occupation, colonization, and bordering, but rather its analysis refers to facts on the ground from the point of view of the ground. This complementary view of geopolitical processes reveals the paradoxical situation of colonial territories such as French Hill. As we have detailed, French Hill is a well-established settlement, "normalized" by different practices such as architecture and infrastructure planning, and at the same time its frontier location on the old border makes it a space of negotiation, unexpected migration, and habitation. The paradox of contested frontier and work-a-day suburb is typical of many Israeli settlements, but French Hill is particularly vulnerable to such a strained dichotomy because of the challenge to the homogeneous Jewish population by its Palestinian residents.

Palestinians are a small minority in French Hill and likely to remain so for the foreseeable future. Nonetheless, their presence carries with it larger implications and even some concrete benefits. The Palestinians do enjoy better housing and municipal services; for some, there is the sense of beating the system, and for others, a form of resistance. The Israeli interests and concerns are more difficult to pinpoint and many would argue that the phenomenon is wholly negative. But at the risk of sounding patronizing, it would be fair to say that the Palestinian residents of French Hill are a small chink in the stone of a politically driven colonial planning system that is one-sided, unjust, and needing of reform. It is also important that Israelis see Palestinians and hear Arabic in a city where many segments of the population never encounter it.

But more to the point would be to look at the Palestinian residents in the neighborhood as it pertains to both groups. Can we talk about shared space under occupation in any way? After all, multicultural cities today in the West are seen as dealing with the Other, particularly where destinies may exist in tandem. To a small extent, public and commercial spaces in French Hill are shared and at a minimal level, some experiences of the neighborhood become applicable to all. This is typical of many middle-class Western cities where, in Bauman's words, "strangers meet, remain in each other's proximity, and interact for a long time without stopping being strangers to each other" (2006, 6). At the same time, Jerusalem is a highly contested city and normal comments on, and aspirations for, multiculturalism seem feeble here. The immigration of ethnic and racial minorities to "white" middle-class neighborhoods is not a peculiar Israeli phenomenon and has been covered widely in the literature; however, the discourses of inclusion and exclusion, borders and boundaries, demographic control, security, and separation attached to it "resonates with a long-standing discourse among the public as well as among scholars and politicians who frame Israel as a regional ghetto"—which is both "refuge" and "island" (Monterescu 2009).

Two interrelated possibilities of sharing may be cited in the French Hill example, possibilities which in themselves are powerful, although it is too soon to understand their impact. First, both groups share the problem of having their private lives regularly catapulted into the public realm and world stage. Yet, both groups are middle class, educated, and living relatively conventional lives in this suburb of Jerusalem. This raises the second point: in many ways these two groups are remarkably similar economically and professionally if not politically. Ultimately, will such profound similarities help to form a quiet if not friendly sharing of the neighborhood? And, would not a middle-class initiative, like establishing a joint Palestinian-Israeli school with instruction in Hebrew and Arabic, go a long way to easing tensions and preparing the next generation for a certain amount of shared space? It is in a neighborhood like French Hill, with its middle-class populations, that such schemes might bear fruit.

Although this research raises many questions at this point, it does make clear that geopolitics in contested cities is happening at the minute and everyday level. As we have discussed, the geopolitics of cities and the shaping of their territorial borders and social boundaries—both externally (the city in relation to its region) and internally (between the city's neighborhoods)—are determined not solely through military acts but rather through the emergence of discourses and forces attached to technologies of control, in our case, planning. At the same time, patterns of migration such as the case of Palestinians moving to French Hill and the flow capital in the housing free market are much more loosely related to formal structures, and they sometimes act as a controlling or unjust policy that has backfired.

Geopolitical perspective is a useful analytical framework for studying planning and the production of urban space that subverts the traditional distinction between domestic and international affairs habitually taken for granted in political geography. We would also conclude that the emergence of Palestinian inhabitants in Jerusalem's colonial neighborhoods that were established after the 1967 war mark new forms of urban dynamics that form inclusion and exclusion as well as some new spatiopolitical possibilities.

Following Holston (1989) we can conclude that the city is a space in which residents oppose and undermine dominant narratives of the state and capital. Simultaneously, communities in the city create alternative local narratives that do not necessarily reflect the rationale of the nation or of capital, nor do they reflect the social hierarchy or the power relations that create it. As this chapter shows, the production of urban space in colonial neighborhoods cannot be understood solely through the binary analysis of top-down processes and policies. Rather, a deeper understanding demands acknowledging the bottom-up initiatives and their roles. As Lefebvre suggests, one can see how a counterspace can insert itself into spatial reality "against the Eye and the Gaze, against quantity and homogeneity, against power and the arrogance of power" (Lefebvre 1996, 382).

At the contested boundaries of Jerusalem, it is not surprising to find radical urban frontiers manufactured by planning apparatus that have dominated the city since 1967. But the frontier neighborhood because of its "front line" geographical location enables, to some extent, negotiation between Palestinian buyers and Jewish vendors, which in turn cracks the demographic homogeneity dictated by the colonial project.

This is the paradox of current colonial urbanism in Jerusalem: on the one hand, the forceful effect of the normalization of occupation was orchestrated by Israeli law and planning and state regulations that privilege Jewish citizens. On the other hand, the opening of the market—to all intents and purposes a normalization process—countered these policies and practices when it started attracting Palestinian population. Indeed, normalization has the potential to not only help the course of Judaization, but also may threaten it by breaking ethnonational dichotomies. To some extent this may be expected and it is worth considering the French Hill situation in a broader context: except in the most rigidly authoritarian cases, cities accommodate, at least to some extent, the flow of different urban populations. Even in heavily contested situations, such as Jerusalem, there are at certain times and places some level of integration of ethnic groups. French Hill appears to reflect a version of this, despite the peculiarities of its own conditions. At the same time, it would be wrong to attempt to idealize such instability or to overestimate the possibilities of interaction achieved from it, especially under conditions of duress such as the Palestinians' experience. Relying on the possibilities offered by free-market housing through the *tosefet Aravi* as a vehicle for achieving the right to the city is problematic, primarily because it overlooks the promise of the city to be a space for neighboring. In this context, we further conclude that neighboring in its modern sense, with the full possibilities and demands of participation in a neighborhood, demands equality, on both a legal and a practical level, which cannot be achieved in present colonial conditions on the one hand and in the context of growing reliance on individuals' socioeconomic mobility on the other.

Notes

This chapter forms a part of the research of "Conflict in Cities and the Contested State," funded by the United Kingdom's Economic and Social Research Council (RES-060-25-0015), and the Marie Curie Intra-European Fellowship "Neighboring and the Geopolitics of Ethnically 'Mixed Cities'" (No. 252369).

1. The figures given in the introduction are confirmed by other sources. Out of approximately seven thousand inhabitants in French Hill, there are around fifty Palestinian Arab families, mainly from Israel's northern region. Also, according to media reports there are four hundred Palestinian families that moved to Jewish neighborhoods—mainly in French Hill, Pisgat Ze'ev, and Neve Ya'akov. For details see Hasson 2009.

2. Palestinian uprisings; the First Intifada began in 1987 and the Second Intifada (or al-Aqsa Intifada) in 2000.

3. Within the scope of this chapter, we are not able to discuss the political dimension of this structure. However, it is important to note that the construction of the wall in Jerusalem/al-Quds represents a special case; it creates a tangible delineation of greater Israeli Jerusalem, including many of its settlements (that is, the area "annexed" by Israel in 1967—illegally, according to international law). It also includes some Palestinian areas that have been "cherry-picked" by Israel. The immediate effect of the wall is to annex de facto the settlements/neighborhoods within the municipal boundaries (in total more than 4 km²). The Palestinian neighborhoods, constituting 3.2 km² within Jerusalem's municipal boundaries, are excluded; that is, they are on the other side of the wall. Thus their inhabitants unilaterally are deprived of their status as Jerusalemites. Around forty thousand Palestinian Jerusalemites are separated from the city and its services, and an additional sixty thousand to ninety thousand Palestinian Jerusalemites living in the areas surrounding Jerusalem are isolated from the city. This spatial distortion is aimed at officially reducing the percentage of the city's Palestinian population.

4. A number of these were concentrated at French Hill bus stops for Israeli buses going to the settlements north and east of the city; see Pullan (2007, 63–64).

5. For example, many mortgages have been available only to people who have served in the Israel Defence Forces. All Jewish Israelis are routinely conscripted but Arab Israelis are exempted.

6. Jerusalem residency identification cards are issued by the Israeli authorities on their own terms. Residency in Jerusalem is based upon an Israeli census carried out in 1967; Pales-

tinians who spend time outside of Jerusalem may lose their status, and those who marry West Bank residents may not obtain Jerusalem status for them. Besides the right to live in the city, they enjoy Israeli social welfare programs. They are not citizens of Israel. On the contrary, Palestinians with Israeli citizenship constitute approximately 20 percent of Israel's population; they are subject to Israeli laws and, like Israeli Jews, are not supposed to pass into the Palestinian areas of the West Bank.

References

Abowd, Thomas. 2007. "National Boundaries, Colonized Spaces: The Gendered Politics of Residential Life in Contemporary Jerusalem." *Anthropological Quarterly* 80 (4): 997–1034.

Appadurai, Arjun. 1996. *Modernity at Large: Cultural Dimensions of Globalization.* Vol. 1. Minneapolix: University of Minnesota Press.

Arendt, Hannah. 1989. *The Human Condition.* Chicago: The University of Chicago Press. [Original edition, 1958.]

Bauman, Zygmunt. 2006. *Liquid Fear.* Cambridge, UK: Polity Press.

Benhabib, Seyla. 2002. *The Claims of Culture: Equality and Diversity in the Global Era.* Princeton: Princeton University Press.

CBS. 2008. *Population Census.* Jerusalem: Central Bureau of Statistics.

Dahan-Kalev, Henriette. 2010. "Zionism, Post-Zionism and Fear of Arabness." In *Fear Itself: Reasoning the Unreasonable,* edited by Stephen Hessel and Michèle Huppert, 163–174. Amsterdam: Rodopi.

Gillette, Howard. 2010. *Civitas by Design: Building Better Communities, from the Garden City to the New Urbanism.* University of Pennsylvania Press

Hasson, Nir. 2009. "The Palestinians in the French Hill Enjoy a High Life-Quality and Get Use to the Racism." *Haaretz,* July 24. http://www.haaretz.co.il/news/education/1.1272704. [Hebrew.]

Holston, James. 1989. *The Modernist City: An Anthropological Critique of Brasília.* Chicago: The University of Chicago Press.

IPCC. 2005. *The Wall.* Jerusalem: International Peace and Cooperation Center.

Katznelson, Ira. 1997. "Social Justice, Liberalism and the City." In *The Urbanization of Injustice,* edited by Andy Merrifield and Erik Swyngedouw, 45–64. London: New York University Press.

Kendall, Henri. 1948. *Jerusalem: The City Plan, Preservation and Development During the British Mandate, 1918–1948.* London: H.M.S.O.

Lefebvre, Henri. 1996. *Writings on Cities.* Translated by Eleonore Kofman and Elizabeth Lebas. Oxford: Blackwell.

Massey, Douglas S., and Nancy A. Denton. 1993. *American Apartheid: Segregation and the Making of the Underclass.* Cambridge: Harvard University Press.

Monterescu, Daniel. 2009. "To Buy or Not to Be: Trespassing the Gated Community." *Public Culture* 21 (2): 403–430.

Pullan, Wendy. 2007. "Contested Mobilities and the Spatial Topography of Jerusalem." In *Contested Spaces: Sites, Representations and Histories of Conflict,* edited by Louise Purbrick, Jim Aulich, and Graham Dawson, 49–73. London: Palgrave Macmillan.

———. 2011. "Frontier Urbanism: The Periphery at the Centre of Contested Cities." *Journal of Architecture* 16 (1): 15–35. doi: 10.1080/13602365.2011.546999.

Rabinowitz, Dan. 1994. "To Sell or Not to Sell? Theory versus Practice, Public versus Private, and the Failure of Liberalism: The Case of Israel and Its Palestinian Citizens." *American Ethnologist* 21 (4): 827–844.

Robinson, Jennifer. 1997. "The Geopolitics of South African Cities: States, Citizens, Territory." *Political Geography* 16 (5): 365–386.

Ron, James. 2003. *Frontiers and Ghettos: State Violence in Serbia and Israel.* Berkeley: University of California Press.

Sandercock, Leonie. 2000. "When Strangers Become Neighbours: Managing Cities of Difference." *Planning Theory and Practice* 1 (1): 13–30.

Smith, Susan J., and Rachel Pain. 2008. "Fear: Critical Geopolitics and Everyday Life." In *Fear: Critical Geopolitics and Everyday Life*, edited by Susan J. Smith and Rachel Pain, 1–19. London: Ashgate.

Tamari, Selim. 2011. "Confessionalism and Public Space in Ottoman and Colonial Jerusalem." In *Cities and Sovereignty: Identity Politics in Urban Spaces*, edited by Diane E. Davis and Nora Libertun de Duren, 59–84. Bloomington: Indiana University Press.

Yacobi, Haim. 2008. "Academic Fortress: The Planning of the Hebrew University Campus on Mount Scopus." In *Urban Universities and Development: The International Experience*, edited by David Perry and Wim Wievel, 257–272. Cambridge, MA: Lincoln Institute of Land Policy.

———. 2009. *The Jewish-Arab City: Spatio-politics in a Mixed Community.* New York: Routledge.

Appendix: The Settlements

In the 1967 War, Israel occupied several territories at the expense of its Arab neighbors: the Sinai Peninsula and the Gaza Strip (previously controlled by Egypt); the West Bank, including the eastern part of the city of Jerusalem (Jordan); and the Golan Heights (Syria). Following the Camp David Accords (September 1978) and the subsequent peace treaty between Egypt and Israel (March 1979), the Sinai Peninsula was returned to Egypt. All the other territories have remained under different scales of Israeli control to this day.

Immediately after the 1967 War, Israel began establishing communities in the conquered territories, commonly known as "Jewish settlements." These communities, some of which are now nearly fifty years old, vary considerably in nature (from agricultural villages and small exurban communities, to full-fledged towns and urban neighborhoods, to "single building" settlements established in densely inhabited Palestinian urban areas); size (from few dozens to the more than sixty thousand residents of the Ultraorthodox community of Modi'in Illit); genesis (from state-sponsored planned towns to the "illegal outposts" established by activist groups formally acting outside the boundaries of Israeli law); and administrative status in the Israeli system of local authorities. Throughout the years, a limited number of these communities were evacuated by Israel. This is the case of the settlements in Sinai (and notably of the town of Yamit in the northern part of the peninsula) in 1982, following the Israeli-Egyptian agreement; of the communities of the Gaza Strip in 2005, in the context of the Disengagement Plan from the area implemented by the then Israeli Prime Minister Ariel Sharon; and of smaller settlements in the West Bank. Overall, however, the settler population has experienced a steady and impressive growth in the last five decades.

Before proceeding further, however, some terminological clarifications are in order. Throughout this collection, the term "settlements" identifies all Jewish communities (towns, villages, neighborhoods) established in the areas conquered by Israel during the 1967 War (sometime referred to as the Occupied Territories), irrespective of their status in international and Israeli law and geographical location. In the terminology adopted in this collection, the terms "Israel" and "West Bank," wherever used to identify specific territories, refer to the armistice lines of the 1949 between Israel and its Arab neighbors (and, for what concerns the West Bank in particular, to the armistice line agreed on by Israel and Jordan, the so-called Green Line): the term "West Bank" therefore indicates the area of Mandatory Palestine controlled by Jordan before the 1967 War (including the eastern portion of the city of Jerusalem); the term "Israel" (or "Israel proper") refers to the de facto borders of the State of Israel in the period 1949–1967. Together with the Golan Heights, Israel, the Gaza Strip and the West Bank will be sometimes be referred to in the book as "Israel/Palestine" to indicate the territory currently under Israeli control. In addition, in the aftermath of the 1967 War, the Israeli government created in the West Bank the territorial entity that is now commonly known as "East Jerusalem," an area of some seventy square kilometers that includes the Old City of Jerusalem and tens of square kilometers of its surroundings. East Jerusalem is (along with the Golan Heights) the only area that Israel has formally annexed and currently constitutes an integral part of the Israeli municipality of Jerusalem.

As of today, we can count 270–280 settlements, including some thirty communities located in Golan Heights and between 240 and 250 settlements in the West Bank (of which some hundred are "illegal outposts").[1] The latest and most accurate data indicate a total settler population of about 585,000–590,000 units (end of 2013), out of a total Israeli population of 8,130,000: the Israel Central Bureau of Statistics (CBS) counted about 356,000 residents in "Judea and Samaria" and 20,000 in the Golan Heights; following estimates based on official figures provided by the CBS and the Jerusalem Institute for Israel Studies, the number of Israeli settlers in East Jerusalem at the same date was about 211,000.[2] Major population centers, each counting more than 10,000 residents, are the "new neighborhoods" established in East Jerusalem (Gilo, Ramot Allon, Neve Ya'akov, Pisgat Ze'ev, Har Homa, Ramat Shlomo, and East Talpiot) and a few large communities in the West Bank (Modi'in Illit, Beitar Illit, Ma'ale Adumim, Ariel, and Giv'at Ze'ev), whose combined population amounted to 330,000 residents in 2011; at the same date, nine other settlements in the West Bank (Efrat, French Hill, Kiryat Arba, Alfei Menashe, Ramat Eshkol, Oranit, Karnei Shomron, Kochav Ya'akov, and Beit El) had a population between 5,000 and 10,000 units (*B'Tselem* 2013)—see maps 1, 2.

Various estimates have shown that the vast majority of settlers (between two thirds and four fifths, depending on the definitions adopted) live in large suburban communities around Jerusalem (Allegra 2013, forthcoming). A large part of this population is constituted by the residents of East Jerusalem and of the five main "settlements blocs"—as they are usually referred to—namely the clusters around the communities of Ma'ale Adumim, Modi'in Illit, Giv'at Ze'ev, Gush Etzion in the area of Jerusalem, and the cluster around the city of Ariel in the northern West Bank. Although the definition of these "blocs" has no administrative or legal standing, it loosely alludes, on the one side, to the sociopolitical fabric of the resident population, which is by and large constituted by the "quality of life settlers"—that is, by Israelis who moved beyond the Green Line in search of better housing opportunities and economic benefits rather than being motivated by ideological reasons. On the other side, the notion of settlement blocs largely coincides with the idea of "consensus settlements"—the settlements whose status is regarded as relatively noncontroversial by the vast majority of Israeli public opinion. Since the inception of Israeli-Palestinian diplomatic talks in the early 1990s, the maintenance of control over these settlement blocs, as well as on East Jerusalem, has constituted Israel's nonnegotiable condition for the definition of a border with a future Palestinian entity—although it should be noted that the vague definition of "bloc" does leave considerable scope for ambiguity in this respect. At the Camp David Summit (2000), in the context of Israeli-Palestinian peace negotiations, U.S. President Bill Clinton proposed Israel's annexation of the main settlement blocs; by his estimates, this would have brought about 80 percent of the settler population outside Jerusalem under Israeli sovereignty.

While our definition of settlements refers, strictly speaking, to human habitation, it should be noted that over time Israeli governments established an extended network of infrastructure of varying nature, destined to service the Jewish communities in the Occupied Territories and the population of Israel proper. Major examples in this respect are the system of military bases and surveillance artifacts (walls, checkpoints, etc.) and the network of dedicated roads connecting them to one another and to the Israeli road system. Furthermore, in the West Bank we also find several infrastructures catering to the interests of a wider audience: this is the case, for example, of the several industrial areas (such as the Mishor Adumim Industrial Park in the municipality of Ma'ale Adumim), and of the touristic infrastructures established within and around the Old City of Jerusalem (such as the tourist park of the City of David). The establishment and maintenance of the settlements has had huge costs so far for Israel, which include expenses for building the settlements themselves and their dedicated infrastructures; for subsidies and tax benefits directed to individual settlers as well as economic activities; and for maintaining a large security apparatus to protect the settlers.[3]

In addition to material infrastructure, and especially since the second half of the 1970s, Israel has gradually extended its legal and administrative system onto the Jewish West Bank. Today, the structure of local government of the settlements is virtually indistinguishable from the one established in Israel proper—although local authorities in the settlements tend to receive a larger proportion of public funds with respect to their equivalent in Israel.[4] As we have noted, the area of East Jerusalem is formally part of the Israeli municipality of Jerusalem. The rest of the West Bank is officially designated by Israeli authorities as "Judea and Samaria Area" (*Ezor Yehuda VeShomron*); "Judea and Samaria" is also the term used by most Israelis to refer to this area. As in Israel, Jewish local authorities in the West Bank are divided between "cities" and "local councils" (independent municipal units, differentiated by size), and "regional councils" (regional bodies governing a number of small and typically rural settlements scattered over a large area).[5] The creation of the Palestinian National Authority, starting in 1994, did not alter this framework, since the Oslo Agreements did not concern the settlements (which were included among the "final status issues" to be settled by a comprehensive peace agreement that never materialized). Israel's continuing control over the areas of the West Bank outside the main Palestinian urban centers guaranteed abundant territorial resources to enable the expansion of settlements and large, growing infrastructural investments. At least from a formal point of view, however, the status of the settlements is not completely uncontroversial for the Israeli legal and administrative system: several settlements (e.g., the "illegal outposts") have been created outside the established administrative procedures and/or (in contravention with the landmark ruling by the Israeli Supreme Court on the Elon Moreh case) on privately owned Palestinian land.[6]

The status of the settlements is even more controversial in relation to international and Israeli law. Most of the international community, including the United States and the European Union, considers the areas conquered by Israel in 1967 as "occupied territories," and therefore sees Israel as bounded by the provisions of the international law governing the conduct of states during and after armed conflict—as codified, among other documents, by the Geneva Conventions. Under the provisions of the Fourth Geneva Convention, Israel would be obliged to maintain the status quo in the occupied areas—and, importantly, forbidden to establish civilian settlements there. Israel, a signatory of the Geneva Conventions, has consistently rejected the applicability of these norms to the West Bank and Gaza, arguing that these areas constitute "contested" rather than "occupied" territories—an argument that, however, has never been accepted by the international community and most legal experts.[7]

As a final consideration, it might be worth noting also that the term "settlement" does not have a univocal Hebrew translation: settlements can be indicated with the term *hitnachalut* (a biblical term indicating the rightful possession of a piece of land) by those emphasizing the political and/or religious dimension of the settlement enterprise; or *hityashvut* (a more neutral term indicating a community, equivalent to the standard usage of the word "settlement" in English) by those who want to emphasize its more mundane, matter-of-fact dimension. At the same time, specific settlements can be indicated by referring to their administrative status in the Israeli system: settlements in East Jerusalem are, for example, commonly known as "neighborhoods" (*shchunot*), while others can be referred to, alternatively, as "towns" (*a'rim*) or, in the case of cooperative settlements, as *kibbutz, moshav* (collectivist agricultural communities), *nahal* (military agricultural communities), or *yishuv kehilati* (exurban, nonagricultural communities). All of these terms (except for *hitnachalut*) are used to indicate communities both in Israel and in the West Bank, although the model of *yishuv kehilati* was originally devised by the national-religious movement of Gush Emunim in the context of its settlement activities in the West Bank in the 1970s.

Notes

1. See for example the data provided by the Israeli nongovernmental organizations Peace Now and B'Tselem (not including the Golan Heights). The methodologies and categories used to count the settlements vary. Peace Now counts 149 settlements (of which 13 are located in East Jerusalem; another 14 settlements in East Jerusalem are listed with no population), to which 99 outposts and 9 industrial areas are added (Peace Now n.d.). B'Tselem counts 138 settlements (of which 11 are in East Jerusalem; another 4 settlements in East Jerusalem are listed with no population), plus 98 outposts and 7 settlers' enclaves in Hebron (B'Tselem 2013). Since the 1990s, the bulk of the data on Israel's settlement policy has been produced by nongovernmental organizations and institutions (such as Bimkom, B'Tselem, the Foundation for Middle East Peace, Al Haq, the Applied Research Institute of Jerusalem, and Peace Now, as well as the U.N. Office for the Coordination of Humanitarian Affairs) devoted to the monitoring of settlements' expansion and its legal and humanitarian consequences.

2. See Allegra (forthcoming). The reader should be reminded that it is difficult to estimate the settler population—and in particular in the area of Jerusalem, since Israeli figures from the Israeli CBS do not distinguish between East and West Jerusalem. The figures presented here are based on CBS (2014, table 2.15) and JIIS (2015, table III.13), although more recent data exists on the population of Judea and Samaria, which the CBS placed (end of 2014) at 371,000 units (CBS 2015, table 2.15). The figure for Golan Heights refers only to Jewish residents—not the local Arab residents with Israeli citizenship. The figure for East Jerusalem does not include a few hundred settlers living in the Holy Basin outside the Jewish quarter of the Old City.

3. There is an increasing awareness of the growing costs of Israel's settlement policy—and more broadly, of Israel's occupation of the West Bank among most Israelis. A precise measure of such costs, however, remains elusive for various reasons. In the first place, it is difficult to separate the costs linked to the settlement per se from Israel's expenses in the field of security. In the second place, the budget of Israel's settlement policy is fragmented along different ministries and agencies involved, as well as the lack of transparency of key players such as the Israeli Army and the Ministry of Defense, whose budgets are not open to scrutiny because of national security considerations. Shir Hever (2010, 51–75) is among the authors that have taken on the Herculean task of estimating the costs of the settlement policy.

4. Israel has formally maintained in the West Bank the Jordanian legal system (with the exception of East Jerusalem, where Israeli law applies); however, the latter has been repeatedly amended by the Military Orders promulgated by the military authority in charge of the administration of the area. The orders referring to the settlements, in particular, have been modeled on Israel's codes, thereby creating a de facto equivalence between the statuses of Israelis on the two sides of the Green Line. Another example of such legal creative ambiguity relates to the status of the Israeli Supreme Court, which has argued that it has no jurisdiction on areas that have not been annexed by Israel, but recognized its jurisdiction on the military agencies dependent on the Ministry of Defense that are in charge of the administration of the territories (Kretzmer 2002, 79–81; Galchinsky 2005). In any case, as Eyal Benvenisti (1989, preface) pointed out at the end of the 1980s, "the pre-June 1967 borders have faded for almost all legal purposes that reflect Israeli interest."

5. Local authorities of the West Bank (and formerly Gaza) are represented by the Judea Samaria and Gaza Council (*Mo'etzet Yehuda Shomron and 'Azza*, usually known as YESHA Council), which defends the interest of the settlers through lobbying and political campaigning.

6. These considerations came first to the attention of the Israeli public opinion with the publication of the special report on the "illegal outposts" authored by Israeli Attorney General Talya Sasson (Sasson 2005).

7. See, for example, Kretzmer (2002, 31–42), E. Benvenisti (1989, 108–114). In 1979, a U.N. Security Council resolution (n. 446 of March 22, 1979) was passed to reaffirm the applicability of the Fourth Geneva Convention to the territories occupied by Israel in 1967, including Jerusalem. In the occasion, the United States abstained from the vote, but did not exercise their right to veto it.

References

Allegra, Marco. 2013. "The Politics of Suburbia: Israel's Settlement Policy and the Production of Space in the Metropolitan Area of Jerusalem." *Environment and Planning A* 45 (3): 497–516.

———. "The Politics of Suburbia: The Suburbanization of Israel's Settlement Policy and the Production of Space in the Metropolitan Area of Jerusalem." *Theory and Criticism.* [Hebrew.] Forthcoming.

Benvenisti, Eyal. 1989. *Legal Dualism: The Absorption of the Occupied Territories into Israel.* Boulder: Westview Press.

B'Tselem. 2013. "Settlement Population, XLS." *B'Tselem.* Accessed January 31, 2016. http://www .btselem.org/download/settlement_population_eng.xls.

CBS. 2014. *Statistical Abstract of Israel 2014.* Jerusalem: Central Bureau of Statistics. http://www
.cbs.gov.il/reader/shnaton/shnatone_new.htm?CYear=2014&Vol=65&CSubject=2.

———. 2015. *Statistical Abstract of Israel 2015.* Jerusalem: Central Bureau of Statistics.

Galchinsky, Michael. 2005. "The Jewish Settlements in the West Bank: International Law and
Israeli Jurisprudence." *Israel Studies* 9 (3): 115–136.

Hever, Shir. 2010. *The Political Economy of Israel's Occupation.* London: Pluto Press.

JIIS. 2015. *Statistical Yearbook of Jerusalem.* Vol. 29. Jerusalem: Jerusalem Institute for Israel
Studies.

Kretzmer, David. 2002. *The Occupation of Justice: The Supreme Court of Israel and the Occupied
Territories.* SUNY Series in Israeli Studies. Albany: State University of New York Press.

Peace Now. n.d. "Settlements and Outposts Numbers and Data." *Peace Now.* Accessed January 31,
2016. http://peacenow.org.il/eng/sites/default/files/settlements database for publication_0.xls.

Sasson, Talya. 2005. *Unauthorized Outposts: Report for the Prime Minister.* Jerusalem: Ministry of
Justice. http://www.pmo.gov.il/SiteCollectionDocuments/PMO/Communication
/Spokesman/sason2.pdf. [Hebrew.]

Contributors

MARCO ALLEGRA is a Research Fellow at the Instituto de Ciências Sociais of the University of Lisbon and Investigador Associado at the Centro de Investigação e Estudos de Sociologia of the University Institute of Lisbon. His areas of expertise include Middle East politics, planning theory, and urban studies; his current research activities focus on Israel's settlement policy in the area of Jerusalem, and on the role of knowledge and professional expertise in the policy process. His publications include articles in *Citizenship Studies, Israel-Palestine Journal, Mediterranean Politics, The Geography Compass, Environment and Planning A, Urban Studies, International Journal of Urban and Regional Research*, and a monograph on the history of Palestinian people (Carocci, 2010).

LEE CAHANER is Chair of the Department of Multidisciplinary Studies and Senior Lecturer in the Department of Geography and Environmental studies at Oranim Academic College of Education. Her book *Modern Ultra-Orthodoxy: The Emerging Haredi Middle Class in Israel* (coauthored, 2012) was published by the Israel Democracy Institute. She has also published various other articles related to the spatial aspects of the Ultraorthodox society in Israel.

HONAIDA GHANIM is a Palestinian sociologist and anthropologist who has published various articles and studies in the fields of political and cultural sociology and gender studies and was a lecturer in different universities in Palestine. She is the author of *Reinventing the Nation: Palestinian Intellectuals and Persons of Pen in Israel 1948-2000* (Hebrew University, 2009). She also served as the editor of *On Recognition of the Jewish State* (2014), coeditor of *On the Meaning of a Jewish State* (2011), chief editor of *Qadaya Israelia* (Israeli Affairs) quarterly journal (2000–2011), and, since 2009, has served as chief editor of MADAR's *Strategic Report*.

RUTHIE GINSBURG teaches photography, visual culture, and visual testimony in the modern era and currently leads the Photolexic research group at the Minerva Center for Humanities at Tel Aviv University. Her research focuses on the visual culture related to human rights, especially from a critical perspective. Her book *And You Will Serve as Eyes for Us: Israeli Human Rights Organizations as Seen through the Camera's Eye* (2014) examines the practices of local Israeli human rights organizations working in the Occupied Territories.

DANNY GUTWEIN is Associate Professor of Modern Jewish History at the University of Haifa, Israel. His work focuses on socioeconomic analyses of various aspects of Jewish modernization, such as Jewish economic elites (Rothschilds, Schiff, Montagus), Jews in economic discourse (Marx, Weber, Sombart, Leon), Jewish nationalism, Zionism, Jewish Socialism, and modern antisemitism. He has also used a socioeconomic perspective to probe the social, political, ideological, and cultural ramifications of the privatization process in Israel (identity politics, settlements).

ARIEL HANDEL is Director of the Lexicon for Political Theory project at the Minerva Humanities Center, Tel Aviv University. His main research interests are critical political geography and political theory. Handel has published numerous journal papers and book chapters on issues of space, politics, power, and violence and is also editor-in-chief of *The Political Lexicon of the Social Protest* (2012).

ASSAF HAREL is a Visiting Assistant Professor in the Department of Anthropology at Rutgers University in New Brunswick. He is a sociocultural and visual anthropologist who conducted ethnographic fieldwork among Jewish settlers and Palestinians in the Gaza Strip and the West Bank.

MIKI KRATSMAN is the former Head of the Photography Department at the Bezalel Academy of Art and Design in Jerusalem (2006–2014) and currently Head of the Photography Department of Basis School of Art. He is the founder, and, since 2005, Chairman of Breaking the Silence (http://www.breakingthesilence .org.il/). He is the fifth recipient of the Robert Gardner Fellowship in Photography, Peabody Museum of Archaeology and Ethnology, Harvard University 2011 and the Winner of the Emet Prize for Science, Art and Culture, 2011.

EREZ MAGGOR is a PhD candidate at the Department of Sociology at New York University and an Israel Institute Doctoral Fellow. His main research interests include political economy, state theory, the politics of late-development, and comparative historical sociology. His research has appeared in *Israeli Sociology*.

DAVID NEWMAN is Dean of the Faculty of Humanities and Social Sciences at Ben-Gurion University, where he holds the chair in geopolitics. His work focuses on the territorial dimensions of ethnic conflict and the changing role and significance of borders in the contemporary world. From 1999 to 2014, he was the editor of the *International Journal of Geopolitics*. His PhD (1982) was the first academic study of West Bank settlement and the Gush Emunim movement, a topic he has revisited throughout the subsequent three decades with an ongoing analysis of the ways in which the settlement network has expanded and taken root.

AMIR PAZ-FUCHS is Senior Lecturer in Employment Law at the University of Sussex School of Law and Associate Research Fellow at the Centre for Socio-Legal Studies, University of Oxford. He specializes in theoretical analysis of employment relations and social-economic rights. His publications include *Welfare to Work: Conditional Rights in Social Policy* (2008).

WENDY PULLAN is Professor of Architecture and Urban Studies and Head of the Department of Architecture at the University of Cambridge. She was principal investigator for "Conflict in Cities and the Contested State" and now directs the Centre for Urban Conflicts Research. Her recent publications include *Locating Urban Conflicts* (coedited, 2013), *The Struggle for Jerusalem's Holy Places* (co-authored, 2013) and *Architecture and Pilgrimage 1000–1500: Southern Europe and Beyond* (coedited, 2013). She is a Fellow of Clare College, Cambridge. For further details visit: www.urbanconflicts.arct.cam.ac.uk.

YAËL RONEN is Professor of Public International Law at Sha'arei Mishpat Academic Center for Science and Law in Israel and Research Fellow at the Minerva Center for Human Rights at the Hebrew University in Jerusalem. Her areas of interest include statehood and territorial status, particularly as they intersect with questions of human rights, humanitarian law, and international criminal law. Her most recent books are *Transition from Illegal Regimes under International Law* (2011) and *The Iranian Nuclear Issue* (2010).

EREZ TZFADIA is Associate Professor of Public Policy and Administration at Sapir Collage, Israel, and his work focuses on spatial policy and politics. In 2015–2016 he was an Israel Institute Visiting Scholar at the Bildner Center for the Study of Jewish Life in the Department of Jewish Studies of Rutgers University. He earned his PhD in geography at Ben-Gurion University in 2002, and was a Lady Davis Postdoctoral Fellow at the Hebrew University in 2003. He is the coauthor of *Rethinking Israeli Space* (Routledge, 2011); *Israel since 1980* (Cambridge, 2008), and the coeditor of *Abandoning State—Surveillancing State: Social Policy in Israel, 1985–2008* (Sapir and Resling, 2010).

HADAS WEISS is a Senior Fellow at the Max Planck Institute for Social Anthropology, where she is part of a research group on financialization. She obtained a PhD in anthropology at the University of Chicago and has held postdoctoral appointments in Jerusalem, Frankfurt, Helsinki, and Budapest. Her dissertation research focused on West Bank settlements, while her subsequent research in Israel and Germany turned to financial issues. Her work has been published in leading anthropology journals, and she is the author of the forthcoming monograph *We Have Never Been Middle Class*.

HAIM YACOBI is an architect specializing in urban-political geography and a member of the Department of Politics and Government at Ben-Gurion University. His main research interests in relation to the issue of urban space are social justice, the politics of identity, migration, and colonial planning. In 1999, he formulated the idea of establishing Bimkom—Planners for Planning Rights, a nongovernmental organization that focuses on human rights and planning in Israel and served as its cofounder. His work has been published in *Environment and Planning A*, *Environment and Planning D*, *Urban Geography*, *City*, *Planning Theory and Practice*, and the *International Journal of Middle East Studies*.

Index

Ibn al-Nadhir, 151
identity politics, 24
ideology, 4, 7, 53; declining significance of, 69, 103; Gush Emunim settlements and, 54; of territorial control, 93; ultraorthodox communities and, 113
In the Land of Israel (Oz, 1983), 14n6
industrial areas/zones, 6, 9, 176; Barkan, 179; labor law in, 188, 191n56; Ma'ale Efraim, 179; Mishor Adumim Industrial Area (Ma'ale Adumim), *xiii*, 5, 11, 213; Nitzanei Shamlom, 172; rights of Palestinian workers in, 181; *Worker's Hotline* ruling and, 177
infrastructure, 6, 9, 25, 78, 96, 106; expansion of settlements and, 162; government funded, 7; interactions of different communities and, 14; tourism and, 213; transportation, 37, 41; in ultraorthodox settlements, 122; unequal distribution of, 197
international law, 42, 60, 61n2, 107n7, 160, 172
Intifada, First, 62n4, 88n5, 163, 174
Intifada, Second, 62n4, 85, 174, 200, 201
Israel, State of: annexation of occupied territories to, 35, 143, 177, 182, 188; Arab citizens of, 30; "development towns," 114; Disengagement Plan, in Gaza, 14n3, 68; educational institutions, 9; establishment/founding of, 156, 158, 196; global market and, 76; immigrants to, 76, 79, 87n1, 87n3; integration with West Bank, 13; "Israel proper," 8–11, 66, 160, 211, 213; as "Jewish democratic state," 13; Ministry of Defense, 42, 215nn3–4; Ministry of Interior, 35, 42, 164; peace treaty with Egypt (1979), 60, 211; political establishment of, 2, 4, 6; settlers' attitudes toward laws of, 166; social/economic inequality in, 23; "two Israels," 7–11; ultraorthodox population of, 112
Israel Defense Forces [IDF] (Israeli Army), 2, 99, 104, 163, 176, 208n5, 215n3
"Israel Our House" (Yisrael Beteinu) Party, 43
Israeli Military Administration, 44
Israeli–Palestinian conflict/relations, 2, 49, 61, 75; Interim Agreement (1995), 172; messianism and, 141; religion and, 137–39; status of Jerusalem and, 48, 50; "unpleasant otherness" and, 57. *See also* settlements, Palestinian descriptions of
Israel/Palestine, 7, 8, 10, 11, 75; daily life of residents, 13; geography of settlement, 37; geopolitics of, 12; "informal outposts" and

colonization of, 92, 97–102, 105; Jewish demographic majority in, 143; social/political/economic fabric of, 13
Issawiya, village of, 196, 197, 199

Jalazone refugee camp, 155
Jalazun refugee camp, 163
Jericho, city of, *xii*, 62n4
Jerusalem, 6, 25, 35, 38, 104; Holy Basin, 50; inner city of, 11, 50, 51, 54, 56, 57; on maps, *xii*, *xiii*; Mevasseret Zion, 54; Moroccan Quarter, 50; "new neighborhoods" of, 5, 10, 12, 195, 196, 212; Old City (Jewish Quarter), *xiii*, 49, 50, 155, 195, 196, 212, 213; Palestinians living in settlements, 193–208; physical relation to the West Bank, 8–9; population growth in, 116; Regional Labor Tribunal, 178, 190n18; residency identification cards for Palestinians, 193, 200, 208–209n5; status as divisive issue, 48, 60; suburbanization of, 48, 50–52, 212; ultraorthodox communities and, 112, 114, 115, 121, 124, 125n1. *See also* East Jerusalem
Jewish settlers: differentiated types of, 55, 104; growth in population of, 4; ideological and religious, 15n9, 34, 35, 46, 113; Israeli public opinion and, 84; Israeli state seen by, 139–141; Knesset representation of, 43; "new age," 103, 135; number of, 10, 15n10, 25, 212; Palestinians as ultimate "others" for, 57; possible return to Israel, 36; reasons for relocation to West Bank, 9; security of, 12–13; stereotypical images of, 2, 93, 102, 163; suburbanization and, 34, 49. *See also* "hilltop youth"
Jordan, 53, 138, 156, 172, 211
Jordan Valley, *xii*, 37, 160, 175, 181
Jordanian law, 176, 178, 179, 181, 183, 184, 188; "Israeli exclaves" and, 187; *Madnabe* case and, 186; maintained by Israel in West Bank, 215n4
Jua'bah, 'Abd Al-Mu'ti, 153
Judaism, 128–29, 131–32, 136, 143, 144n2
Judaization, 102, 105, 106, 194, 207
Judea and Samaria, 97, 104, 107n11, 136, 213; number of settlers in, 212, 214n2; Order on Employment of Workers in Certain Places (1982), 177; as Palestinian land, 138; Settlement Council for Judea and Samaria, 35; theological discourse about, 101; tourism and, 15n9; Yesha Council and, 14n5, 42, 129, 215n5

peripheries, 30, 31, 46; development towns in, 41; of Jerusalem, 53; "new," 40; "real," 39–40
Persico, Tomer, 135
Petah Tikva, *xii*
pioneering, notion of, 36, 38, 75, 94
Pisgat Ze'ev, *xiii*, 9, 51, 200, 212
place attachment, 52–53
Planning and Construction Law (1965), 195
population dispersal, 36, 39, 46
Porat, Rabbi Hanan, 131
Portugali, Juval, 10, 36
postmodernity, 135
poverty, 24, 29
Precariat ("precarious class"), 29, 30, 31
"Price Tag" actions, 136, 144n9, 164, 165, 166
privatization, 21, 22, 24, 27, 77; false separation from Occupation, 22–24; Israeli settlement policy and, 53; "privatized peace" of the Left, 27–29; of the welfare state, 25
property rights, 55, 77, 94, 98, 99, 100
public opinion, Israeli, 49, 84, 215n6
Pullan, Wendy, 9, 197

Qalqilya, *xii*
Qusra, 164–65

Rabbis for Human Rights, 55
Rabin, Yitzhak, 7, 28, 133
Rabinowitz, Dan, 202
Ram, Uri, 78
Ramallah, *xii*, 70, 155, 163
Ramat Beit Shemesh, 119
Ramat Eshkol, *xiii*, 5, 212
Ramat Shlomo, *xiii*, 212
Ramot, *xiii*, 54
Ramot Allon, 212
Rawabi, 70, 86
real-estate developers, 6, 7
Real-Time: The Al-Aqsa Intifada and the Israeli Left (Ophir, 2001), 23
Regev, Miri, 31
Regional Labor Tribunals, 175, 178, 179, 183, 190n18
Reichman, Shalom, 36, 39, 40
Reichman, Shlomo, 11
Right, Israeli, 32, 82; economic gap and, 28; hegemony of, 21, 22, 24; lower-class supporters of, 25, 27; "Loyalty Regime" and, 29–31; neoliberalism and, 31; privatization policy of, 23; ultraorthodox communities and, 23, 112, 118, 119–120, 123; Yitzhar settlement and, 135

Rishon LeZion, 64, 65
Rogers' Plan (1969), 196
Ron, James, 197
Rosh HaAyin, 64
Roy, Ananya, 95
rurbanization, 34, 38, 39

Sandercock, Leonie, 198
Sarta, village of, 165
Sasson, Talya, 96, 215n6
Savion, 66
sector-system, 29
sefirot, 137, 145n10
Segev, Tom, 10, 15n10
Separation Barrier, 65, 67, 88n6, 162, 164; effects on employment of West Bank residents, 175; in Jerusalem/French Hill, 197, 208n3; Palestinian self-sustenance hindered by, 174
settlement blocs, 81, 100, 131; "consensus settlements" and, 212; "illegal outposts" distinguished from, 166; majority of Palestinian land controlled by, 168; proximity to Green Line, 45
Settlement Council for Judea and Samaria, 35
settlement evacuation, 13, 36, 43, 45; cost of, 81; in Gaza Strip, 14n3, 45, 68, 79, 87, 211; settler refusal of, 46; in the Sinai, 60, 211
settlement policy, Israeli, 1, 3–4, 8, 61; allies of settler movement, 5–6; conflict of laws and, 172; flexibility of, 125; "informal outposts" and, 92; Israeli-Palestinian relations and, 48, 49; media debate over, 2; motivations for participation in, 3; social conditions created by, 7; suburbanization of, 48, 50–52; teleological explanation of, 13; territorial implications of, 51, 52–53; two Israels and, 10
settlements: Arab-Israeli War (1967) and establishment of, 211; border discourse and, 45–46; bourgeoisification of, 141; changed appearance of, 64; clusters of, 36–37; compensatory mechanism of, 24–27, 28; defined, 211; expansion of, 13; geographical factor in settlement, 37–42; heterogeneous population of, 8; history since 1967 war, 77–79; "ideological" versus "quality of life," 116, 124; as "legal exclaves," 186, 187, 188; on maps, *xii*, *xiii*; marketing of houses in, 104; Mizrahi population of, 9; municipal and administrative structures, 42–45; neoliberalism and, 31; "normal," 12; Palestinian families in, 9; panoramic

www.ingramcontent.com/pod-product-compliance
Lightning Source LLC
Chambersburg PA
CBHW030647270326
41929CB00007B/252